Don Benito Wilson

From Mountain Man
to Mayor
Don
Benito
Wilson
Los Angeles 1841 to 1878

To Robert Quintero
A fellow student
of Southern California
history. With the best
wishes

10-8-09

Nat B. Read

Don Benito Wilson
From Mountain Man to Mayor, Los Angeles, 1841 to 1878
Copyright © 2008 by Nat B. Read

Designed by Amy Inouye, www.futurestudio.com

10 9 8 7 6 5 4 3 2 1

ISBN-13 978-1-883318-83-3 / ISBN-10 1-883318-83-1

LIBRARY OF CONGRESS CATALOGING-IN-PUBLICATION DATA

Read, Nat B.
 Don Benito Wilson : from mountain man to mayor, Los Angeles, 1841 to 1878 / by Nat B. Read.
     p. cm.
 Summary: "Don Benito Wilson (née Benjamin Davis Wilson) is remembered as the namesake of Mount Wilson. Few know he was the second mayor of Los Angeles. Twenty-six State Senators divvy up the district that Benjamin Wilson once represented. Southern California will never again see anyone who made such a mark on so many different fields as Don Benito Wilson" —Provided by publisher.
 Includes bibliographical references and index.
 ISBN 978-1-883318-83-3 (hardcover : alk. paper)
 1. Wilson, Benjamin Davis, 1811-1878. 2. Mayors—California—Los Angeles—Biography.
 3. Pioneers—California, Southern—Biography. 4. Pioneers—Southwest, New—Biography.
 5. Los Angeles (Calif.)—Biography. 6. Los Angeles (Calif.)—History—19th century.
 7. California, Southern—History—19th century. 8. Frontier and pioneer life—California, Southern. 9. Frontier and pioneer life—Southwest, New. I. Title.

F869.L853W557 2008
979.4'9404092–dc22
[B]
                              2008006192

Printed in the United States of America

ANGEL CITY PRESS
2118 Wilshire Blvd. #880
Santa Monica, California 90403
310.395.9982
ANGEL CITY PRESS   www.angelcitypress.com

To Linda

Contents

Acknowledgments

One of the most pleasant tasks in writing this book is to celebrate for the record those without whose help this work could not have been researched and written. At the top of this list must come the name Paddy Calistro, the publisher who doggedly insisted that I fill the conspicuous gap on the Southern California reference shelves where a biography of Benjamin Davis Wilson had for so long been missing. I pleaded that I had other things do with my spare time for three years of my life, but she was relentless, and I'm glad she was. Don Benito deserved his due. William Deverell, the eminent Southern California historian, was a constant source of information, guidance and encouragement. I was also encouraged by the Huntington Library's President Steven Koblick and Director of Research Robert C. Ritchie. My second home for these past years has been the stacks and reading rooms of the Huntington Library, where I've been helped by William Frank, Jennifer Watts, Laura Stalker, Jill Cogen, Kate Henningsen, Meredith Berbee, Christopher Adde, Juan Gomez, Phil Brontosaurus and many others.

I was guided by countless librarians and staff members at numerous libraries and institutions, including the Los Angeles Public Library, Pasadena Public Library, Beverly Hills Public Library, San Marino Public Library, State of California Library, State of California Archives, Pasadena Historical Museum, City of Los Angeles Archives, County Board of Supervisors office. Kevin Hallaran, archivist at the Riverside Metropolitan Museum, and Judith Carter of the San Marino Historical Society were especially helpful. Jim Hardee, director of the Fur Trade Research Center, shared generously his time and expertise on nuances of mountain-man lore. Jeannette O'Malley and Patrick Conyers were most understanding when my moving deadline overturned plans at their Pasadena Museum of History.

Individuals who helped included David Meshulam, Peggy Hendricks, Johan M. Sandstrom, Midge Sherwood and John Watkins. I am especially indebted to the Honorable Barbara Vucanovich, former U.S. Congresswoman from Reno, and her daughter, Patricia D. Cafferata, the first woman elected to a statewide position in Nevada. These two elected officials are the great-great granddaughter and great-great-great granddaughter of Don Benito Wilson and Ramona Yorba. They heard about my project and graciously shared their family archives.

I have saved for last the person who has helped the most, Linda Anne Read. Through courtship, wedding and marriage she has encouraged me, rearranged her own priorities and (sort of) understood my insane hours of seemingly endless obsession with this work. For this she has my undying appreciation and it is to her I dedicate this book.

—NAT B. READ

CHAPTER 1

Beginning–
Early Life

Benjamin Davis Wilson was born on December 1, 1811 in what was then the westernmost of the seventeen United States: Tennessee. John Adams and Thomas Jefferson were still alive. So was King George III, the target of the American Revolution. James Madison, the nation's fourth president, sat in the new White House and "The Star Spangled Banner" had not yet been composed.

Beyond Wilson's native Tennessee lay a wilderness that President Jefferson had bought from Napoleon eight years earlier. Five years before Wilson was born, Lewis and Clark had completed their trek to learn what they could about the part of the map that was still blank. A continent away lay the King of Spain's empire along the Western coast of North America. Within that Spanish realm sat a tiny, thirty-year-old hamlet called la Reyna de los Angeles (Queen of the Angels) with a population of about three hundred souls.

This is the story of how Benjamin Wilson connected those dots. This is how he rode the crest of the frontier wave and made a life outside the United States, only to have the tide of his native country overtake him as a middle-aged man decades later. Meanwhile he had written himself into the history of that vast, uncharted American wilderness, had settled and raised his family in what was then Mexico, and had played a key role in the new American state of California and its still-small pueblo of Los Angeles. He died a revered leader of a much larger Los Angeles in 1878, a city which was beginning to take a form that could be vaguely recognized by today's residents. His Los Angeles had become a city with downtown brick buildings, streetcar tracks, telegraph wires and street lighting. But that's getting ahead of our story.

Benjamin Davis Wilson was born in Nashville, into a family who had lived on the frontier for two generations. His grandfather, Adam William Willson (spelled sometimes with two l's), Sr., was born about 1727 and may have come to the Colonies from Scotland. Adam Willson married twice and sired thirteen children, including John G. Wilson, Benjamin's father, who was born on November 15, 1772.[1] Benjamin said later that his father was born in a fort in what is today Wilson County, Tennessee, but there were no settlers in that part of the country in 1772, and no forts. His father came in the first wave of permanent settlers, shortly before the turn of the century. The closest fort around would be Fort Nashborough in what is today the city of Nashville, but that fort was not built until 1780, seven years after his father's birth. Perhaps Benjamin Wilson's autobiography contained a misstatement or maybe he meant that he himself, rather than his father, was born in a fort. Since Benjamin Wilson was born in Nashville, this would have been quite possible, and would place his nativity in Fort Nashborough. Alas, birth records were not filed in county courthouses in those frontier days, so we can't be sure.

Wilson County was named in 1799 for Major David Wilson, a Revolutionary war veteran from Pennsylvania who had settled in North Carolina on land given him for his military service. He shares no kinship with Benjamin Wilson's family. Wilson County sits in the great Silurian basin of Middle Tennessee. After the Revolutionary War the State of North Carolina (which then included this region) gratefully gave land in what is now Wilson County to a number of its veterans, some of whom settled there and some of whom sold their plots. Other settlers rushed in, locating on the rich soil along the various creeks in the area.[2] One of the original Stoner Lick Creek settlers, shortly after 1799, was the recently married John Wilson.

John Wilson had risked his fortune trying to increase it and lost it all before dying in 1819 when Benjamin was eight. He left his wife, Ruth, and young Benjamin to cope with frontier life without resources. Benjamin's older brother, Wylie Ritchie Wilson, was eighteen when their father died. Young Benjamin later said that he got some education from his grandfather, perhaps his father's father, Adam, before setting out at age fifteen to open a small trading house at Yazoo City on the Yazoo River north of Vicksburg, Mississippi, to trade with the Choctaw and Chickasaw Indians.

While in Mississippi Wilson suffered a breakdown in his health and his doctors told him that he would die if he did not move out of that area. It is hard to imagine what kind of ailment he could have suffered in his stationary occupation, because for the sake of his health he then became a trapper, testing his limits of survival and endurance against an unforgiving wilderness and aggressive Indians and had no more complaints about health during his younger years. He joined a company of frontiersmen at Fort Smith, on the very edge of the white man's world, but when the Arkansas River did not rise in time for the party to set out as planned he joined the Rocky Mountain Fur Company out of St. Louis instead.

Fur trappers attacked the West from the American launching site of St. Louis or from Taos and Santa Fe in the nation of Mexico. Wilson's party, under the leadership of James Kirker, left St. Louis to make Santa Fe its base. For all of his physical risk in this venture, Wilson, like most other employees of trapping parties, ended up broke, so he switched employers in 1833 and explored the country of the Gila and Apache Indians, where his party was quite successful in bringing beaver pelts back to Santa Fe after two years in the mountains. Wilson then outfitted his own party of trappers.

Thus, Benjamin Wilson was, in his early years, one of the legendary mountain men. To understand the man Benjamin Wilson became we must understand the anvil on which he was shaped. To review who the mountain men were, what drove them and what their day-to-day life was like we must freeze the frame of Benjamin Wilson's chronology to better understand that remarkable breed.

NOTES FOR CHAPTER 1

1 Most of what we know of Wilson's life prior to 1850 comes from an 1877 interview by Thomas Savage, who was working for Hubert Howe Bancroft to collect memoirs from California pioneers still living at the time. A copy of this narrative is preserved in the Bancroft Library, and was published, with commentary by Arthur Woodward in the 1934 annual publication of the *Historical Society of Southern California Annual* under the title of "Benjamin Davis Wilson's Observations on Early Days in California and New Mexico."

2 Cooley, *The Goodspeed History of Wilson County,* Tennessee, 1971.

CHAPTER 2

The Mountain Men

The mountain men wrote one of the most colorful chapters of American history. They were few in number and they did not have an important impact on American history, but their heroic life-style in the mysterious Indian wilderness west of the existing states made them legends in their time and ours. Like the Pony Express riders who came later, their saga was brief, but dramatic.[1]

In his time the mountain man was an Army Ranger, Hell's Angel, Viking and pirate wrapped into one cultural mutant. He left the comforts of the nineteenth century for Stone Age survival in a mostly unmapped, alien landscape of B-movie hazards. With the exception of his guns, his steel beaver traps and a few other odd metal objects, he lived off the land exactly as the Indian had survived in the same environment for thousands of years. He ate what he killed—and wore what he killed as well—if it didn't kill him first.

Mountain men were traders and fur trappers, more specifically beaver trappers, who fed the lucrative market for men's beaver hats that were the fashion rage in Europe and the civilized centers of the New World. There is a certain irony in the fact that this most primitive and dangerous exploit in the West was undertaken for the most refined fashion in the safest of European and North American cultures, in the East. The mountain man viewed the risk as a gamble to become one of those rich gentlemen who could afford the beaver hats he was so painstakingly supplying. Often, men with little education or advantage who'd been raised on a farm with gun in hand[2] trapped the beaver as a hoped-for stepping stone to a position of comfort in polite civilization far from the dangerous wilderness.

Benjamin Wilson did acquire wealth, but not by fur trapping.

The core of the mountain-man era was only about twenty years long, from about 1820 until about 1840. Lewis and Clark had made their celebrated trek on behalf of President Thomas Jefferson in 1804 to 1806, to find out what lay in the blank part of the continental map between the new United States and the Pacific coast. They reported seeing an awful lot of beavers on their way.

The white man had been trading with the Indians for beaver and other furs for over a hundred years, but the wealth of beaver that Lewis and Clark reported inspired the Euro-American to go out in the wilderness and trap the valuable little animal himself, instead of waiting for Indians to bring pelts to the trading post.

Let's fit the mountain-man era into the timeline of American history. What is now the Western United States remained mostly unexplored by the White population from the time of Columbus through about 1820. The American and European mountain men filled in that map in a rough sort of way during the two colorful decades from 1820 to 1840, even though the land remained in the hands of Native Americans. The cascade of Western settlers in their covered wagons followed the mountain men from about 1850 through 1870. By about 1870 the West was permanently the land of the white man.[3] By then, the days of the free-roaming Indians and mountain men were long gone.

During the mountain-man era Indians inhabited the lands in the West almost exclusively. One day those lands would become a little more than fifteen American states: Missouri, Iowa, Minnesota, North Dakota, South Dakota, Nebraska, Kansas, Colorado, Wyoming, Montana, Idaho, Utah, Nevada, Oregon, Washington, and the California Rockies. There were no American settlers. It was wilderness and the home of dozens of nations of Native Americans.

Throughout this era there were only about a thousand mountain men scattered throughout the Rocky Mountain fur regions. The maps of the region were mostly in the heads of the fur trappers themselves. Imagine wandering on foot or horseback through a million square miles and fifteen Western states knowing just about where you were at any given time.

Mountain men fascinated us over the years because these men lived human life at testosterone's edge. Historian Stanley Vestal quotes mountain men as claiming that only cripples and Army soldiers slept in tents. A mountain man slept in the open, in cold, pouring rain, except in the winter camps. His clothes might not be waterproof but his skin was, he reasoned.[4]

He lived in a world where there were no doctors and no police. First he had to survive on what he could kill. Then, to trap the beaver he had to wade in water close to freezing. He knew only three months in his world—July, August and Winter.[5] He set his traps in an environment of dangerous animals, especially grizzly bears that killed a number of mountain men. And then there were the Indians who used all of their stealth and power to steal the horses and the traps and kill the mountain men. The few of them scattered throughout the West were the toughest of the tough. Still one of them died every ten days on the average, according to historian Vestal.[6] Percentage-wise, their chances of survival were the same as those for U.S. Marines in World War II.

The mountain-man era was short. Shortly after Lewis and Clark returned, a man named Manuel Lisa followed the model used in the East and built an armed post for trading with the Indians. But Lisa soon discovered that his own men could trap beaver as well as the Indians. The partners in his new company included William Clark (the Clark of Lewis and Clark). At about the same time an immigrant from Waldorf, Germany, began the American Fur Company that was to make more money than any other. His name was John Jacob Astor and he sent men out to trade with the Indians from fixed posts.

In the early 1820s three things happened to create the mountain-man phenomenon. In 1821 Astor convinced the U.S. government to privatize the business of trading with the Indians, freeing the enterprise for the profit motive. The following year, 1822, William Ashley and Andrew Henry formed a company around the concept of white men doing all of the trapping, then rendezvousing at a fixed time and place to sell their furs in return for provisions for the next season. Their first expedition included men who would become legends as mountain men, Jedediah Smith and Jim Bridger. And the year after that, 1823, an improved steel beaver trap was invented, increasing the white man's productivity significantly. Benjamin Wilson entered the fur trapping business in 1833 under a famous mountain man, James Kirker, and working at the same time as another who was to become the most famous of all, Kit Carson.

The mountain man had to wade upstream in the freezing mountain stream so the beaver wouldn't smell his presence. He set a steel trap, then bent a sapling or stuck a broken-off branch in the mud near the trap. He dipped the end of this stick in a substance from beaver castor glands that attracted the beaver from a great distance. The beaver, curious about another of his species being in his territory, came to investigate the smell near the trap. The trap worked by drowning the beaver, which instinctively fled to deeper water when panicked. The trap with its chain rode along a stake that was firmly planted in deep water. The stake contained a notch near the stream bed that allowed the chain to move down, but not back up. Thus when the beaver was caught and carried the trap and chain to the "safety" of deep water, the chain slipped over the notch, keeping the beaver from returning to the surface. The steel trap was a great improvement over the methods used by the Indians to kill beaver. The mountain man carried about six of these traps,[7] which were about all he could set and recover in a single day. After he recovered the beaver from the trap he carefully removed the odorous gland and stored it for use with his next trap.

Mountain men typically traveled in groups for safety. The lone trapper was often a dead trapper. They ate virtually nothing but meat while they were in the mountains. The economies of the mountains were such that it was almost impossible to leave the mountains with money after trapping. The mark-up on goods hauled into the wilderness was as much as one thousand to two thousand percent. No wonder so many mountain men went bankrupt. As in the gold fields of California, those who became millionaires were not those who gathered the produce, but those who sold them their goods.

There were three levels of mountain men. At the base level was the *engagé*, a direct employee of the fur company, who was outfitted at the company's expense and paid about two hundred dollars a year as what amounted to a day laborer. Whatever he trapped belonged to the company. The next step in the hierarchy was the *contract trapper*, who was bankrolled by the company. He operated on his own but was obligated to buy his trade goods from the company and sell his furs exclusively to the company. At the top of the food chain was the *free trapper*, who owned his own outfit, bought from anyone he pleased, sold his furs as he chose and was free to go wherever he wanted. For safety, free trappers organized into brigades, and chose a leader, whom they sometimes called a *partisan*. There were a few hundred free trappers at work in the mountains at any one time. After working with Kirker, Benjamin Wilson went out on his own at the age of twenty-six as one of the free-trapper elite.

Misconceptions have it that mountain men were shaggy guys in buckskin clothing. Some did wear the scruffy beards associated with prospectors, but many mountain men shaved. And mountain men did wear buckskin clothing, but often only after their store-bought clothing wore out completely. Traditional European/American clothing was far superior to buckskin. Rawhide became waterlogged and clammy and it shrank painfully when it got wet, becoming very uncomfortable in the crotch. But after their Eastern clothes wore out fur trappers often had to live off the land.

The annual rendezvous started by William Ashley in the Rocky Mountains became wilder over the years as more bands of Indians showed up. The mountain-man era had begun because of high society and its demand for beaver hair hats for hundreds of years. (More than half a million beaver hats were made in Europe some years even prior to 1800.) During the mountain-man era there may have been one hundred to four hundred million beavers living in the present continental United States. The mountain-man era ended as the market flooded with the much cheaper South American river mammal, the nutria, as high society switched to silk hats (think Abraham Lincoln) and as settlers began to destroy the wilderness with permanent communities. By 1840 buffalo robes had replaced beaver pelts as trade ware in the Far West.[8]

It is misleading to think of what is now the Western United States in the mountain-man era as a dichotomy of Whites vs. Indians. It is more accurate to think of the region as occupied exclusively by Indians, with the fur trappers being essentially another of the many Indian clans roaming the lands. The model of Whites vs. Indians was true when Whites built permanent communities on lands contested by Indians. The mountain man, though, was as alien to white settlements as the Indian was. The mountain man's skin turned to leather in the sun, and he often wore the same animal skins for clothes. He survived using the same skills and techniques as Indians. Travelers in the area sometimes mistook the mountain man for an Indian, a mistake that flattered the fur trapper.[9] The mountain men were genetically almost exclusively non-Indian, but sociologically mountain men and Indians lived almost exactly the same, in cultures shaped by their common environment.

Many, if not most, mountain men were not Anglo Americans. French were numerous in their bands, but many other nationalities and ethnicities were also represented. Any party of mountain men was likely to include many Indians. Indians were not united against the Whites, and Indian nations were friendly to some other nations and enemies of others. Mountain men were like another tribe. The cultural traits of the mountain men set them apart from other tribes, just as Indian tribes differed greatly from each other. There were about 360,000 Indians in the West at that time and only about a thousand mountain men,[10] so the mountain men were not a significant tribe in terms of numbers, but they had an inordinate significance in Indian country because of their access to weapons and metal tools, which were fervently sought by the Indians.

The dozens of Indian nations differed greatly from each other. Their languages could be as different from one another as English is from Chinese. Friendly tribes included the Nez Perces, Flatheads and Snakes. At the other extreme, the Blackfeet and Comanches were the fiercest adversaries to the mountain men. The Crows were the tallest Indians on the

Plains, the best dressed and had the largest teepees. Their women were very attractive by white standards. And the Crows had two other distinctions, among Indians and mountain men alike: They were the best horse thieves and supreme in the corollary—the hardest to steal horses from.

Warfare between mountain men and Indians followed a certain pattern. A party of mountain men at full strength was almost immune from attack by hostile Indians.[11] But to trap beaver, the men had to divide into small bands, with only two or three trapping any one stream together. The smaller the group of Whites, the more convenient they were as an Indian target.

The Indian strategy for larger warfare was based on the differences in the weapons being used. The mountain men often used flintlock rifles. The mountain rifle had a barrel that was shorter and heavier than the Kentucky rifle of Daniel Boone's day. Back in the Eastern United States the percussion cap rifle was in use, but in the West the mountain man was slow to give up his reliable flintlock, because flint percussion could be improvised in the mountains. But if you lost your percussion caps, your gun was useless.[12]

Mountain men sometimes lived with Indians, participated in their rituals, and adopted, to some degree, their religion, seeking blessings from their holy men for their hunting trips. And Rocky Mountain trappers sometimes took Indian brides. There were no white women in the wilderness country at that time until 1836.[13]

It was the king of the mountain-man economy, the free trapper, who could afford to take one or more Indian wives in the mountains, which he did primarily in the winter months. One downside of marrying an Indian was that by acquisition came a family, and every kinsman, no matter how remote, felt free to come live with you for as long as he chose. A white fur trapper could have as many wives as he could afford, as was the tribal custom. And when he grew tired of the arrangement he had only to tell his wife to leave him, and back home she would dutifully go, the divorce final.

The fur trapper in the mountains had to be on guard not only against Indians, but against the lord of the land, the grizzly bear. Some mountain men were killed by bears, and those who weren't usually had tall tales of close encounters. Mountain men, being the macho extremists they were, could not resist trying to kill a grizzly when they came across one. The problem was that only a precise shot would kill a grizzly. To miss meant it took twenty to thirty seconds to reload and fire a flintlock, and that was a big advantage to a bear. There are records of fifty shots being fired into a bear before bringing it down.[14] Like other mountain men, Benjamin Wilson had a fascination with this lethal adversary. Twice he was almost killed by a bear . . . and it was the same bear both times, as we shall see. He named a part of California after the grizzly bears he found there (Bear Lake) and he was on his way to a sporting bear hunt when called into the conflict with Mexico.

The Rocky Mountain trappers, the mountain men who used St. Louis as a jumping-off place to the upper Far West, differed in important ways from the mountain men like Wilson who used the Taos area as their base. The trappers of the Central Rockies operated out of U.S. points of departure in and around Missouri and in a territory mostly claimed by the United States. They were beholden to U.S. law, although they modified it to fit their circumstance. The Rocky Mountain trappers lived in the Indian Country claimed by the United States. In doing so they both trailed and led American law. The Southwest trappers operated out of Mexico and under Mexican law as they probed what is now Colorado, Utah, Arizona and Nevada, sometimes ending up at the annual rendezvous with the St. Louis-based trappers.[15] In fact, four of these historic rendezvous were staged at rallying points south of the forty-second parallel, ignoring Mexico's legal jurisdiction in the mountain wilderness.

The Rocky Mountain trappers out of St. Louis lived with, traveled with, allied themselves with, and fought against, Indians. They married Indian women, sometimes more than one at a time, although these marriages were generally not long-lasting relationships. The Southwest trappers, like Wilson, also interfaced with Indians, but these Indians' relations with the Mexican government and people colored their relationships. Trappers operating out of the Southwest tended to marry Mexican women, not Indians. Wilson himself would take a Mexican wife, but not until he'd left Mexican Santa Fe and settled in Mexican Alta California.

The trapper out of St. Louis lived a harder life than his New Mexico counterpart. The St. Louis trapper lived at the end of a longer supply line and therefore he needed a greater investment. As a result, this trade was in the relatively few hands of men who tended to be gamblers. The New Mexico trapper tended to combine trapping with trading to a greater extent than his St. Louis counterpart. In his trading he skirted Mexican law to avoid the red tape and to gain a greater payoff for the effort. Virtually all Americans operating out of Taos and Santa Fe were smugglers of brandy, stolen horses or other contraband.

Before 1821 New Mexico, and all of Mexico, was ruled by Spain, which kept foreigners outside its borders except in very controlled circumstances. With Mexican independence the new government loosened the tough restrictions and began to allow Americans and Europeans into its territory. The regular overland trade between St. Louis and Santa Fe can be traced to the year that Mexico became independent, 1822.[16]

In addition to their trade with the United States through St. Louis, Santa Fe traders also opened a trading link with California, bringing stolen horses as well as beaver pelts across the desert. California, like New Mexico, was a part of the nation of Mexico. American traders were no strangers in Alta California, but prior to the overland business, Yankees had reached that territory from the sea. Mountain man Jedediah Smith had been the first American to reach California by land, arriving to the surprise and horror of Mexican officials in 1826. Richard Campbell, Sylvester Pattie and Ewing Young were among the mountain men whose search for new beaver grounds brought them overland to California. The increasingly familiar path between Santa Fe and Southern California along the Old Spanish Trail would be the escape route that Benjamin Wilson and 133 others would use to flee Santa Fe some years later.

NOTES FOR CHAPTER 2
  1 For a more in-depth view of mountain-man lore, read Bernard DeVoto's classic work, *Across the Wide Missouri*.
  2 Laycock, *The Mountain Men*.

3 A note is necessary on terminology that will be used throughout the book. In differentiating Indians from non-Indians, the author has used terms such as "white man," or "Whites," or "Americans" as antidotes for the endless repetition of "non-Indian" in discussing the mountain-man era. The reader should understand that these generalized terms for non-Indians in the country at this time included Americans, Canadians, Mexicans, Europeans, Africans and perhaps others. An even greater semantic problem arises in discussing Alta California in coming chapters, where the Indians and the Spanish-speaking population of Hispanic and Black ancestry were joined by a wave of humanity that included Americans, Caucasian variants, Chinese and Blacks. The problem is compounded by the fact that California was Mexican on one day and American on the next, and that many of the same leaders participated in both systems. Thus, literally, "Mexicans" could include American and European expatriates who had taken up Mexican citizenship prior to the Mexican War, "Americans" (as counterpoint to "Mexicans") could include non-Latinos who were from Europe or elsewhere. And where do free Blacks, Indians and racial mixtures fit? The author has attempted, through context, to make clear the group being referenced, trusting that the reader will accept the lack of absolute preciseness. To be clinically precise would make the prose sound like a legal treatise and destroy the rhythm and flow of the story.

4 Vestal, *Jim Bridger—Mountain Man*, 12.

5 Ibid., 43

6 Ibid., 95.

7 Laycock, *The Mountain Men*, 10.

8 Hafen, *Fur Trappers and Traders of the Far Southwest*, xvii, 12, 14.

9 Vestal, *Jim Bridger—Mountain Man*, 121.

10 Ibid., 95.

11 DeVoto, *Across the Wide Missouri*, 22.

12 Ibid., 393.

13 Ibid., 247.

14 Ibid., 96.

15 Ibid., 47.

16 Ibid., 3.

CHAPTER 3

Wilson in Santa Fe

Wilson joined a trapping party of the Rocky Mountain Fur Company, left Missouri and reached Santa Fe in the autumn of 1833. Wilson was broke, so he signed up with a trapping party headed by James Kirker and headed out that winter to look for beaver in the country of the Gila River and the Apache Indians.[1] Kirker was an Irishman who'd been a pirate off the coast of Brazil and a copper miner in Mexico as well as a fur trapper. Running afoul of Mexican authorities for skirting their laws, his furs had been seized on an 1824 trapping expedition. Kirker had signed on with copper miner Robert McKnight when McKnight's goods were confiscated by the authorities. The governor of Chihuahua put a bounty of nine thousand dollars on Kirker's head for stealing livestock in his state and selling them through Apache friends in New Mexico. To get out of that jam, Kirker turned against the Indians and agreed to bring as many Apache scalps as he could to the Mexican authorities for the reward of fifty dollars apiece. He said later that he had killed 487 Apaches.

Although Wilson was part of Kirker's party for two years, there is no evidence that he took part in Kirker's treachery. Wilson was in New Mexico as a self-admitted "interloper and smuggler" to be sure, but he did not share Kirker's savagery towards the Apaches nor Kirker's trait of double-dealing. Kirker's turn against his former Apache friends came long after Wilson's association with him.

After two years under Kirker, Wilson returned to Santa Fe, organized his own small company, refitted and returned to the same Gila River area. He was now twenty-three years old.

During the winter of 1835-36 Wilson undertook another expedition to the Gila River area and experienced the kind of hunger and thirst that cursed many mountain men in their life as they roamed the wilderness. Wilson and five other men went six days without food, and the men grew so weak that Wilson took the only alternative left to him, shooting the faithful mule that had served him for over a thousand miles. The memory of this act bothered him the rest of his life. Later on, his party went five days without water. With no water for so long the men wasted away to shriveled skeletons with painful joints, their eyes sunk back deeply into cadaverous skulls. Wilson recounted later that the hunger of six days was nothing compared to the absence of water. As they stumbled along the sandy plain between two mountain ranges they saw, in their thirst-crazed state, a bizarre and tantalizing sight far ahead of them. They could see a large building, and as they got closer they saw that it was a perfectly preserved church, surrounded by the crumbled ruins of a town long extinct. But alas, there were no people and there was no water. They spent an entire day searching for traces of water at the ghost church, before finding the remains of an abandoned aqueduct. They spent another full day following this dry water canal to its source in a gorge, where at long last the men found water.

Wilson had stumbled onto *La Gran Quivira*, a half-fabled place that was probably a Piros Indian community. Coronado had sought *La Gran Quivira* believing it to be a city of gold, but he never found this village. The Spanish first came here in 1581, built a church at the place in 1628, and in 1644 built the larger version that Wilson found. Some time between 1670 and 1675 Apaches drove the Spanish away from the site.[2]

Wilson, like other Americans, enjoyed good relations with the Apache chief, Juan José, a highly educated Indian leader who had trained for a career in the Catholic church. But when the Mexicans killed Juan

José's father, he went back to his own people and made bitter war on the Mexicans. The Gila Apaches he led had been brought up in the church, but when Mexico gained its independence in 1821, the government's care and protection of Indians fell into chaos, and the Indians felt abused by the local Mexicans. So the Indians rebelled against Mexico and Mexicans, and fell in behind Juan José, their leader. Though he was a constant menace to the Mexicans he welcomed the friendship and trading of Americans, and would return any horses or cattle that his warriors had stolen from the *yanquis*.

Juan José was a leader, but not a warrior. His people felt him too valuable to risk in battle, so he lived behind the lines of skirmish, protected by a guard of twenty to thirty young fighting men. The Mexicans were determined to rid themselves of this constant thorn in their side. They arranged with an American known to have access to his camp for his murder. The American was James Johnson. Chief Juan José was warned that Johnson was on his way to assassinate him, but the chief waved off the warnings because Johnson had always been a trusted friend. Once in the chief's camp, Johnson offered gifts of pinole, a food staple, which the guards took away to distribute to the people in the clan. Johnson then led Chief Juan José to the chief's mule under the pretense of wanting to buy it. There, upon a pre-arranged signal, Johnson killed the chief while Johnson's men slaughtered the young warriors with a blunderbuss loaded with balls and chains.

A noble, kind-hearted chief had been murdered in the worst kind of betrayal at the hands of an American. A war party of Indians was gathered by smoke signals and other methods to pursue Johnson's party into the town of Oposura. The Indians then found a party of twenty-two American trappers headed by Charles Kemp camped on the Gila River. The Indians, mad with revenge for the dastardly action of Americans, killed every person in this innocent party.

Benjamin Wilson had been camped about thirty miles from Chief Juan José's encampment and was making his way to intercept a caravan bound for Missouri. As Wilson and his party of five others were making their forced march to overtake the caravan, the rampaging Apache party came upon him. Wilson, of course, was entirely ignorant of the tragedy than had befallen his friend, Chief Juan José, and was incredulous over this hostile behavior of the Indians who had been such comrades in the past. Three of Wilson's party managed to steal away, but the Indians captured Wilson and two others, taking everything they had and marching them back to camp as prisoners. Wilson, with his comrades Maxwell and Tucker, were stripped of their clothing and confined naked by Chief Mangas while the Indians kept up a war dance and prepared wood for burning the prisoners alive.

The old chief who tried to reason with the hot-tempered warriors of his camp was against sacrificing the trio. These Indians' relations with Americans had been positive up to that time, and Mangas wanted to keep that relationship open. The night wore on. The warriors continued their war dance as the hour for the execution by fire grew closer and Mangas knew he had to act quickly. He suggested freeing one of the Americans for an escape, as a way to save the three. Wilson was the only man capable since Tucker was an invalid and Maxwell had a sprained ankle. Wilson, still naked, was able to snatch up a small buffalo robe and shoes before stealing off.

Wilson scurried up a small mountain behind the camp and had barely left when he heard the turmoil over the discovery of his escape. He crawled into a fissure in the rocks and froze in silence as Indians on horseback swarmed the countryside trying to find him. Giving up the search for the night, they returned to their camp. Wilson now faced an epic challenge. The closest friendly settlement he knew of was one hundred twenty miles away, and he would have nothing to eat on his forced march. Meanwhile, the only place on that broad plain where he could hide was a deep canyon about twenty miles away. He would be discovered in the daylight if he tried to remain hidden on his small, rocky mountain and the plain was so flat that a man could be seen many miles away. So he must make it to the canyon before daybreak. He forced himself to run and walk, run and walk, and was finally able to sit down in exhaustion at the ledge of the canyon as the day was breaking. Hearing the Apaches, he then slid down the deep side of the gorge into a chasm covered by vines and brush. There he passed the day, wracked by hunger.

After night fell he began another perilous forced march across the stark plain, to the safety of a spur of the Rocky Mountains where he rested for a while before continuing his odyssey by daylight. That night he rested for a little while once again, then resumed his trek. By now he had walked and run across perhaps seventy miles of hostile terrain with no clothes and had not eaten in three days. Just before daybreak of the third night he stumbled onto a sheep ranch that he had known nothing about. By now his shoes were all but useless and his feet were bleeding. The herder fed him mutton and atole (a cornmeal drink) and fashioned some moccasins out of raw, untanned sheep skin with the wool still attached. A grateful Wilson spent a day with the shepherd before taking up his journey once again, finally reaching the first settlement, where he was able to secure a pair of shoes and some food.

He then continued walking another three or four days, covering a hundred miles, to Santa Fe. He arrived with no money and no clothes. He didn't know a single soul in the town.

James Johnson's town of Oposura was overwhelmed by the Apaches, driving Johnson out of business and forcing him to sell his commercial holdings to escape with his life, leaving his family behind. For his dastardly deed, Johnson never even got the reward he expected from the Mexican authorities. The blot he left on the pages of Southwest history was entirely for naught. The Apaches had been friendly to Americans, but Johnson's treachery, and similar offenses by other Americans, turned the Apaches into a fierce enemy. Among those cited for actions that turned the Apaches from friend to foe was Wilson's early trapping party leader, James Kirker.[3] Chief Mangas and Wilson remained friends, and Mangas often visited Wilson in Santa Fe. Mangas's plot had worked perfectly. Wilson had escaped and his two companions, Maxwell and Tucker, were spared, although Wilson never saw either again. In eternal gratitude, Wilson provided a pension for Mangas.

Wilson had been in Santa Fe only two days after his ordeal when news reached the town of a massacre of the American Keykendall Party one hundred fifty miles to the south. This action by the Apaches was another retribution for Johnson's murder of Chief Juan José. Wilson agreed to go with a work party of three or four Americans to bury the dead in exchange for clothing and an animal to ride. They found twelve decomposed bodies and a host of burnt wagons.

Back in Santa Fe, Wilson found work as a store clerk for twenty-five dollars a month, plus food. Three or four months later he left that job to tend the goods that Dr. Josiah Gregg would leave in Santa Fe while he traveled on with his remaining ware to Chihuahua. Dr. Gregg, who was pleased with Wilson's work in Santa Fe on his behalf, would later become noted for his book, *Commerce on the Prairies*.[4] Wilson ran Dr. Gregg's affairs for two years, then paid the doctor for the rest of the goods and ran the business under his own name.

Two years after coming to Santa Fe, a revolutionary party headed by Manuel Armijo swept into town, killing Governor Alvino Perez and everyone who had been associated with him. With severed heads raised on pikes, the marauders marched through Santa Fe yelling, "Death to the Americans! Death to the Gringos!" Wilson was one of about seven Americans in the town at the time and this small colony sealed itself in Wilson's store for six days waiting for the riot to subside. The mob once tried to force its way into the store, and Wilson was convinced that his life was at its end. But an Indian friend of Wilson, Chief Pedro Leon, convinced the rioters that the Americans were not there, so the thugs moved on.

This was the second time an Indian had saved Wilson's life.

Armijo issued a call for leaders from throughout the territory to assemble in Santa Fe. When they arrived, he had thirty-two of the top officials shot, and Armijo, a former low-life sheepherder, declared himself governor.

Spain had been careful to keep foreigners out of its borders, and it had done so rather effectively in the Territory of New Mexico. After Mexico gained its independence in 1821 the new government at first courted foreign participation in its economy. But Mexico had grown alarmed at the number of foreigners flowing into its borders and at the outsiders' pattern of flaunting Mexican laws and bypassing the country's duties.[5] Texas had gained independence from Mexico in 1836 and in the spring of 1841 some Texans began to talk of coming to New Mexico to "liberate" that territory, as well. There were rumors that Wilson and other local foreigners were in correspondence with the plotters. A French-American gambler named Tiboux made some very public and very insulting remarks and a force that Wilson labeled "rabble" moved on the Americans. Governor Armijo called them back, but the mood in New Mexico toward Americans was ugly, and getting worse. So Wilson and others decided to get out while they still could. Wilson sold his store and made plans to make his way to China.

NOTES FOR CHAPTER 3

1   Woodward, "Benjamin Davis Wilson's Observations on Early Days in California and New Mexico," 128-132.

2   Ibid., 139.

3   Ibid., 131.

4   Ibid., 131-134. Woodward writes that "An article by Henry S. Brooks in *The Californian*, October 1880 states that it was John Johnson, not James Johnson, who perpetuated this bloody deed." Woodward also notes that although Wilson believed that Johnson died in great poverty near Gilroy, California, Brooks wrote that Johnson had later met with financial success in Sonora.

5   Rowland, *John Rowland and William Workman: Southern California Pioneers of 1841*, 19, 21,

CHAPTER 4

The Rowland-Workman Party

Wilson threw in with John Rowland and William Workman, who were making plans to flee the anti-American hysteria in the Territory of New Mexico and travel to a distant territory of Mexico—California. Rowland and Workman had both been mountain men and both were naturalized Mexican citizens. Rowland was born around 1791 in Maryland and Workman was born in northwestern England in 1799. Workman's brother, David, ran a saddlery store in St. Louis, where fifteen-year-old Kit Carson had apprenticed. In New Mexico the two abandoned fur trapping for more stable, less risky businesses. Rowland started a flour mill and Workman ran a store and a distillery.

Rowland and Workman formed a party of foreigners with plans to make their way to California. The trail Rowland and Workman planned to use was called the Old Spanish Trail, although it was neither ancient nor Spanish. It was a relatively new route linking New Mexico and California, forged by Anglo traders in the late 1820s. By the time Rowland and Workman used it as their exit lane in 1841 Anglo traders were using the route on an annual basis. The traders had made their way to California on horseback, leading pack animals and driving sheep, carrying blankets, serapes and woolen goods west, and returning with goods from the Far East and with California horses and mules to be sold in New Mexico.[1] It is quite possible that one or both of the expedition leaders had visited California as traders before the 1841 expedition.[2]

Although used frequently it was by no means a leveled road. To maneuver the Old Spanish Trail's ups and downs Rowland and Workman used pack mules rather than the ox-drawn covered wagons that would become such icons of Western migration a decade or so later. The travelers drove sheep to California, living off their flock for food.

The party assembled in Abiquiu, forty-eight miles northwest of Santa Fe. In addition to the Santa Fe Europeans eager to flee the possible violence to come, there was a small group of travelers that had reached Independence, Missouri, too late to join the Bidwell-Bartleson Party, and had decided to head to Santa Fe rather than strike out across the hostile West alone. Short on provisions, this group was helped by the Santa Fe travelers. Not long after members of this combined group left Santa Fe, about twenty-five New Mexicans caught up with them, asked to join the party and were invited in.[3] Altogether 134 persons ended up making the journey.[4] They followed the Old Spanish Trail through the southwest corner of Colorado, through southern and central Utah, through the deserts of Nevada and the tiny crossroads of "las Vegas," across the Mojave Desert and through the Cajon pass into Southern California.[5] Accounts vary greatly about the difficulty of the trip. Some would write later about great hardships in the journey; others remarked that the trip was routine. Perhaps their reactions had to do with their different appetites for survival. Benjamin Wilson noted only that "we met with no accidents on the journey." At one point in the journey Wilson was fishing in the Sevier River in Utah Territory with Dr. J.W. Lyman, when a ball shot by an Indian hit the ground near the doctor. The physician said, "That fellow can't hit me so far, therefore I will stay and get this fish before I leave." And he did.

After arriving in Los Angeles, Rowland prepared a list of his party members for an official in Los Angeles:[6]

William Workman and family; William Gordon and family; James D. Mead, physician; Benjamin Wilson; [William] Knight; Jacob Frankfort, tailor; William Gambel, naturalist; Tomas Linsay, mineralogist; Hiram

Taylor, musician; Wade Hampton, gunsmith; Isaac Givens, engineer; John McClure, esquire; James Doke; L. Lyman, physician; [Daniel] Tibeau; Albert Toomes, carpenter; [Daniel] Sexton, carpenter; William Moore, cooper; [Fred] Bachelder, cooper; Francisco Bediley, carpenter; Francisco Guinn, blacksmith; Miguel Blanco [Michael White]; Lorenzo Trujillo and family; J. Manuel Baca and family; Ygno [Ignacio] Sallazar and servants; John Rowland.

In an interesting coincidence of history, the first two overland settlers' parties reached California only a day apart, one in the Bay Area and the other in Southern California. The Bidwell-Bartleson Party completed its six-month, 1,200-mile trip from Independence, Missouri, to Conta Costa County, California, on November 4, 1841, and the Rowland-Workman Party ended its western trek at the San Gabriel Mission the following day. The former party was the first group of settlers to reach Northern California; the latter was the first group of settlers to reach Southern California. But there were important differences between the two. The thirty-four-person Bidwell-Bartleson Party was exclusively white, and was all-male except for one woman and one child.[7] On the other hand, Wilson's Rowland-Workman Party was multi-cultural and included Jacob Frankfort, a German tailor in the group, who became the first Jewish resident in Los Angeles.[8] While the Bidwell-Bartleson Party came west for the agreed-upon purpose of settling, the Rowland-Workman Party included people with a variety of motives.

As the first overland parties of settlers to reach the West Coast the Bidwell-Bartleson and the Rowland-Workman parties were the first tentative drops in what would become a flood of two hundred thousand settlers to cross the plains in the next twenty years. They found a handful of Americans already settled along the West Coast, but most of these had arrived by ship or had defected from fur-trapping parties to settle in this part of Mexico. Those arriving in the Rowland-Workman Party included many of the early leaders of Southern California and Los Angeles specifically.

Wilson had no intention of settling in Southern California. Instead, he was fleeing a hostile New Mexico, and his dream was to get to China. He traveled to San Francisco three times seeking a ship to the Orient, but was unsuccessful each time and he gave up on his dream and settled among the California Mexican population, called Californios. Alta California was too sparsely populated at this time to qualify as a state of Mexico, and was classified as a territory.

The native Indians had been subjugated by the Spanish in earlier years and turned into virtual slaves for the Franciscan missions. A few generations later a secular Mexican society had replaced the mission-dominated culture of Spain, and the former mission Indians now served as the army of manual laborers that made possible the immense cattle ranches on the Spanish and Mexican land-grant cattle ranches, or ranchos, of the owners, called *rancheros*. The ranch hands for these cattle estates were horsemen called *vaqueros*, the profession known by Americans in later years as cowboys.

Benjamin Wilson fell into the California lifestyle and economy as a *ranchero*.

NOTES FOR CHAPTER 4

1 Beattie, "San Bernardino Valley Before the Americans Came," 113.
2 Rowland, *John Rowland and William Workman: Southern California Pioneers of 1841*, 55-56.
3 Spitzzeri, "'To Seduce and Confuse': The Rowland-Workman Expedition of 1841," 37.
4 Lawrence, "Mexican Trade Between Santa Fe and Los Angeles, 1830-1848," 34.
5 Spitzzeri, "'To Seduce and Confuse': The Rowland-Workman Expedition of 1841," 40.
6 Rowland, *John Rowland and William Workman: Southern California Pioneers of 1841*, 54-55.
7 Spitzzeri, "'To Seduce and Confuse': The Rowland-Workman Expedition of 1841," 46.
8 Vorspan, *History of the Jews of Los Angeles*.

CHAPTER 5

Jurupa Ranch

Some time during his stay in New Mexico or early in his Southern California life, Benjamin Wilson became known in the Spanish-speaking community as "Don Benito," ("Mister Benjamin"). He would be known by the names B.D. Wilson and Don Benito Wilson for the rest of his life. Many Americans in New Mexico and California had renounced their American citizenship and had become citizens of Mexico to enjoy the benefits and protection of the government in the land they had chosen to live in, but not Wilson. He never took Mexican citizenship and never converted to Catholicism. So, unlike his friends who were now Mexican citizens, he was not eligible for a land grant from Mexico. Foreigners were allowed to own property far away from the seacoast, though, so in late 1842 or early 1843, Wilson began discussions with Don Juan Bandini, mentioned in Richard Henry Dana's *Two Years Before the Mast*, to buy part of Bandini's *Rancho Jurupa*, an area now known as the City of Riverside. [1] Bandini had received the land in a grant from the government of Mexico a few years earlier, in 1838.

Wilson closed the deal with Bandini on May 6, 1843, a year and a half after arriving from New Mexico, paying a thousand dollars for the land.[2] Bandini was motivated to sell the properties to this rugged ex-mountain man since it would protect his remaining properties from the sheep-stealing Indians who were such a menace in the area. Indeed, when Wilson left his ranch a few years later, Bandini had to depart the area as well for his own safety.[3] Chief Cuaka, known at the time as Walker, lived as though the rancheros were building their stock for his personal taking, and he would emerge from the mountains during full moons to drive herds into the canyons, over the mountains and into the desert. From there he would drive them to Salt Lake City where he'd sell his booty.[4]

Don Juan Bandini, who sold the land to Wilson, was a *ranchero* mentioned in Richard Henry Dana's *Two Years Before the Mast*.

In Wilson's own words:

> After many unsuccessful efforts to leave California, and receiving so much kindness from the native Californians (Mexicans) I arrived at the conclusion that there was no place in the world where I could enjoy more true happiness and true friendship than among them. There were no courts, no juries, no lawyers, nor any need for them. The people were honest and hospitable, and their word was as good as their bond, indeed, bonds and notes of hand were entirely unknown among the natives. So . . . I settled upon the Ranch and led a *ranchero's* life for some years.

Wilson insisted that Bandini also give nearby land for a community of New Mexicans for added safety, since Indians raiding from the desert had been a dangerous nuisance to the New Mexicans who had begun to raise cattle there. A few New Mexicans from the Rowland-Workman Party, and even more from a group headed by Santiago Martinez, settled in 1843 on the 2,200 acres set aside for them by land barons Bandini and Antonio María Lugo at the northern end of the Jurupa Ranch. The settlement with its seventy-three inhabitants was known as Politana, although it appears in the records of the time variously as Politan, Apolitan, Land of Apolitan, Napolitan, Epolitana and Hypolitana, according to George Beattie writing in the *California Historical Quarterly* in 1934. The community was named for a man named Polito, who had brought a large party from near Taos.[5] The settlement sat high above the Santa Ana River, and was made up of eight adobe houses in a compact formation, or perhaps there were eight sections in one large building. There may even have been an outer defensive wall around Politana.

But the New Mexicans were soon gone. Vincente Lugo, a young family member whose land was adjacent to the New Mexicans' community, blocked the water from his Politana neighbors to care for his own stock. The New Mexicans suffered not only from lack of water but by Vincente's cattle flattening their crops. After they left, the Lugo family then offered the land to Indian chief Juan Antonio, who kept the marauders at bay with the help of forty or so of his Cahuilla warriors.

The New Mexicans who'd left the Lugo land came back to Don Bandini and accepted the original offer of Wilson of 2,200 acres in the "Bandini Donation." The New Mexicans' leader in this switch of land was Lorenzo Trujillo, a Comanche[6] Wilson had hired to accompany him on the Rowland-Workman trip from Santa Fe. Trujillo had gone back to New Mexico to collect his large family and cattle. Wilson and Trujillo had remained friends, and now Trujillo was bringing his family close to Wilson's ranch for their mutual defense against the cattle-stealing Indians. In one of the pursuits of Indians who were retreating with settlers' cattle, the Trujillo family caught up with the Indians in the mountains southeast of present-day Highgrove. Three Trujillo sons were injured. Doroteo caught an arrow in his back, Teodoro was shot in his right foot and Esquipula was shot through the nose, disfiguring him for life. All three survived, though, and the settlers recovered their cattle. Trujillo was an industrious leader and devout Catholic, who worked tirelessly to build a small church in the simple plaza faced by the New Mexicans' homes.

As history would evolve, Trujillo would save Don Benito Wilson's life, and the Lugo neighbors would try to kill Wilson.

Don Benito was asked to be the *alcalde* of the district. Although non-citizens were not required to accept such offices, and not even allowed to hold such posts by Mexican law, Wilson took the position because of the urgings of his friends and because it suited his own interests as well. The *alcalde* was the senior official of a civilian Spanish or Mexican town. This government title was taken from the Arabic/Moorish *Al-Cadi*, meaning village judge. *Alcalde* is perhaps best translated into English as justice of the peace, an official combining executive, legislative and judicial powers. [7]

This official combined the executive and judicial roles, but not the legislative. There is no direct equivalent in the American government model. Some translate the term as "mayor," but the *alcalde* was generally appointed, not elected.[8]

A year after buying the Jurupa Ranch Don Benito married his neighbor's daughter, Ramona Yorba, on February 20, 1844.[9] His neighbor, Don Bernardo Yorba, owned the 150,000-acre *Rancho Santa Ana*, a domain that is now Orange County. Wilson was thirty-two; Ramona, the youngest of four children, was fifteen.[10]

Father-in-law Don Bernardo Yorba's eighty-room mansion was two stories high with sweeping verandas. In and about it were shops, stores and rooms for gold and silversmiths, for leather toolers, saddlemakers, weavers and tailors. There were also wine cellars and presses, distilleries, mills, granaries, soap and tallow vats, chapels and residences—a whole *adobe pueblo*.[11]

On his Jurupa Ranch Wilson kept three hundred head of cattle and thirty horses[12] and grew grapes. An inventory at the time reflected stores of wheat and beans. Wilson built an adobe house seventy-two feet long and twenty-two feet wide with a deep and sturdy wine cellar for his wine and brandy. He installed bars on his windows for safety.[13]

A few months after marrying Ramona Yorba in 1844, Wilson went into the woods after a large bear that had killed one of his milk cows. He followed the bear's tracks past the carcass of the cow and he and his horse became entangled in some wild vines, when the bear came out of a nearby hiding place and brought Wilson and his horse to the ground. The bear bit Wilson on his hip and on his shoulder and into his lungs before his dogs caught up and scared it off. A ranch hand came to Wilson's aid and found Wilson's horse lying still on the ground. But as the *vaquero* approached the horse the animal jumped up and ran home at full speed. Wilson was carried home in a blanket, bleeding so profusely that he lost his sight and speech, although he could still think clearly. He kept the scar on his shoulder the rest of his life.

The bear continued to kill Don Benito's cattle almost every night, so as soon as Wilson recovered he was obliged to go looking for the bear again. He ordered a ranch hand to kill a calf and drag it to the area where the bear had been hanging around. Then Wilson and a servant armed themselves and waited in a sycamore tree near the bait for the bear to show up. Sure enough, around the hour of darkness the bear found the calf and began to dine. The two men opened fire, both hitting the bear. Wilson's shot entered the bear behind the shoulder and the servant's shot hit the animal's hind leg. Three times the bear tried to reach the men in the tree, but because of the wound to its leg was unable to reach its would-be assassins. When the bear had left, the two men returned home. The next morning Wilson collected all the neighbors and dogs available for bear hunting duty and went to finish off the beast once and for all. They followed the bear's trail to a marsh, where they looked high and low, but found no sign of him and were ready to give up, when Wilson, the one-time mountain man, spotted a tiny clue. A curious object "no larger than a black bird" was breaking the surface of the mud. Bears sought out mud to heal their wounds, Wilson was told later. Wilson was convinced that it was the tip of the bear's nose and he dismounted twenty feet away to make sure of his shot to the bear's brain, a place where a bullet could kill a grizzly bear. Before he could shoot, however, the bear leapt with lightning speed from its therapeutic mud bath and charged Wilson, coming close to mauling him a second time. A shower of bullets from the hunting party finally killed the bear once and for all.

Between 1846 and 1848 Wilson sold Jurupa as the casual, carefree lifestyle of Southern California *rancheros* came to an end. Louis Robidoux bought the *Rancho Jurupa* and his name (later spelled Rubidoux) is prominent today as a Riverside-area place name.

Notes for Chapter 5

1 Woodward, "Benjamin Davis Wilson's Observations on Early Days in California and New Mexico," 136.

2 Gunther, *Riverside County, California, Place Names: Their Origins and Their Stories*, 260.

3 Beattie, "San Bernardino Valley Before the Americans Came," 111-124.

4 Hornbeck, *Roubidoux's Ranch In the 70's*, 64-65.

5 Beattie, "San Bernardino Valley Before the Americans Came," 111-124.

6 Judge Benjamin Hayes thought him to be a pure Pueblo Indian. Whelan, "Eden in the Jurupa Valley: The Story of *Agua Mansa*," 419.

7 Grivas, "Alcalde Rule: The Nature of Local Government in Spanish and Mexican California," 11-32.

8 Ibid., 11-32.

9 Wilson-Patton Bible, B.D. Wilson papers.

10 Stephenson, *Don Bernardo Yorba*, 39.

11 Conde, "Santa Ana of the Yorbas, which might have become Pastoral California's Greatest Semi-Feudal Hacienda," 70-71.

12 Account of property taken by the Insurgents at Jurupa belonging to Benjamin D. Wilson. Certification by Abel Stearns, Eulogio de Célis and Charles William Flügge, Joseph L. Perdu. May 5, 1847, Wilson Correspondence Collection, Huntington Library, San Marino, California.

13 Klotz, *Adobes, Bungalows, and Mansions of Riverside, California.*

CHAPTER 6

Governor Micheltorena

After his defeat by the Americans under Sam Houston in Texas, Mexican president Antonio López de Santa Anna was leery of Americans and determined to keep them from claiming California as well. He directed his new governor of California, Manuel Micheltorena, who had fought with him in Texas, to keep a force in Alta California that was large enough to discourage any thought of American adventurism. Micheltorena, having no place else to raise such a force, emptied the prisons and surrounded himself in California with an army of dregs and ruffians, landing with his force of riff-raff in San Diego in 1842. So wretched was this band of thieves that they came ashore with their scroungy families with no uniforms—in fact, with practically no clothing of any kind—hiding their dirty bodies with filthy blankets. At least that's how Micheltorena's critics described them.

Once in Los Angeles, then the capital city of California, Micheltorena tried to govern as a responsible official, while his army of misfits, in uniforms at last, fanned out through the area like ravaging ants, stripping chicken coops, orchards and vineyards of every item of value, or so it seemed to the involuntary donors. Since the sordid soldiers received little or no salary, they paid themselves with what they could steal. In 1844 a revolution ignited in Santa Clara and Micheltorena marched with five hundred men to quash it. He was aided by Captain John A. Sutter (later of Gold Rush fame) and Sutter's company of militarily trained Indians. The rebels, under former Governor Don Juan Batista Alvarado and former civil commander José Castro, retreated with ninety men to Los Angeles. The Los Angeles political leadership voted to "depose" Micheltorena and replace him with former Governor Pío Pico. Micheltorena marched slowly towards Los Angeles to capture the city and rid himself of the shadow government. Los Angeles residents knew that Micheltorena's ruffians would plunder the city once again if they could capture it.

As the *alcalde* of his area, Wilson was directed to bring every able-bodied man in his district to Los Angeles to take up arms against Micheltorena and his hooligans. Wilson gathered twenty to thirty men and joined an excited crowd in Los Angeles making provisions and preparing ammunition for a defense of the city. The following morning the force of about fifty men marched to the Cahuenga Valley about fifteen miles from Micheltorena's forces which were camped in Encino. The two armies, both about four hundred strong, wasted shot at extremely long range, the only casualty of the day being either an unlucky mule or a horse (the accounts vary). Wilson had friends among the Americans on the other side and he knew that most of them were fighting because they expected land grants for their effort. He arranged for a white flag of truce and met with Americans who were fighting for Micheltorena. He told them that they were enlisted under a man who was opposed to Americans and whose minions were "rabble." Confirming that none of the Americans were Mexican citizens he explained to them that their land grants under Micheltorena were invalid under Mexican law. He further offered to protect their land titles tentatively and guarantee them under Governor Pío Pico if they would become Mexican citizens. Governor Pío Pico was nearby and Wilson summoned him to confirm what he had said, while Wilson translated. The Americans abandoned Micheltorena's cause, and Micheltorena then surrendered, marched his hooligans to San Pedro and boarded a ship for Mexico. Wilson's diplomacy had forged a successful revolution.

CHAPTER 7

Renegade Indians in Bear Lake and Palm Springs

Now governor of California once again, thanks in large part to Wilson, Pío Pico turned to Wilson for military, rather than diplomatic, help. In July or August of 1845 Governor Pico asked Wilson to lead a major campaign against the Mojaves and other Indians who had been such a constant threat to ranches in the area. In doing so, Pico imitated the Hollywood stereotype of a frustrated chief of police who calls in Superman when his own forces fall short. Governor Pico, unable to bring the lawless Indians under control, offered Wilson a force of eighty well-armed mounted men for the expedition into the San Bernardino Mountains. It is a tribute to Wilson's leadership skills that the governor would enlist a foreigner, who had only owned his ranch in the area for two years, to lead such an important expedition—one which apparently included Mexican soldiers.

Wilson organized a pack train and sent it up through the Cajon Pass, while he and twenty-two young *Californios* climbed the mountains up the Santa Ana River (then known as the San Bernardino River).[1] Wilson's party came onto an Indian village which had been abandoned shortly beforehand, except for two elderly Indian women and some children. Two days into the expedition, in the evening, they came to a lake teeming with bears. This lake was probably the lake known today as Lower Bear Lake, a body of water that separates Bear Valley from Baldwin Valley. The twenty-two men with him went out in pairs and each of the eleven pairs came back to camp with a captive bear. Wilson gave the body of water the name Bear Lake. Today's names of Big Bear Lake and Bear Valley derive from the name Wilson impulsively gave the shallow, swampy Lower Bear Lake that day.[2] (The lake we know of today as Big Bear Lake was created in 1884 by the founders of the town of Redlands, who needed more water for their farms).

Wilson and his party of twenty-two continued down the Mojave River joining up with the rest of the command and pressing on for another four days. Wilson had gone out in advance of the troop, using his mountain-man skills to look for signs of Indians. Wilson spotted four Indians coming along the path in their direction before the Indians saw him, so he ducked down into the river bed and continued to a point which he guessed to be even with the Indians. Planning to take them alive and interrogate them, he called out in a friendly way, and they called back in a likewise friendly manner. Wilson then recognized one of the quartet as the very ringleader his expedition was after, a man Wilson later referred to as Joaquin. This Indian had been brought up as a page at the San Gabriel Mission and years later had been punished for wrongdoings at the *Rancho Santa Ana del Chino* by having his ear cut off and an iron brand seared into his hip. As Joaquin talked to Wilson he spotted others in the expedition coming towards them, and the Indian immediately knew that this party had come for him and his gang.

There followed a moment worthy of the most dramatic Hollywood western. In super-slow motion, we can see Joaquin's smile turn to alarm and, instinctively, the Indian, in one fluid motion, reaches over this shoulder for an arrow which he brings to the string of his bow, pulling the arrow in one uninterrupted motion. Wilson, on his mule, recognizes in that split second the hostile act unfolding and reaches for his pistol. In this Hollywood cliché Wilson has no time to bring his pistol to shoulder height for a proper shot and must fire from his hip the instant he can turn his gun. The two antagonists fire at precisely the same moment, and arrow passes bullet half-way between the two heroic figures. Both find their mark. We can hear the "thwack" as the arrow embed itself in Wilson's shoulder, causing him to drop his firearm, and the bullet buries itself in the Indian's chest, both men gravely wounded. Joaquin will die an agonizing death from his wound using his final energy in a tirade of the most vulgar Spanish directed at the Spanish-speaking race.

Wilson dismounted to pick up his pistol and ordered his men to overtake the three remaining Indians who were escaping on the open plain and to bring them back alive. Eighty men took off in pursuit, but the Indians, preferring not to be taken prisoners, fought the legion of pursuers to their deaths. Some of the men returned to find Joaquin still alive, and they finished him off.

The arrow that had struck Wilson turned out to be poisoned. Indians prepared their poison from rotting meat and blood, which they dried into sticks to be carried in leather cases. They then rubbed the deadly sticks onto their arrows, softening the sticks in the fire if they'd gotten too dry.

To dress his wound Wilson rode down to the river, about five hundred yards away. His arm and shoulder had already swollen alarmingly and were causing Wilson great pain. Lorenzo Trujillo sucked the poison from his wound. Trujillo was the trusted Comanche Indian who had come with Wilson in the Rowland-Workman Party from New Mexico to California and who had installed the community of *La Placita de los Trujillos* next to Wilson's *Rancho Jurupa* land.

Wilson was too ill to travel and stayed where he was with five of his men. The pain finally disappeared after three or four days, but Wilson carried a piece of the arrow in his shoulder for the rest of his life. Meanwhile the expedition had proceeded under the second in command, Enrique Avila, a *Californio* who was to become the *alcalde* of Los Angeles two years later. Under Avila's command the men chased the Indians into the mountains, where the Indians fortified themselves and badly wounded several of their attackers before Avila led his party back to camp. With the wounded men to care for and with the horses ridden to the limit of their endurance, Wilson abandoned the campaign.

The expedition returned to Wilson's *Rancho Jurupa* for new provisions and fresh horses. The injured left the party there, as did some others, leaving about sixty men to continue the campaign against the Mission Indians turned bad. The refreshed party headed up through the San Gorgonio Pass and into the blazing hot low desert, a region now known as the Palm Springs area, after two Indian ringleaders who had traded their neophyte mission past for a life of violence and plunder and were living among the Cahuilla Indians. The Cahuillas had been friendly to the Whites but their leader, Chief Cabazon, intercepted the Wilson party in a place then called Agua Caliente, probably the site of present-day Palm Springs. This Chief Cabazon was one of two Cabazon chiefs of the period 1840 to 1870.[3] He had maintained friendly relations with the Whites, refusing to ally his people with the Colorado River Indian clans who were hostile to the Whites. Wilson told the chief that their mission was to seek out the refugee thieves, but Chief Cabazon told Wilson he would not allow the party in Cahuilla territory for that purpose. Wilson replied that he had no desire to make war with the Cahuillas, but was determined to find the individuals who'd been causing havoc with his people. The chief tried to discourage Wilson, warning that his party and its animals would surely die in the wilting desert heat where there was no grass or water. He was trying to reason with the wrong man, though. Wilson had lived for years among Indians and knew that if the natives could exist in those parts, the White Man could also. The conversation see-sawed back and forth until a frustrated Don Benito ended the discussion by ordering his men to seize the chief and his twenty chosen followers and hold them hostage. The chief cried and protested that he had always been a friend to the white man.

Wilson stood firm, offering Chief Cabazon two alternatives. Either Wilson's expedition could proceed through Cahuilla territory as a hostile army on the march, or the chief could dispatch a few of his warriors to bring back the pillaging Indians Wilson was seeking dead or alive. When the old chief continued to argue, Wilson made plans to mount war against the Cahuilla Band. Only then did Chief Cabazon consult with his followers and relent, asking that the chief's brother, Adan, and twelve other chosen associates, be released. Two days would be needed for the mission. The chief and six or seven of his men would remain hostage in Wilson's camp. Don Benito agreed.

The heat was the worst Wilson had ever experienced. The men found the searing desert floor too hot to sit on so they stood all day long fanning themselves with their hats. In the evening of the second day the Indian party could be heard returning to the camp, and the chief said that he could tell by the singing of his men that they had fulfilled their mission. Wilson, ever wary, sent half his men out to meet the returning Cahuillas, lest they be returning to make war. As the Wilson party waited, fully armed and ready for any deception, a delegation of forty to fifty warriors stopped a quarter of a mile from camp and Adan, the chief's brother, approached with another Cahuilla and happily threw the severed heads of the wanted men at Wilson's feet. Adan described a heated battle with the renegades and their followers in which several men had been wounded and Adan had been struck in the thigh by an arrow. None had been killed, however, except the two thief leaders. The expedition had ended successfully, and, as dawn of the third day was breaking Wilson presented to the chief as a goodwill gift the immense supply of stores which the expedition had brought along in anticipation of an extended campaign. The party then returned to Wilson's Jurupa Ranch before beginning the next phase of their eradication campaign. Chief Cabazon lived to be ninety or so and, as an old man, turned his leadership over to his son, who was also remembered by the Cahuillas as a revered leader.

When Wilson told a group of ten or twelve visiting mountain men how his campaign in the Bear Lake area had ended in victory for the Indians, the trappers were incensed and wanted to go with him to finish the job. Wilson persuaded his friend Don Enrique Avila to join him with ten picked men. The combined party of twenty headed along the Mojave River, once again bent on cleaning out the Indian stronghold. The Mojave River runs today north of present-day San Bernardino roughly parallel to Interstate 15 from Crestline to perhaps forty miles northeast of Barstow.

As they trooped down the Mojave River they came to the home village of the Indians who had staved off their expedition in the mountains. Splitting up, Wilson's men surrounded the village and demanded that the Indians surrender. No deal. Instead, the Indians shot in the back one of those trying to reason with them. Wilson ordered his men to fire, and when the battle was finished, every single Indian man in the village lay dead. Wilson took the women and children prisoners and marched them to the San Gabriel Mission, where he left them in the care of the resident officials. Thus, in three campaigns Wilson had wiped out the colony of marauding thieves who had so tormented settlers in the area of present-day San Bernardino and Riverside.

NOTES FOR CHAPTER 7

1   Core, *Big Bear Grizzly.*

2   Ibid.

3   Woodward, Arthur, "Benjamin Davis Wilson's Observations on Early Days in California and New Mexico," 137-138.

CHAPTER 8

The
Mexican War

In the mid-1840s the United States was torn on the subject of slavery and an equal number of slave and non-slave states had been admitted as part of the Missouri Compromise. Annexing California, geographically a Southern state, could keep the balance if a geographically northern state was to be admitted. Americans had been taking up residence in California in growing numbers since Mexican law had allowed their immigration in 1824. They were coming, not to become Mexican citizens but in the belief that manifest destiny would extend the United States to their new California home. American Commodore T.A.C. Jones had raised the Stars and Stripes in Monterey in 1842 thinking that war had broken out between his country and Mexico, then hauled it down, with apologies, the following day when he realized his error. On May 13, 1846, the United States declared war on Mexico, but California would not know about that act until months later. On June 14, 1846, an independent California was proclaimed in Sonoma under the homely design of a Bear Flag. A few weeks later Commodore John Drake Sloat declared California part of the United States as he raised the American flag in Monterey. There were soon rumors in Southern California that American military units were marching toward Los Angeles.

Wilson's friend, Governor Pío Pico, asked him to raise troops to help repel these foreign troops. Wilson was a settled member of the Mexican community of Southern California. He spoke the Spanish language fluently, was married to a Mexican wife, his daughter bore a Spanish name and he held office as the senior official in the district where he lived. Different American expatriates took different sides in this conflict that pitted their adopted country against their native country. Wilson bore a grudge the rest of his life against fellow ex-pats like Abel Stearns, who'd come to California from the sea and had amassed more wealth and position in Mexican Los Angeles than any other American. Wilson wrote,

> In 1846 when the American flag was raised in California the great majority of the Americans . . . took pride in offering their services to the American cause, but their (sic) were a few . . . who took pride in vowing that they were Mexican Citizens and refused to aid the American cause . . . Amongst the latter was Don Abel Stearns. For Stearns by every act showed every possible hatred towards [the] American cause.[1]

So, when Governor Pío Pico pressed Wilson to take up arms with his neighbors, Don Benito turned the governor down, noting that he was an American citizen. He also protested that he was not a military man, a disingenuous claim, since he'd led expeditions against renegade Indians at the request of this same Governor Pico and had raised a contingent of armed men to fight the forces of Governor Micheltorena on behalf of Pico.

About a dozen Americans gathered at Wilson's ranch because it had become unsafe for them elsewhere in the current climate of saber rattling. A *Californio* called at Wilson's ranch to warn that Wilson would be arrested if he did not throw in with the Mexican side. Wilson's machismo boiled. He countered that no one should try to arrest him for he would resist. He pledged his word that if allowed "to remain quietly on my ranch" he would "be peaceable, and do no act hostile to the country."

When Commodore Stockton's squadron arrived in San Pedro for a campaign against Los Angeles, Governor Pico called Wilson to his office asking him to convey to the commodore that he was leaving California for Sonora, that General Juan José Castro "had broken camp and left" and that Los Angeles was an open city. Pico asked Wilson to request that Stockton "not ill treat my people." As Wilson met Commodore Stockton he also presented the favorite saddle horse of a member of the Dominguez family, one of the leading *rancheros* of Southern California. After pleasantries, Wilson invited the commodore to mount his new horse and ride with him to the center of Los Angeles, with Wilson guaranteeing the naval commander's safety. As Wilson was taking his leave from Los Angeles a few days later the commodore said, "I don't think we ought to place too much reliance on Castro's actual leaving for Sonora. . . . he may go only to the frontier and await for a rabble of Sonoranians, to come back and retake the country."

The commodore then said he wanted Wilson in military command to guard against such a threat. Again Wilson protested that he was not a military man, to which Commodore Stockton said, "That is nonsense. You have a ranch on the frontier. There is no other person . . . I can trust who knows the people or understands their language."

Stockton knew Wilson's ability to inspire other Americans to serve under him, so he offered Don Benito a commission in the U.S. Army as a captain. Wilson accepted on the condition that he not be required to serve outside of Southern California where his family and business interests were. Captain Benjamin D. Wilson, U.S. Army, gathered twenty-two men to serve in his new company. Wilson later confirmed that Castro had, indeed, fled to Sonora, crossing at Yuma with his small force. Satisfied that the danger had passed, Commodore Stockton sailed away, leaving Marine Lieutenant Archibald Gillespie at the head of the provisional American government in Los Angeles and in charge of a token military force. Bad choice!

Gillespie turned victory into defeat. With a harsh dictatorial style he alienated a community which had accepted with easy grace the coming of American rule. Gillespie designed regulations to irritate the people and he arrested some of the most respected men in the community on the flimsiest of pretenses, apparently for the sole purpose of humiliating them.

While Wilson undoubtedly knew of Gillespie's unpopularity, he apparently saw no threat to the public peace. With nothing to do as leader of his military company, he went to visit some Indian friends and enjoy some hunting and fishing. A few days into his holiday an urgent message was delivered to him telling of a general revolt in the city. Wilson traveled all night and arrived at his ranch by daybreak. On September 25, 1846, a number of American families had gathered at his Jurupa Ranch and others at the home of Louis Robidoux for safety. Wilson had squandered most of his ammunition supply on his hunting trip, but found a letter waiting for him from Colonel Isaac "Don Julian" Williams urging Don Benito and his men to come to his *Rancho Santa Ana del Chino*, adding that he had plenty of ammunition. The horses of the Wilson party were fatigued, but the *Californios* had cleaned out Wilson's fresh mounts, so the party of Americans hobbled along on tired animals, according to an account by Matt Harbin, one of Wilson's men.[2] About ten miles into their forty-mile trek across a treeless plain the *Californio* cavalry formed up at long range on both sides of the Americans and kept up a distant barrage. One American, Evan Callaghan, was wounded, but returned fire and hit Captain José Diego Sepúlveda in the thigh.

Known simply as the Chino Ranch, its ranch house was located about three miles southwest of present day Chino Hills just outside the southeastern end of today's Boy's Republic school for troubled youngsters. When Wilson and his men showed up at the ranch abode, though, they found that U.S. soldiers had taken away all of Williams' ammunition.

In recounting the events that followed, Wilson would later go into considerable detail, the kind that people painstakingly weave into their memoirs as they explain away some ignoble chapter in their history, lobbying historians of the future to absolve them of faulty judgment. Wilson was in command, but he wanted future generations to understand that he saw clearly the coming doom and would have avoided it entirely but for the bravado and poor judgment of his men. Even though he was their commander, he yielded again and again to their misguided assessment of the military situation, he would have us believe. Don Benito was used to leading men in pitched battles. He'd been doing it as a mountain man and frontiersman most of his life, but mountain men and frontiersmen follow only where they want to go, and do not blindly follow a superior officer in the way that drilled military men do. Wilson bowed to the strong conclusions of his men out of loyalty, or so he later said.

Wilson says that he pointed out to them that they had little hope of withstanding a siege with so little ammunition, and that they should make their way to Los Angeles along the safety of the mountain foothills, but the men were new to Southern California and had a condescending view of the *Californio's* courage and battle skills. They accused Don Benito of cowardice. Wilson agreed to stay with them and even agreed not to try to exercise command over them. They were, after all, volunteers. Wilson then crafted a note to Gillespie explaining their tenuous position, their lack of ammunition and the improbability of their coming to the Army's aid in Los Angeles. He hid the note in the false heel of a trusted employee of his host, Colonel Williams, but Williams called the servant back and instructed him to deliver the note to the Mexican forces under Captain Flores instead of to the American forces.[3] As night fell, Wilson's men could see a force of Mexicans on horseback. Wilson estimated their number at eighty to one hundred. Robidoux said two hundred; Harbin said 330. Wilson's account attributes the arrival of Mexican cavalry to this messenger, yet Harbin's account described a cavalry force dogging the Americans all the way to the ranch.

Wilson counseled his men that the coming night would allow them to steal away to safety. Once again his men said, "No! We can whip all they can bring against us."[4] By daybreak the cavalry all but surrounded the house. The adobe house was built in the typical plan, with rooms built around an inner patio, the outer wall having a door or two large enough for carts, and a few windows, but basically blank. A blacksmith's shop stood in one corner. The blacksmith was a deaf Englishman who was kept busy cutting copper rods into slugs for the guns, since the men were short on ammunition. According to Harbin, the Mexicans who died expired from poisoning from this metal. The attackers had only to dash to the windowless outside walls where they were safe from gunfire from those inside. The defenders had only muzzle-loading guns, so they were not able to fire more than two or three shots as the attackers rushed to the safety of the outer wall. Knowing that Wilson and the defenders were trapped inside, the attackers set fire to the cane and tar roof and the house burned rapidly, filling with smoke and a foul odor. The attack had lasted only about an hour.[5]

Harbin defended the blacksmith shop, losing two men to wounds. Lieutenant Carlos Ballesteros, a good friend of Wilson, commanded the troops opposite Harbin. Harbin and Ballesteros rose on opposite sides of the window at the same time and they fired simultaneously. Harbin's hand was injured for life and Ballesteros died of a wound to the head. The commander of the troops, Cerbulo Varela, came to the large door and called for his friend, Wilson, guaranteeing the safety of the men if they would surrender. The defenders really had no choice. Wilson heard the firing around the blacksmith shop and came to order a cease fire and surrender.

These *Californio* troops who had tried to kill Wilson and the Americans and had taken them prisoners were his neighbors, the same former New Mexicans whom he had implanted alongside his rancho for their mutual defense. Wilson had sought them out, to fight with him, but the Lugo family had already rounded up about twenty of them to join with compatriots from Los Angeles into a fighting force for the locals.

The role of the ranch owner, Colonel Williams, is curious. He had asked Wilson to bring troops to his ranch, promising ammunition, then directed a messenger to alert the Mexican troops, according to the messenger's own testimony later. It is unclear why he would alert Mexican fighters and remain with the defenders during a pitched battle. Now, as the choking smoke filled his house he climbed to his roof with his three children and shouted his allegiance to the Mexican cause. "Don't shoot me! Don't shoot me!" he called. Some of the Mexican troops called him a coward in return.

Cerbulo Valera, the Mexican commander, allowed Wilson to keep his own horse and ride at his side while Wilson's men were marched ahead as a group, a few of them injured, two of them badly. Captain Sepúlveda, who had been wounded in the running battle the day before, lined up the Americans to shoot them, but Valera spotted the attempt and rode forward to intercede by putting himself between his troops and the Americans. He told them in a commanding voice that he had given his word for their safe treatment and if they must shoot someone, shoot him.

The Americans, about twenty in number,[6] were marched to an adobe in Boyle Heights which would serve as a prison. When a priest arrived with a cross Louis Robidoux panicked, believing the father to be there for last rights, which turned out not to be true. Wilson was taken to the *comandante general* Don José M. Flores and asked to write a message to Captain Gillespie, noting that with the Wilson party prisoners the

American cause was hopeless. Flores would allow Gillespie to march to San Pedro with their arms and leave the area by ship. Otherwise, General Flores said he could not be responsible for the certain attack by his drunken troops. Gillespie accepted the terms, leaving town with his men the following morning. Flores then made plans to send his trophy prisoners to Mexico City, but a number of *Californios*, perhaps fearing the retribution of Americans when they came to power, thwarted him from shipping off the *yanqui* prisoners to an unpleasant fate the night before they were to begin their trek. The American POWs remembered the unpleasant fate of Texas prisoners who had been marched from New Mexico to Mexico City, suffering so much that half of their number died on the road. So, Wilson and his fellow prisoners pooled their money to help influence Flores' removal from office. The general was able to resume his command only after he promised to keep the POWs in town.[7]

From the Boyle Heights jail Wilson and his men were transferred to one of the most notable locations in Los Angeles, an 1835 adobe building which would later be known as the Bella Union Hotel. Many important chapters of early Los Angeles history would be written in this building. In fact, Wilson himself would own it for some time. Here a doctor first visited the injured Americans. He was an Irish physician, Richard Den. The venerable American expatriate, Abel Stearns, never lifted a finger to help Wilson and his men and never once visited them. The men were in miserable condition until a Spaniard, Eulogis Celis, acting out of charity, came by to survey the prisoners' needs and returned with blankets, clothing and tobacco and a rebuke to the harsh Mexican guards who were treating the Americans as common criminals rather than prisoners of war. The authorities threatened the POWs every day and Wilson had little hope of surviving the ordeal.[8]

About two months after the battle of Chino, in November of 1846, the temporary Mexican commander Don Antonio José Carillo marched the prisoners to Cerritos and made a plan for Wilson to play a further role in the war. Wilson was to stand on the San Pedro landing, raising a white flag, upon the arrival of Commodore Stockton with his enlarged force. Wilson would communicate that the American interests in the city were safe and that commodore should not try to take the city by force because of the blood that would be shed as a result. Meanwhile Carillo's four hundred to five hundred horse soldiers made a great dust cloud. This show of force worked too well. The commodore fled the scene entirely.

A few months after that, in January, 1847, prominent *Californios*, including Don Andres Pico, came to parole the prisoners. Commodore Stockton was making his way toward Los Angeles from the south, and General Kearny was approaching from the east. The *Californios* had no troops to spare as prison guards. If the POWs did not steal away the rabble would do them in. Pico offered Wilson and Rowland two of the finest horses in the country. Wilson's horse was equipped with its regal silver-trimmed saddle, bridle and spurs. Wilson was able to reunite with his family, staying with his father-in-law, Don Bernardo Yorba, and Rowland joined his family at the *Rancho La Puente*. The rest of the men dispersed through nearby vineyards rather than risk recognition on the streets and roads.

Wilson rode to where he could see the battle between the two forces, eager to know the fate of the country, and his own, which depended on how the Americans fared. Wilson then was met by two prominent *Californios* from Monterey, Joaquin and Gabriel de la Torre, and interceded successfully on their behalf with Commodore Stockton in Los Angeles.

Then Wilson met General Andres Pico, whose noble horse he had been riding. Pico, also, asked Wilson to take him to Commodore Stockton. In a major breach of military procedure, Pico had surrendered his troops to the grandstanding Colonel John C. Frémont, instead of to the senior enemy commander, Commodore Stockton. Though Stockton was most unhappy with Pico, he graciously accepted his abject apologies.

Commodore Stockton retired to his ship with all of his men, leaving the official American command in the hands of General Kearny. General Kearny was in a ticklish position. Colonel John C. Frémont was ignoring the command structure in accepting the surrender of the Mexican army (for which he was later court-martialed). The general's fifteen- to twenty-man personal guard was no match for the number of fighting men loyal to the ambitious and unpredictable Frémont. General Kearny kept Wilson close to him, as someone he could trust and someone who knew the local people well. General Kearny left Los Angeles to avoid a show-down with Frémont and kept Wilson by his side all the way to the Santa Ana River, well south of Los Angeles. Wilson even recruited a few *Californios* to ride with them for additional protection. Wilson never saw General Kearny again, although he would become quite involved with Frémont in the years ahead.

Notes for Chapter 8

1 Wilson, Benjamin D., fragment of writing, perhaps c. 1853. Huntington Library.

2 Lewis, "'I Surrender Nothing!' Matt Harbin at the Battle of Rancho Chino," 10-15. Harbin's account of the events surrounding the Battle of Chino come from his petition to the federal government for a pension, as a veteran of the Mexican War. His account of the events was written about forty years after the encounter and he seems to take personal credit for actions of the entire force, so the details of his narrative may not be entirely accurate.

3 Wilson, "Observations."

4 Ibid.

5 Weber, "Louis Robidoux: Two Letters From California, 1848," 107.

6 Wilson, Benjamin D., fragment of writing, perhaps c. 1853. Huntington Library.

7 Weber, "Louis Robidoux: Two Letters From California, 1848," 107.

8 Wilson, Benjamin D., fragment of writing, perhaps c. 1853. Huntington Library.

CHAPTER 9

The Move to Los Angeles

Wilson's young wife, Ramona, had given birth to a daughter, María de Jesús, on December 30, 1844, nine months and ten days after their marriage. Ramona had conceived when she was fifteen and given birth when she was sixteen. The daughter bore the name of María de Jesús Alvarado, Ramona's mother, who had died two days after Ramona's birth.[1] In the years to come, growing up in an increasingly American culture, María Jesús became known as Sue. Ramona was pregnant again when her husband was captured in the Battle of Chino and she gave birth to a son while he was in prison. The son, John B., was born on December 30, 1846.

In 1847, now thirty-six years of age, Wilson was living under the American flag for the first time since he started out from St. Louis as a mountain man at age twenty-two. Now out of prison and free of his abortive military career, he resumed making his way in the frontier world. His original three hundred head of cattle had grown to two thousand, but he had become a merchant once again, with a place of business in "the pueblo," as Los Angeles was called in those days.[2] He built a handsome house on Alameda Street (An *alameda* is a public walk lined by shade trees) just east of the plaza, where Cesar E. Chavez Avenue now separates the old Terminal Annex post office and Union Station, cater-cornered from the north end of Olvera Street.[3] He described his location as "not in town . . . only on the edge of town." He wrote that it was "all enclosed where I am quite retired if I choose to be."[4] His house was one of the first frame buildings in Los Angeles.[5] On his land he grew grapes and a variety of other fruit.[6]

In moving to Los Angeles, Wilson disposed of his cattle by driving them north to Sutter's Fort, near present-day Sacramento. In the fall of 1847 he proceeded through the *Cajon de las Uvas* (Grapevine Canyon), which is known today as simply "The Grapevine," and is the route today used by vehicle traffic on the I-5 Interstate. In his journey up the state he did not encounter a single white person living in his path. He arrived only a few months before gold was discovered at Sutter's Fort.

That discovery caused a frenzy that brought hundreds of thousands of people, mostly men, to California to seek their fortune. The population of the state ballooned, almost overnight, from about twelve thousand to over 107,000.[7] With this flood came the dregs of human detritus and some of the riff-raff drifted down to Southern California, which was still virtually uninhabited.

After the Mexican War and his months as a POW, Wilson had given up cattle ranching and re-entered a trade he knew well: merchandising and trading. Among his clients was John C. Frémont, the colorful and controversial Army officer who would become one of the original California senators and the first presidential candidate of the new Republican Party. Frémont asked Wilson to buy cattle for him, and then had trouble paying his debt to Wilson. He also asked Wilson to buy him "a property some where (sic) in the vicinity of the Pueblo," sensing that land was a good investment in this fast-growing state.[8] After retiring from the U.S. Senate in 1851, Frémont wrote to Wilson, saying he still was not able to repay what he owed.[9]

In the waning years of the 1840s Wilson did business as B.D. Wilson & Company, but began to do more and more business with Albert Packard. By late 1849 Wilson had bought fifty-thousand dollars worth of goods in separate accounts for himself and Packard, "mostly Mexican," although Wilson complained that competition had begun to make business less profitable in Los Angeles.[10] Wilson suggested that the two of them buy from Pío Pico, a store in San Diego, but Packard evidently didn't agree to the offer.[11] In 1850 Wilson entered a formal partnership with Packard and began doing business as Wilson & Packard on New Year's Day.[12] Together the men built a forty-two-square-foot store in the pueblo on the southeast corner of *La Calle Principal* (Main Street) and *La Calle Commercial*[13] with ten-foot-high walls, five feet of adobe on top of five feet of stone. They paid the firm of Granger and Brier twelve hundred dollars to build their new fifteen-door, eight-window emporium.[14] There turned out to be a problem with this location, in that ox-cart *carreta* drivers cut the corner, driving on the walkway by his store as they wheeled around his building, so Wilson devised a novel solution. Wilson half-buried two cannons in the street at the corner, preventing the wagoners from coming too close to his establishment.[15] Wilson said that Pío Pico had buried these heavy cast iron cannons during the Mexican War and had disclosed their location to Commodore Stockton as a gesture of good will. When Stockton said he had no use for them, Wilson sent men to retrieve them for his own use.[16]

From their downtown store Wilson and Packard bought hides and tallow and sold the kinds of things Los Angeles residents needed for their daily lives: [17]

Foodstuffs, such as sugar, cocoa, rice, arrowroot, coffee, chocolate, and cinnamon

Tools, including crowbars, axes, hatchets, butcher knives, manila rope, and paint

Fabric and clothing, such as stockings, flannel, muslin, aprons, beaver overcoats, mantillas (fine silk shawls), scarves, silk hose, "fine morning gowns," shoes, buttons, and silk vests,

Luxuries, such as bundles of tobacco, "segars," pale ale, claret, gin, and monte cards

Bibles in both English and Spanish[18]

But their business was more than that of a retail general store. Away from the store the partners also sold horses and jackasses and invested in mining operations and other business ventures.[19] Inside the store the facility served as the Los Angeles post office, with a tub on the counter containing mail for patrons to sort through for themselves.[20]

On December 1, 1851, the partnership of Wilson & Packard dissolved, and Packard moved to Santa Barbara to practice law.[21] The two embittered businessmen went their separate ways, but the acrimony continued in court and correspondence for years.[22] In 1853 Wilson leased the store to S.R. LaBatt, who offered imported goods from China in his *Tienda de China*.[23] Wilson grew even richer, but he never again worked as a merchant.

In 1850, Don Benito Wilson was one of the four richest men in Los Angeles County, listing his property value at fifty thousand dollars in the 1850 Census. Two other men, John Temple and Juan Luis Vignes, listed the same real-estate net worth, and only one man, Abel Stearns, at eighty-thousand dollars, declared more wealth. Temple was a native of Reading, Massachusetts, who had sailed to California from the Sandwich Islands (Hawaii) in 1827 to open the city's first general merchandising store. By the time Wilson opened his own store in the pueblo, Temple had moved on to land speculation and building and ranching, amassing so much money that he was able to purchase the mint of the nation of Mexico. Vignes, a native of France, also came by way of the Sandwich Islands. He brought with him a stock of religious ware that he sold at great profit and settled down to become a vintner and the area's first commercial orange grower.[24] Both Temple and Vignes are remembered in downtown Los Angeles street names today.

Don Abel Stearns was the only man in Los Angeles wealthier than Don Benito Wilson, and one of the only men to challenge Wilson for the title of most influential man in the early city of Los Angeles. Stearns, a native of Salem, Massachusetts, had moved in 1828 from within Mexico to a Los Angeles whose non-Indian population was only 764. He was one of perhaps ten or fewer expatriates in town.[25] He established himself as a middleman in the first rudimentary port facility at San Pedro. He bought and warehoused the hides, tallow, horses, soap, horns and other products of the local rancheros and traded them to the passing ships for goods that he could sell to the local population from a retail store in the pueblo. Prior to his centralized process, a ship's officer known as a "supercargo" rode from rancho to rancho trading the ships' goods for the *rancheros'* hides and tallow in a time-consuming process.[26] Stearns' dealings in the difficult system imposed by Mexican officialdom led to charges against him of smuggling. It was said that Steans was only bettered in a trade once, when he was offered twenty donkeys. The seller brought the animals to Stearns one at a time, and Stearns inspected each of them carefully, only to discover later that he had bought the same ass twenty times.[27] Stearns almost died in a fight with a Kentucky saloon keeper named William Day. Day's knife slashed Stearns' hand and shoulder and almost completely severed his tongue. The fight left Stearns disfigured and with a lifelong speech impediment,[28] but his wealth outweighed his physical presence and in 1841, just as Wilson was arriving in the area with the Roland-Workman Party, the forty-three-year-old Stearns married Arcadia Bandini, the strikingly beautiful fourteen-year-old daughter of Don Juan Bandini, the *Californio* who would sell the *Rancho Jurupa* to Don Benito Wilson two years later. Despite their difference in age, the Stearns-Bandini marriage of thirty years appears to have been a happy one. Stearns built the grandest house in the city, *El Palacio de Don Abel,* for his wife, where they entertained famously. Arcadia Bandini is remembered today as the namesake for the City of Arcadia.[29] It was Stearns who forwarded gold to Washington, D.C., from the first discovery of the precious mineral in California. The gold strike was in 1842, not 1848, and the discovery was made in the north San Fernando Valley region near Los Angeles, not in Northern California.

Stearns amassed enormous land holdings, beginning with the 28,512-acre *Rancho Los Alamitos* in 1842, and became the largest landholder in Southern California. His empire came crashing down, threatening him with bankruptcy. In desperation he subdivided two hundred square miles in 1868, stretching from the Santa Ana mountains to the Pacific Ocean. Thus he became the first of the major sub-dividers who broke up the old ranchos to make possible the wider ownership that has characterized Southern California ever since.[30] This move would later make his widow an immensely wealthy woman. Stearns held leading positions in the government of Mexican and American Los Angeles. During one two-month period he was, de facto, the acting governor of California.[31] After he died in San Francisco on August 23, 1871, his metal casket was so heavy, at eight hundred pounds, that the ropes broke while lowering it into the ground and the casket and its contents tumbled into the grave, causing his distressed widow to utter an "unearthly shriek."[32]

On March 21, 1849, Don Benito Wilson's wife, Ramona, died after five years of marriage, at the age of twenty, leaving four-year-old María Jesús and two-year-old John in his care. In census information taken two years later, two miners from England, Richard Alderson, thirty-eight, and Thomas Joy, twenty-six, are listed in his household, along with a twenty-four-year-old bookkeeper, Hiram Nimmo. A twenty-two-year-old woman, Ann, from England, was also listed plus a two-year-old boy, who may have been the young woman's child. Perhaps Ann was the nanny for Wilson's two small children, and perhaps one of the English miners was her husband. Possibly the men who listed mining as their profession were working the agricultural plot on his land and performing handyman duties for his large house.

After the Mexican war, California was a possession of the United States, but not a territory and not a state. Its American overseers left the Mexican *alcalde* system of governance in place alongside U.S. martial law. The last of these caretaker governors, Brigadier General Bennett Riley, called for a constitutional convention, to let the people form a government of their own shape and rid the Army of the responsibility. Wilson was one of the delegates at a meeting in Los Angeles to select representatives to this convention and to pass along instructions. The *Angelenos* chose José Antonio Carrillo, Manuel Domínguez, Stephen Foster and Abel Stearns as their delegates to the state convention. As instructed by Wilson and the others, the Southern California delegation opposed statehood for California, preferring the status of a U.S. Territory. The Southern California faction saw that the here-today-gone-tomorrow northerners wanted to use their greater numbers to control the state, but have the more stable southerners, who owned most of the taxable land, fund it. The *arrigeños* (Northern Californians) easily outvoted the strident *abejeños* (Southern Californians) approving a constitution and seeking Washington's endorsement as a state. The Southern

Californians then held a convention in Santa Barbara to make known to Congress the strong feelings of the southern part of California. Wilson was chosen president of the Los Angeles section, and given the power to choose his fellow delegates. When the full delegation voted to confirm his status as president, though, he declined, accepting the vice-president role.[33] The Santa Barbara delegates declared that if Washington insisted on admitting California as a state, then California should be severed at San Luis Obispo with the *abejeños* living in a territory. Their plea was ignored by Washington. California was, indeed, made a state, and kept intact. And as a state, California divided itself into counties. Those counties held elections, and the voters of Los Angeles County elected Benjamin Davis Wilson as its first County Clerk, with the responsibility for forming American government. In that sense, Wilson is the man who invented Los Angeles.

NOTES FOR CHAPTER 9

1   Stephenson, Terry E., *Don Bernardo Yorba*, Los Angeles: Glen Dawson, 1941, 38-39.
2   Carpenter, *Benito Wilson—Yankee to California*, 31-43.
3   de Packman, "Landmarks and Pioneers of Los Angeles," 73.
4   Letter from Wilson to his brother Wiley R. Wilson, April 12, 1854, B.D. Wilson papers.
5   de Packman, "Landmarks and Pioneers of Los Angeles," 73.
6   Letter from Wilson to his brother, Wiley, April 12, 1854, B.D. Wilson papers.
7   Newmark, *Census of the City and County of Los Angeles For the Year 1850*, 25.
8   Letter from Martin Montgomery to Wilson, December 22, 1849, B.D. Wilson papers.
9   Letter from John C. Fremont to Wilson, December 10, 1851, B.D. Wilson papers.
10 Letter from Wilson to Albert Packard, October 6, 1849, B.D. Wilson papers.
11 Ibid.
12 Invoice book for Wilson & Packard begins January 1, 1850, B.D. Wilson papers.
13 de Packman, "Landmarks and Pioneers of Los Angeles," 90.
14 Agreement between Wilson & Packard and Granger & Brier, April 8, 1850.
15 de Packman, "Landmarks and Pioneers of Los Angeles," 90.
16 This account is disputed in Reid, *History of Pasadena*.
17 Receipts, January 9, 1848, April 10, 1849, April 15, 1849, October 20, 1849, February 9, 1850, B.D. Wilson papers.
18 Taken from various Wilson accounts, B.D. Wilson papers.
19 In Los Angeles Superior Court, First District, Civil Case #679, Wilson sued J.J. Tomlinson and William F. Wood for payment of a Sanford and Wilson debt of five

thousand dollars for 208 horses, one jackass and one American stallion, which was to have been paid on May 1, 1857. Stanford had sold Wilson his interest in the note on December 29, 1856.

20 Guinn, *Historical and Biographical Record of Los Angeles and Vicinity*, 121.

21 *Los Angeles Star*, notices in December 1851 and January 1852 issues.

22 Letter from Albert Packard from San Francisco to Wilson, April 10, 1856, B.D. Wilson papers. Correspondence from Packard to Wilson in 1848 and 1849 is addressed to B.D. Wilson & Company. Correspondence is directed to Wilson & Packard 1850 through 1855. In 1856 correspondence between the two, and to third parties about each other, is acrimonious.

23 de Packman, "Landmarks and Pioneers of Los Angeles," 90.

24 "Pioneers of Los Angeles," 33, 35.

25 Woolsey, "A Capitalist in a Foreign Land: Abel Stearns . . .," 104.

26 Wright, *A Yankee in Mexican California: Abel Stearns, 1798-1848*, 10, 29,

27 Workman, *The City That Grew*, 28.

28 Wright, *A Yankee in Mexican California: Abel Stearns, 1798-1848*, 69.

29 Durham, *California's Geographic Names*, 1231.

30 Wright, *A Yankee in Mexican California: Abel Stearns, 1798-1848*, 146.

31 Ibid.

32 Newmark, *Sixty Years in Southern California 1853-1913*, 430.

33 *San Francisco Daily Herald*, October 26, 1851.

CHAPTER 10

Los Angeles Before Don Benito

B enjamin Wilson had simply relocated from one part of Mexico to another. The territories of New Mexico and Alta California were remote extremities of the mother country, loosely governed by Mexico. In New Mexico, Wilson had been part of an economy of trappers and traders. In Alta California he settled into the life of a gentleman rancher. While non-Indians in New Mexico were congealed into compact communities for protection from hostile natives, the non-Indians of Alta California were relatively safe from Indian attack, because the Native Americans had long ago been uprooted from their ancestral lifestyles and, in effect, enslaved, for the benefit of the missions and the landed gentry. It was this essentially slave labor that made the carefree rancho lifestyle of Southern California possible.

Missions were entrusted with land but held no ownership. Spain, then Mexico, had rewarded their subjects, primarily former soldiers, with large tracts of land, which they were required to put into productive use. These original grantees passed their holdings to family members, sold them to non-family members or lost the property because the grantees could somehow not turn their plots into paying concerns. Wilson came to California twenty years after Mexico won its independence from Spain. Within a decade of the secularization of the missions and settled in as a *ranchero*.

There was an Indian community called Yang-na on the spot where Los Angeles was founded long before the Spanish settlers put down roots there. Yang-na was inhabited by natives who the early Europeans found to be "the cleanest we ever saw."[1] Europeans had first come to Southern California on October 8, 1542, when Juan Rodriguez Cabrillo anchored in San Pedro Bay, and named it *Baia de los Fumos*, (the Bay of Smokes), anticipating a reputation that Southern California would have in centuries to come. This was fifty years almost to the day after Columbus made landfall in the New World.

More than two centuries passed before Europeans set foot in Southern California. Franciscan Padre Junípero Serra established a mission in San Diego in 1769. Spain was nervous that Russia or England might move into San Diego and Monterey harbors so it named Don Gaspar de Portolà governor of California and commander-in-chief of the military forces. Portolà moved north from San Diego towards Monterey with an overland expedition of twenty-seven soldiers and thirty-seven other men later in the same year. On August 2, 1769, the day of indulgence of Our Lady of Los Angeles de Porciúncula, the expedition camped near a river, which they named the Porciúncula (known later as the Los Angeles River). Their camp was near the spot where Broadway crosses the Los Angeles River today. And, wouldn't you know it? Large earthquakes struck the camp. Nevertheless, the place was flagged as a potential site for a future mission, although history is silent about the location for the next twelve years.

In 1775 Felipe de Neve y Perea became governor of California and began planning for farm communities to supply his military presidios. After all, the presidios were located for their military importance and were not self-sustaining like the missions were. As Neve moved his capital north from Loreto in Baja California to Monterey in 1777, he kept an eye out for places to establish pueblos (farm communities). One promising site was on the banks of the Los Angeles River, the same place Portolà's party had noted in 1769. Neve ended up establishing two pueblos in Alta California. The first was the Pueblo of San José in November of 1777 and the second was to be la Reyna de los Angeles (Queen of the Angels) on the Porciúncula River.

In 1779, Governor Neve sent a party into Sinaloa and Sonora to recruit soldiers for a Santa Barbara presidio and twenty-four families for the pueblo of Los Angeles. The soldiers and settlers left for the north in two parties. Indians wiped out one entire party. The other reached the San Gabriel Mission on August 18, 1781, and a week later Governor Neve ordered the founding of Pueblo de Nuestra Señora de Los Angeles, a secular community under the control of the Santa Barbara Presidio, not the San Gabriel Mission.[2] On September 4, 1781, the settlers left the San Gabriel Mission to inhabit their new city. Although lore has grown up describing a procession of flags from the Mission to the new town site, no specific ceremony is described in existing records. In fact, the townspeople drifted to the site over a period of weeks.

Fourteen heads of household had been recruited in Sonora and Sinaloa, but two had deserted and one was left in Baja California. Of the eleven heads of household and their eleven wives, ten people were listed as Negroes or mulattoes (European and Negro parents), nine were Indians, one mestizo (European and Indian parents) and two were Spaniards. Both Spaniards were married to Indians, thus there were no pure European settler families among the founders. Los Angeles was a multi-cultural community from its first moment.

The founders of Los Angeles were:
Spanish/Indian with three children
Mestizo/Mulatta with three children
Indian/Mulatta with six children
Negro/Mulatta with two children
Spaniard/Indian with one child
Indian/Indian with one child
Indian/Indian
Indian/Indian with one child
Mulatto/Mulatta
Negro/Mulatta with five children
Mulatto/(female)

After building huts for their dwellings and digging a *zanja* for their irrigation, the new citizens of Los Angeles began work on their fields.[3] The original pueblo of Los Angeles was about 111 square miles.[4] Thus, Los Angeles had been established in 1781, sixty years before Wilson arrived, and only five years after the Declaration of Independence was signed in the other North American nation, on the other North American coast.

Within a year three of the families had been expelled, being "useless to the village and themselves," and found their way to Santa Barbara. Blacks headed two of these families, the other was headed by a Spaniard.[5] By 1791 the population of Los Angeles had swelled to 139, in twenty-nine adobe households.[6]

There were three kinds of Spanish communities in Alta California, missions, presidios and pueblos. The missions were religious, presidios were military and the pueblos were secular. The missions were at the core of the Spanish master plan. Four military presidios provided muscle for the missions, at locations chosen for their strategic advantage: San Diego, Santa Barbara, Monterey and San Francisco. Three pueblos, located near water and fertile land, were established as farming communities to supply food for the presidios. The first Alta California pueblo was San José, established in 1777. Los Angeles was the second, in 1781 and Branciforte, a smaller pueblo, technically a villa, was formed in 1797. Four other pueblos followed, in Sonoma, San Juan Bautista, San Juan Capistrano and San Luis Obispo. The Northern European tradition left the founding of new communities to individuals and to the vagaries of economic roulette.[7] In the Spanish tradition, the government carefully planned all new communities, including Los Angeles.

Pueblos were overseen by one or more *alcaldes*. Assisting the *alcalde* was a sort of city council, called the *ayuntamiento*. A flood overwhelmed the original plaza in the pueblo of Los Angeles in 1815, so a new plaza was laid out in 1818 and the town's center moved to the new location.[8] This was the plaza that Benjamin Wilson came to know and the plaza that exists to this day.

The first American had arrived in Los Angeles in 1818, twenty-three years before Wilson arrived. This was a pirate named Joseph Chapman, or

José Huero (Blond Joe) in Spanish. Chapman and two companions were captured in Monterey and Chapman was sent to Los Angeles, where he married into the Ortega family and became a productive citizen.[9]

In 1826 an American fur-trapping party under Jedediah Smith alarmed local authorities when it showed up at the San Gabriel Mission. Governor José María de Echeandía had them arrested, understanding all too well the implications of Americans being able to reach this Mexican coast by overland routes. Two years later another American fur-trapping party, headed by James Ohio Pattie, showed up. Three of its members gave up trapping and stayed in Los Angeles: Nathaniel Pryor, Jesse Ferguson, and Richard Laughlin. Two years after that, fur trapper Ewing Young showed up on a mule-buying expedition in 1830. Some Americans came to Los Angeles from the sea, leaving ships that traded along the coast or were shipwrecked. A few men deserted fur-trapping parties. By the time Benjamin Wilson arrived in Los Angeles in 1841 there were dozens of Americans already established in the area.

NOTES FOR CHAPTER 10

1 Kelsey, "A New Look at the Founding of Old Los Angeles," 328.
2 Starr, *Inventing the Dream*, 13.
3 Kelsey, "A New Look at the Founding of Old Los Angeles," 335.
4 16 square leagues. Nunis, *A Southern California Historical Anthology*, 63.
5 Layne, "Annals of Los Angeles: Part I," 200.
6 Starr, *Inventing the Dream*, 13.
7 Williams, "Mission, Presidio and Pueblo: Notes on California Local Institutions Under Spain and Mexico," 24-29.
8 Layne, "Annals of Los Angeles: Part I," 206.
9 Ibid.

Benjamin Wilson and his second wife, Margaret, seated, are flanked by their two
daughters, Anne (left) and Ruth (right). Wilson's daughter, María de Jesús, stands in
the center.

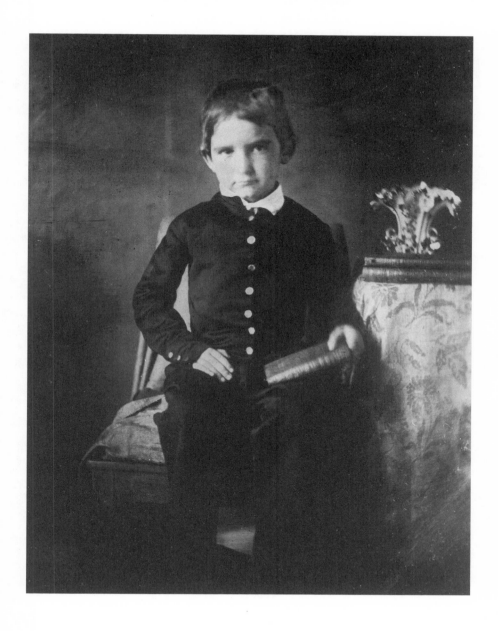

John B. Wilson was Don Benito Wilson's son with his first wife, Ramona.
Don Benito hoped that he and son John would one day be business partners.

Unfortunately, John B. Wilson grew up to be a drinker and a bitter disappointment to his father, and it was Don Benito's son-in-law James De Barth Shorb who became his lasting business partner. John B. Wilson eventually committed suicide at the Bella Union Hotel in Los Angeles.

This portrait of Margaret Hereford Hereford Wilson and daughter Maggie was painted shortly before the child died at age three.

Benjamin Davis Wilson stands on his porch at the far right and his wife Margaret is
on the far left. Their daughter Anne stands between them. On the steps is Wilson's
daughter Sue, and her husband James De Barth Shorb, in the black hat, pets Nero,
one of the family dogs. Daughter Ruth Wilson Patton is the tall figure on the
far left. At the foot of the stairs is friend Mary Stone and in front of her are four
children and a baby. Left to right, the first three are children of the Shorbs: Inez,
Edith and James De Barth Shorb, Jr. The fourth is identified as Sally Flannagan.
The baby is Ramona Shorb, a child who is said to have inspired author Helen Hunt
Jackson to title her famed book, *Ramona*.

María de Jesús was the firstborn of Don Benito Wilson by his first wife, Ramona. Her mother had been part of the *Californio* aristocracy before the region lived under an American flag. María came to be known as Sue in American Los Angeles.

When Sue grew up, she married James De Barth Shorb and together they had eleven children.

Ruth Wilson, like her half-sister Sue, married well. Her husband, George S. Patton II, was a respected community leader, and their son, George, grew up to be the celebrated World War II general, who achieved more fame than both his successful father and grandfather.

Reproduced by permission of The Huntington Library, San Marino California.

Annie Wilson, the devoted older sister of Ruth Wilson, lived a spinster's life and never stopped loving her sister's husband, George S. Patton II.

In a beautiful portrait of the era, Wilson's daughter María de Jesús, right, poses with her maternal aunt, Medora Hereford, who died tragically after an explosion of the ill-fated transfer steamer, *Ada Hancock*. Medora is buried in the Wilson family plot in San Gabriel.

Don Benito Wilson married his second wife, the former Margaret Hereford
Hereford, on February 1, 1853, when she was thirty-three and he was forty-one.
He wrote to her mother, ". . . [it] is natural that I should have loved your daughter,
the only thing that has been strange in the whole event was that your daughter
should have loved me."

A monument to the life of Benjamin Davis Wilson stands in the cemetery next to
The Church of Our Savior in the San Gabriel Valley. He is remembered as "honest,
pure, brave and incorruptible."

Author photo.

CHAPTER 11

The Los Angeles of Don Benito

The Los Angeles that Wilson helped shape in the 1850s was a tiny, dusty Mexican pueblo on the far American frontier surrounded by virtually empty land in all directions. The population of Los Angeles in 1850 found only 1,610 people in town, with men outnumbering women fifty-six to forty-four percent.[1] About half of the people in the huge County of Los Angeles lived in the City of Los Angeles. Four out of five people in the pueblo spoke Spanish, the other twenty percent spoke a variety of languages, of which English was but one.[2] In fact, the French were more numerous than Americans in this Mexican pueblo.[3] As late as 1850 there were only three American "families" (American-born husband and American-born wife) in Los Angeles[4] and Wilson was not one of these since he had not yet remarried after the death of his Mexican wife. The Los Angeles of that time was a young city. A fourth of the residents were under twenty years of age and only three percent were over sixty. Almost a third of the population was illiterate.[5] There were far more residents born abroad, in countries other than Mexico, than there were Americans born in states other than California.[6]

It was a Mexican town of mostly one-story adobe cottages[7] built around a public plaza. The plaza of Benjamin Wilson's time was not the original 1781 town square, but Los Angeles was still a town centered on its town square, and the plaza of Wilson's time can be visited today, just north of Olvera Street. This model of town layout dated back to at least Roman times and was followed by German and other European cultures, and even the New England Puritan villages.[8] The plaza concept was the common Spanish formula, and had been followed in the layout of the original Angeles pueblo. Adobe dwellings vibrated out from the pueblo center, diffusing into private farm plots and community grazing areas. The town's bullfights had been moved out of the plaza to a site near the present-day north Chinatown intersection of Hill and College Streets to separate the commotion from the church, which had complained about the disruption.[9] Still, this was no pristine public space. So much rubbish was heaped in the plaza that work crews might need a few days to clean the public square for a holiday celebration.[10]

Los Angeles was a town of dust and mud and flies and dogs. There were so many flies that Frenchman John La Rue would simply dip his fingers in to fish out a fly before serving the cup of coffee to a guest in his eating joint.[11] Although Los Angeles did not have the rat problem of San Francisco, it was legendary for its fleas.[12]

There were more wild dogs than humans in Los Angeles. Roving in large noisy packs, they hounded carts, killed humans with their rabies, and created an awful din. Said the Los Angeles Star, ". . . it is astonishing they are suffered to exist while powder, lead and strychnine are so plentiful and cheap."[13] Indeed it was common for frustrated residents to throw poison in the streets to reduce the canine population. Tragically, this poison would also kill treasured pets as well as the feral dogs. The dead dogs would float down zanjas, the water canals that provided the city's drinking supply.

There were no paved streets or sidewalks in the pueblo.[14] There was no hospital or school, and only one teacher in town. There were no carriages, only the noisy ox-drawn carretas with their huge solid wooden wheels, the curiosity so commonly used as décor in front of Mexican restaurants today.[15] The shrill squeaking of the *carreta* wheels would attract twenty-five to fifty barking and howling dogs as they clunked through the streets of Los Angeles.[16]

There was practically no money in town, cattle and cattle hides being the medium of exchange. Other than the willows found in the river bottom there were exactly two trees in all of Los Angeles, one pepper tree and one sycamore.[17] The town was laced with *zanjas*, which fed off the *Zanja Madre* (Mother Canal) that, in turn, lifted its water out of the Los Angeles River, with a huge *toma* (water-wheel).

Los Angeles soil was the same gripping clay that made such good adobe. Thus the streets were suction traps when wet and rock-hard formations when dried.[18] Observers reported that the dust on the streets in the summer was "knee deep." Trash and old clothing were thrown into the streets. Sometimes Indians would claim the cast-off clothing and would cut up the dead animals for food.[19] One livery stable was chided by the newspaper for dumping loads of its manure into the alleys or along the sides of the street.[20]

Gambling dens and saloons were numerous in the Los Angeles of the 1850s,[21] and, as a result, the town's only secular public building was a jail.[22] The adobe houses—and every house except Wilson's was made of adobe[23]—didn't have the postcard appeal of San Francisco's elegant brick-and-frame buildings, but, on the other hand, Los Angeles couldn't burn to the ground again and again like its northern cousin. All but three of the pueblo's 274 houses were one-story, and all but five had flat roofs instead of tile.[24] The second stories were reached from the outside. The houses were generally rectangular and were built around patios and corridors.[25]

Los Angeles of 1850 was not yet served by stagecoach or telegraph.[26] Wilson settled in a quiet, backwater Mexican pueblo in the 1840s and he helped mold the town into an American town in the 1850s.

NOTES FOR CHAPTER 11

1 Census of the City and County of Los Angeles For the Year 1850.

2 de Packman, "Landmarks and Pioneers of Los Angeles," 58.

3 Starr, Inventing the Dream, 13.

4 Layne, "Annals of Los Angeles: Part II," 314.

5 1118 illiterate of the 3530 total in the 1850 Census.

6 118 born in the U.S. in states other than California; 181 born in foreign countries other than Mexico.

7 Barrows, "Los Angeles Fifty Years Ago," 204.

8 Nunis, A Southern California Historical Anthology, 57.

9 de Packman, "Landmarks and Pioneers of Los Angeles," 62. The author cites "Castelar and College," which no longer cross.

10 Newmark, Sixty Years in Southern California 1853-1913, 97-98.

11 Ibid., 27-28.

12 O'Flaherty, An End and a Beginning: The South Coast and Los Angeles 1850-1887, 60.

13 Los Angeles Star, August 14, 1852.

14 Barrows, "Los Angeles Fifty Years Ago," 205.

15 O'Flaherty, An End and a Beginning: The South Coast and Los Angeles 1850-1887, 12.

16 Newmark, Sixty Years in Southern California 1853-1913, 84-85.

17 Layne, "Annals of Los Angeles: Part II," 311.

18 O'Flaherty, An End and a Beginning: The South Coast and Los Angeles 1850-1887, 145.

19 Newmark, Sixty Years in Southern California 1853-1913, 34.

20 Southern Californian, December 14, 1854.

21 Newmark, Sixty Years in Southern California 1853-1913, 29-30.

22 Layne, "Annals of Los Angeles: Part II," 301.

23 Ibid., 311.

24 Ibid., 310.

25 Newmark, Sixty Years in Southern California 1853-1913, 113.

26 Starr, Inventing the Dream, 13.

CHAPTER 12

Crime

The film library of Hollywood overflows with Wild West movies about dangerous frontier towns in Arizona, Nevada, Wyoming and Colorado. Yet no town in America, before or since, was as wild and deadly as the frontier town of Los Angeles. The murder rate in greater Los Angeles for September 1850 to September 1851, when Benjamin Wilson was mayor, was 1,240 per 100,000, an all-time record for an American town.[1] That homicide rate would translate to exactly 319 times the current Los Angeles County murder rate of 3.89 per 100,000 residents. The 2006 murder total in Los Angeles County was 402,[2] or slightly more than one homicide per day. At the murder rate of 1850-51 in the Los Angeles area, there would be 351 murders *every day* in Los Angeles County, for an annual total of 128,144. The annual dead of Los Angeles County would equal the living population of Thousand Oaks. To look at it another way, in 1850-51 it was said in those days that there was a murder a day in Los Angeles.[3] There still is about one murder a day, but look at the difference in population!

Townfolk would ask one another over breakfast, "Well, how many were killed last night?"[4] A newspaper account of the time reported, "The week past has been comparatively quiet; four people have been killed it is true, but it has been considered a poor week for killing; a head or two has been split open, and an occasional case of cutting has occurred, but these are miner (sic) matters and create but little feeling."[5] (Yet the same issue of the newspaper contains articles about serious crimes, one of them near Wilson's house.) Another edition of the same newspaper said, "Sunday passed away rather quietly; but one person was killed during the day."[6] The killing of an Indian or "half breed" was so common that it was hardly noticed by the general population. Only the murder of regular citizens caused outrage.[7] But even the known murders represent an enormous number considering the small population of the area at the time. A record was set when Wilson was mayor of the city. On October 20, 1851, the County coroner held eleven inquests in a single day.[8] So much for calling this the City of the Angels.

The high crime rate was the result of several factors. The Gold Rush in Northern California had been a magnet for low life from the United States, and elsewhere. Ne'er-do-wells had oozed their way to California in hopes that lack of ambition, lack of skills and lack of ethics would be no bar to easy fortune. When the established order in San Francisco had shown little humor for their depravity, the thugs had wandered to Southern California in search of a more crime-friendly environment. Also contributing to the high crime rate was the sparse distribution of residents throughout the area. Criminals could pick off the remote farmhouses with relative impunity. Then there was the weak central government of Los Angeles, which had a small tax base for supporting an organized police force. The Los Angeles Star complained that the permanent residents of the city were never involved in crime, but that the "criminalized" state of Los Angeles was due to outsiders.[9] Many travelers avoided Los Angeles because of its reputation for rampant crime.[10]

One example of just how lawless Los Angeles was comes from the curious story of David Brown. Brown had murdered his companion, a man named Clifford, and was arrested in 1854. A crowd of men gathered to hold a kangaroo court and to lynch the suspect, believing that the court system was not capable of dispensing proper justice. Mayor Steven C. Foster found out about the meeting, hurried into the room and jumped onto a table. He argued that Los Angeles had to become a civilized city and pointed out that the sheriff had already appointed a grand jury to bring charges against the suspect. The men responded that the government's court system too often allowed an attorney to overturn a verdict, and which is why they had to take responsibility for justice. Mayor Foster proposed a deal. Let the fledgling justice system proceed, and if some attorney was able to overturn the guilty verdict, then he would resign his office as mayor, would lead the men to the jail, would hang the murderer, and he'd seek his office again in a special election. Skeptically, the men agreed.[11]

As predicted, the court sentenced David Brown to be hanged for the murder, but just as the men had feared, attorneys for the accused won a stay at the appeals level. Shortly after the steamship from San Francisco arrived with the news, an excited crowd of almost six hundred persons gathered to press for action. Foster kept his promise and resigned the post of mayor of Los Angeles. The following morning, he marched with other leaders to the jail, where they broke down the doors, removed David Brown's manacles and hanged him from the corral beam across the street.[12] Brown had protested that he didn't mind being hanged, for although he didn't remember killing Pinckney Clifford, he supposed that he had done it, but he did object to having "greasers" (Mexicans) as his executioners. The crowd happily complied with his last wish, supplied Anglo noosemen and dispatched him at the hands of his own countrymen.[13] In order to get newspapers to the steamship that was scheduled to leave six hours before the lynching, the account of the hanging was printed in detail in advance. In this way the executioners read about their acts at the same time they were performing them.[14] A special election was held the following week, in which Steven Foster was restored to the post of mayor of the city, there being no other candidates in the field.[15] The city marshal, who had argued against the extra-legal hanging, was forced to resign.[16]

By the mid-1850s crime was so rampant that a gang of about one hundred men was able to rob and kill along the roads of Southern California with little fear that a larger force could overpower it. Sheriff James R. Barton and a posse of five men left Los Angeles on January 22, 1857, to confront the gang, which was operating around San Juan Capistrano at the time. The sheriff was outnumbered about eight to one, but was confident of his skills and his cause. In the gun battle that resulted, Sheriff Barton and three of his men were killed. The other two managed to escape and relay the alarming news back to Los Angeles. An act they committed shortly before killing the sheriff and his men signaled the depravity of the outlaws. The thugs came upon a German store-owner who had closed his establishment for the night and had cooked a supper for himself. They killed the merchant and placed his body on his table. Then the gangsters sat down and casually ate the man's dinner seated around their dead host.[17]

The incensed citizens were shocked into strong action. A public meeting was called and two committees were formed, one for public safety and one for retribution. The city of Los Angeles was placed under martial law under the supervision of Wilson's future real-estate partner, Dr. John S. Griffin, and funds were requested from the state legislature. Fifty U.S. Army troops joined the hunt. Men went into the countryside around Los Angeles rounding up about fifty suspicious local characters. Other men rode off in pursuit of the bandits. General Andres Pico, who had led the Mexicans against the Americans in the Mexican-American War, 1846-48, now led native *Californios* against a common enemy.

Justice was meted out in many quarters in the days, weeks and years that followed Sheriff Barton's murder. General Andres Pico captured two of the most notorious gang members and hanged them from trees on the spot. Fifty-two men were locked in the city jail, eleven of whom were hanged.[18] An extra-legal process followed. As news that another suspect had been brought into town, the Vigilance Committee would assemble and Judge Jonathan R. Scott would preside as its chairman. Scott would ask the crowd for a "motion," and someone would yell out the suggestion that the culprit be hanged. Judge Scott would then say something to the effect of, "Gentlemen you have heard the motion; all those in favor of hanging So-and-So will signify by saying Aye!" The vote was inevitably unanimous, and the committee would proceed across the street to overpower the jailor, relieve him of his charge, lead the prisoner to the high ground behind the jail and carry out the decision of the vigilantes. Then the committee members dispersed until word of a new capture rippled through town.[19] Pancho Daniel, the leader of the gang who murdered Sheriff Barton, was captured, jailed, and then released on bail. A public enraged at the criminal justice system lynched the bad guy.[20]

As crime increased, so did the efforts to build a law enforcement system with enough muscle to respond. There was an elected sheriff for Los Angeles County from the first day of American government. While on the Common Council in the city's first year under American government, 1850-51, Wilson and his Police Committee suggested forming a Los Angeles Police Department for crime suppression in the city, but the full council rejected the idea. The following year, as mayor, Wilson appointed the first City Marshal, and authorized him to recruit deputy marshals to fight crime in the city. In addition to the marshal's position, the Common Council, with Mayor Wilson's encouragement, created a volunteer "police force" under "Chief" Alexander W. Hope. In 1853, a year after Wilson was mayor, a larger force called the "Rangers" was created, with financial help from the state legislature to respond to the pandemic crime that was engulfing Los Angeles.[21] Wilson was one of the fifty or so volunteer Rangers, about half of whom were mounted. The Rangers were pressed into service almost daily.[22] Three years later, in another effort "to prevent crime, and to organize in defense of the lives and properties of the citizens," Wilson was named to a committee of twenty citizens to arrest and disarm any suspicious armed persons around Los Angeles.[23]

From 1850 to 1870, seventy-seven people were hanged in Los Angeles and thirty-seven of the hangings were outside the legal justice system.[24] The first judicial hanging did not take place until February 13, 1854, four years after Los Angeles became an American city.[25] Compare the forty legal executions in Los Angeles during those two decades to the statistics of recent years: The population of Los Angeles during those years ranged from 1,610 in 1850 to 5,614 in 1870. The population of the entire state of California was 36,457,549 in 2006[26] and there were only thirteen executions between April 22, 1976, and January 17, 2006, statewide.[27]

The lynchings of "frontier" California continued into the next century, with five men being hanged in Modoc County in May of 1901.[28] In forming one particular vigilance group in Los Angeles in 1856, the *Los Angeles Star* had this to say:

> One look at the immense crowd in front of the rooms of the Vigilance Committee, yesterday, awaiting an opportunity to enroll their names as members, was sufficient to satisfy us that the recent shocking outrage in this community will be redressed by the *right sort* of men. . . . They come forward to take the law into their own hands not because they are not law-abiding men, but because they know from a sad experience that it cannot or will not be properly administered in cases of public assassinations. . . . All human patience in this community has been lost upon cases which now 'drag their slow length along' in our courts of justice, or disgrace our criminal record over the *'acquitted!'* Then who are we to look to in such an emergency but the People. Into whose hands shall the law go, when it has been smiled at and trampled upon in the presence of our judges? We answer most emphatically the People's.[29]

Another newspaper published an anonymous letter with similar thoughts:

> Errors in juries, errors in indictments, blunders of Sheriff's Clerk's Prosecutors, and judges have been the order of the day . . . the prisoners have escaped; rather by absence of witnesses, or by some *friendly hole* in the roof floors or walls of our jails. . . . Are criminals to be punished by our constituted courts, or are we to form ourselves into one good *Vigilance Committee*, and Judge Lynch to visit every crime, with prompt . . . punishment? . . . let us be ready, when the time arrives, to act.

A vigilance group once boarded a ship on which the sheriff was taking eight prisoners to the state prison at San Quentin, seized a prisoner who'd been sentenced to "only" ten years, hanged him and threw his body overboard weighted with stones the mob had brought aboard.[30]

A year after Wilson was mayor, civic patriarch Abel Stearns held a party on Washington's Birthday in 1853. Wilson would probably have been among the town's elite at a party such as this. Some townspeople complained about not having been invited to the party. (Their actions confirmed to history why they hadn't been. As the night wore on some fifteen or twenty of the uninvited hauled the cannon out of the plaza and fired it outside Stearns' compound. The mob then began setting off Chinese firecrackers, ringing gongs and bells and beating tin pans. A gun battle followed, in which two party guests shot and killed two of the disrupters. Judge Myron Norton shot and killed Dr. J.T. Overstreet, a clerk to the Board of Land Commissioners, and Colonel Watson killed party crasher Elias Cook. Judge Norton and another man were injured in the fight. Judge Norton and Colonel Watson were charged with murder, but Judge Benjamin Hayes ruled that both killings had been justifiable homicide.[31]

The wildest, most dangerous, most notorious section of early Los Angeles was a single block, forty feet wide and less than five hundred feet in its one-block length,[32] known as Calle de los Negros, meaning "street of the dark people." Americans called it "Negro Alley," or more commonly, "Nigger Alley," and even the newspapers used that term, which was as derogatory then as it is today. Its name was not a reference to people of African descent, but to the wealthy Spanish or Mexicans who once lived on the street. In the days before American influence a man named Don José António Carillo had posted a sign there reading "Calle de los Negros," referring to the darker-skinned elite who lived on the block. He was hauled before the *alcalde* by the street's residents but, in his defense, he pointed to the dark skin of his accusers, and the complaint was dismissed.[33] The nickname stuck, though.[34] The wealthy were now long gone, and the street had become the address of bars, gambling joints and houses of prostitution. Most of the city's legendary "one every day" murders took place on this street. Foot for foot it was one of the most dangerous and corrupt hellholes on earth. Armed ruffians presided over the money on the gambling tables and settled any disagreements immediately, by beating or shooting the complaining party and simply throwing the body out into the infamous street.[35] It was the land of the quick and the dead. Some were quick; others were dead. As time went on the neighborhood turned Chinese. The street name was later changed to Los Angeles Street. This street lay almost directly in the path Wilson walked daily from his home to his general merchandise store around the time he was mayor of the city.

The courts of early Los Angeles were as colorful as the crime.

The first courts of Los Angeles County met in Wilson's Bella Union Hotel. Crimes heard by that early court included crimes that are seldom prosecuted today, such as counterfeiting gold dust, dueling, selling liquor to Indians and torturing cattle. In the first crime of bigamy in the county, a woman was the defendant.[36]

Judge Benjamin Hayes' court had to adjourn for the day more than once because the judge was too much under the influence of adult beverages.[37] In one case, opposing counsel got into a gunfight inside the courtroom. Judge William G. Dryden dove into his chambers, yelling behind him, "Shoot away, damn you. And to hell with all of you!"[38] Judge Dryden once realized that the defendant in a case against a gang of horse thieves was his own brother-in-law, and found the accused guilty, gave him a stern lecture and said, "I declare you a free man, and you may go about your business." This so flabbergasted the courtroom that someone yelled out, "What is his business?" Judge Dryden, nonplused, retorted, "Horse-stealing, sir! Horse-stealing!"[39] Judge Dryden tried to bring some respect to the court in frontier Los Angeles by ordering that attorneys in his court ". . . will not be allowed to rest their feet on the tops of tables, or whittle or spit tobacco juice on the floor or stove."[40] Dryden was once called to task by a court for "performing an autopsy in the absence of a coroner" and for his "failure to inter the body" so that "it decayed and was eaten by animals."[41]

The fledgling court system of the new American government was a tentative sprout trying to grow strong in a climate of lawlessness that saw crime win over punishment again and again. Appellate courts reversed the Los Angeles judges and juries so many times that the law-abiding folks in town lost faith in the system, and time and again lynched the accused instead of waiting for official justice, or when the system did not agree with their conclusion of guilt. The fledgling court system just couldn't seem to dot the i's and cross the t's to prevent reversals. In 1852, a frustrated district court annulled all of the criminal business of the court of sessions.[42]

Thus Wilson's time in early Los Angeles was a period of extreme danger and bewildering crime. While much of the crime was focused in the sin section of Calle de los Negros, most of the fights were between the rougher class of men, and much of the violence inflicted between and upon Indians, early Los Angeles could nevertheless be a dangerous place for the established gentry. This was the environment in which Wilson lived, made his name and governed. One cannot appreciate the life of Benjamin Wilson or the times he lived in without considering this climate of violence and danger.

NOTES FOR CHAPTER 12

1 Starr, *California: A History*, 84-85.

2 LACountyMurders.com Web site of the Los Angeles County Sheriff's Department, statistics for 2006.

3 Guinn, *A History of California*, 188.

4 Ibid.

5 *Southern Californian*, November 16, 1854.

6 *Southern Californian*, June 6, 1855.

7 Guinn, *A History of California*, 188.

8 Ibid., 288.

9 *Los Angeles Star*, October 22, 1859.

10 *Southern Californian*, November 30, 1854.

11 *Southern Californian*, October 19, 1854.

12 *Southern Californian*, January 18, 1855.

13 Newmark, *Sixty Years in Southern California 1853-1913*, 139-140.

14 Ibid., 141.

15 *Southern Californian*, February 1, 1955.

16 Guinn, *A History of California*, 188.

17 Newmark, *Sixty Years in Southern California 1853-1913*, 205.

18 Guinn, *A History of California*, 189.

19 Newmark, *Sixty Years in Southern California 1853-1913*, 207.

20 Ibid., 223.

21 Bell, *Reminiscences of a Ranger: Early Times in Southern California*, viii.

22 *Los Angeles Star*, February 11, 1854.

23 *Los Angeles Star*, July 26, 1856.

24 Hamilton, "The Toughest Little Town," *Los Angeles Times*, H9.

25 *Los Angeles Star*, February 18, 1854.

26 U.S. Census Bureau.

27 "Capital punishment in California," Wikipedia.org Web site.

28 Starr, *California: A History*, 85.

29 *Los Angeles Star*, May 24, 1856.

30 *Los Angeles Star*, December 12, 1863.

31 *Los Angeles Star*, February 26, 1853.

32 Nunis, *A Southern California Historical Anthology*, 68.

33 Newmark, "Calle de los Negros and the Chinese Massacre of 1871," 97.

34 Ibid.

35 Krythe, "Daily Life in Early Los Angeles," 29.

36 Cameron, "Crime in the Early Pueblo Days," *Los Angeles Times*, B5.

37 Newmark, *Sixty Years in Southern California 1853-1913*, 46.

38 Spalding, *History and Reminiscences: Los Angeles City and County, California*, Vol. 1., 140.

39 Newmark, *Sixty Years in Southern California 1853-1913*, 51-52.

40 "Pioneer Courts and Lawyers of Los Angeles," 221.

41 Ibid., 93.

42 Woolsey, "Crime and Punishment: Los Angeles County, 1850-1856," 85.

B

CHAPTER 13

Early Los Angeles Government

P olitics in Wilson's Los Angeles were as rough and tumble as life in the violent little frontier town. And Wilson was as tough a survivor in the political thicket as he had been in the life-and-death Western wilderness of fur trapping and Indian fighting. After he opened a general merchandise store in the city of Los Angeles and moved to the pueblo from his Jurupa Ranch in 1847 he dove into the politics of the city with manic energy. In eight runs for public office over the life of his political career he lost only once, a sign of his temperament in that cutthroat political environment.[1]

In those tempestuous early years of Los Angeles politics, Mexicans who neglected to take out American citizenship yet were not eligible to vote, and Indians were not yet recognized by the U.S. government as citizens of this country, yet both groups were hustled to the polls by either party that could get them there. Indians or new immigrants from Sonora, Mexico, would be offered free liquor, then locked in a corral in East Los Angeles for the evening and kept well supplied with booze all night long before being carted in stages or wagons to the polls, sometimes two or three times, to cast bloc votes. In at least one case this strategy backfired.

Republicans locked up about a hundred Sonorans in a corral near what is now Macy Street and Mission Road, but prominent Mexican politicians (most establishment Mexicans were Democrats) came to the corral in the middle of the night and delivered passionate speeches in Spanish, and most of the "captive voters" ended up voting Democratic as a result.

Ballots with candidates' names were not printed by election officials. Instead, the political parties, or individual candidates, printed their own slates on ballots of different colors and different sizes and voters dropped a pre-printed ballot of their choice into a soap or candle box. Naturally there were many irregularities and many challenges to the election results. Sometimes a voter had to struggle just to reach the ballot box because of the phalanx of a particular party blocking the way. The outright sale of votes was common and practiced openly by both sides in an election.[2] The standard price was two dollars per vote, paid after the ballot of the proper color was deposited in the box. Some crafty voters managed to get paid by both sides.[3] Voters would vote more than once by changing clothes or by shaving off beards or mustaches before returning to the ballot box.[4]

In 1854 a candidate for justice of the peace made a novel campaign promise. In this frontier town of unmarried men he promised to marry all bachelors who would vote for him for half price. And to smooth his press relations (he went by his initials, P.R.), he offered to marry newspaper editors for free. The local editor did, indeed, support him.[5]

The numbers in these early elections were small, as evidenced by the following news account:

> The election in San Pedro resulted in another Whig victory. Mayor Banning was elected by a majority of one, having received two votes.[6]

For the election of Los Angeles mayor and other offices in 1854, nine versions of printed tickets were deposited, and a number of votes were cast for persons not announced as candidates. Still, the total number of votes cast was only 281.[7]

The original American municipal City of Los Angeles was about twenty-eight square miles,[8] and the need for a city government was called into question again and again in the early days. In 1860 the newspaper urged that city and county government be combined, reflecting the conclusion of at least two petitions.[9] The grand jury took a similar view the following year.[10]

The affairs of early government in Los Angeles were conducted in Spanish. English-speaking elected officials were sworn-in in English and Spanish-speaking officials were sworn-in in Spanish.[11] The official government records were in Spanish, but were translated into English as well. Ninety percent of the population of Los Angeles County spoke only Spanish in 1850.[12] Spanish and English continued to be the dual official languages in Los Angeles until 1879,[13] despite the fact that it caused confusion. Augustin Olvera was elected to the post of county judge. Olvera spoke no English and one of his two associate judges spoke no Spanish.[14] It should be noted, however, that Judge Olvera quickly became proficient in English.[15] The state legislature conducted its affairs in English, so Judge Benjamin Hayes worked late into the night translating the new acts of the state legislature into Spanish for the Los Angeles officials who did not speak English.[16]

February 18, 1850, one of the first acts of the new state government was to divide the state into twenty-seven counties. Los Angeles County hugged the coast between two enormous counties: Mariposa County, which then included the town of Santa Barbara, on the north, and San Diego County on the south. In 1851 the size of its two neighbors was reduced and the size of Los Angeles County was increased to stretch from the Pacific Ocean to the Colorado River and from the Tehachapi Mountains in the north to San Juan Capistrano on the south. [17] The boundaries of the original counties were sometimes vague, sometimes overlapped, and sometimes left unclaimed parts of the state where white men did not venture. The original boundaries of Los Angeles County, for example, were set down as

> Beginning on the coast of the Pacific at the southern boundary of the farm called Triunfo, and running thence along the summit of the ridge of hills called Santa Susana to the northwestern boundary of the farm called San Francisco; thence . . . to the farm called Pico . . .[18]

and so forth in that vein.

Two months before California became a state, the county and city of Los Angeles held the elections that launched the American government system. As the date for that first local American election drew near, a group of community leaders gathered in secret at the home of Judge Augustin Olvera on the north side of the plaza, and conspired on a complete slate for the various local offices. The slate of this junta included Benjamin Wilson as the original county clerk with responsibility for setting up American government in the newly-formed Los Angeles County, and this prearranged slate won the election of July 1, 1850.[19] In the last election of the Mexican system Wilson ran for the office of *regidor* (alderman) and won, with 129 votes,[20] serving to the very last day in the Mexican system and from the very first day of the American system. Three of the newly elected officials could neither speak nor write English. Wilson and the other new government officials signed a constitutional oath in their native languages and knelt on a cushion at an altar beneath a large crucifix. This arrangement was deemed appropriate by the newly elected county recorder, Don Ignacio del Valle, in the Mexican tradition, but the more democratic Americans thought it a bit too regal for their sense of office holding.[21]

Over his political career Wilson was elected as a Whig, a Know-Nothing and as a Democrat. In his time the Democrats were the country's conservatives and the Republicans were the liberals. Wilson was an unswerving conservative. Benjamin Wilson began his political career as the county clerk as a member of the waning Whig Party, a party that had risen out of hostility to President Andrew Jackson's power grab in his fight against the Bank of the United States. The Whigs held sway for only a decade and a half, from the mid-1830s till the early 1850s. Whigs elected two presidents, William Henry Harrison and Zachary Taylor, both of whom died shortly after taking office. Wilson chaired the first Whig meeting in Los Angeles,[22] and was a Whig when he was elected mayor in 1851 and when he ran unsuccessfully for the State Assembly later that same year. Wilson and Andres Pico were elected delegates from Los Angeles County to the Whig state convention in 1851[23] and the two ran as candidates for the state legislature from Los Angeles County later that year, although the Democratic newspaper, *Los Angeles Star*, supported the two with the claim that they were independents.[24] Wilson was elected to the state Senate as a Whig, although he may well have been a Know-Nothing as he went to

Sacramento. Being a party of national solutions the Whigs were torn apart over the question of slave state admissions, and by the end of his two-year term as state senator Wilson was serving in an official capacity for the Democratic Central Committee of Los Angeles County.[25]

As the first county clerk, it was Benjamin Wilson who set up American government in Los Angeles.[26] Wilson was tapped by the founding junta for a job of strict legal writing and paperwork despite the fact that those were not his gifts. In fact, he did not perform the work of the office but hired Dr. Wilson W. Jones to do the real job, giving Jones the salary he received in his position.[27] At the time Wilson was focusing his energies on his growing real-estate fortune.[28] Neither Wilson nor anyone around him knew just what they were supposed to do, so they wrote the governor seeking instructions.[29] Governor Peter Burnett responded quickly and, as clerk, Wilson immediately called the new Court of Sessions together for its historic first meeting on June 24, 1850. One of the first items of business was to choose a temporary county courthouse, and the judges decided on Don Benito's Bella Union Hotel. So, in addition to his many other distinctions, Benjamin Wilson became the county's first landlord. The hotel adapted rooms for the county's first courtroom, a jury room and Don Benito's clerk's office, staffed by his double, Dr. Wilson Jones. Wilson charged the county one hundred dollars a month and the Bella Union remained the courthouse until May 1, 1851.[30]

The original Los Angeles County of Benjamin Wilson's clerkship, with its population of 3,530, was strikingly Lilliputian. On April 1, 1850, a grand total of 377 people cast votes in the first Los Angeles County election, sweeping into office the slate decided in advance by the junta in Judge Olvera's home:

> County judge, Augustin Olvera
> County attorney, Benjamin Hayes
> County clerk, B.D. Wilson
> Sheriff, G. Thompson Burrill
> Treasurer, Manuel Garfias
> Assessor, Antonio F. Coronel
> Recorder, Ignacio del Valle

Surveyor, J. R. Conway

Coroner, Charles B. Cullen

These men served the county on a part-time basis. In fact, in the entire state of California in 1850, only eighty-four people listed their occupation as employees of city or county government. Of the 77,631 men in the state, 57,797 were miners.[31]

The one recognized city in the county was Los Angeles, which had been an American city since the Treaty of Guadalupe in 1848, but the traditional Mexican style of government had been kept intact up to that time. With the election of July 1, 1850, a county structure was put into place to comply with the state legislature's new American government. The government of the City of Los Angeles, however, was little changed. The name of the chief executive was changed from *alcalde* to mayor, and the governing body was now to be known as the Common Council instead of the *ayuntamiento*. The new Common Council received from the *ayuntamiento* its public lands,[32] archives[33], its cache of arms[34] and its book of registered cattle brands.[35] There was so much for the new Common Council to do that it met on average almost every other business day during that first month.[36]

The original Common Council meeting of the City of Los Angeles was held on July 3, 1850, seating the councilmen who'd been elected two days earlier. The original seven members of the Common Council were a mixture of *Californios* and *Americanos*: David W. Alejandro (Alexander), Alejandro Bell, J. Temple, Manuel Requena, Julian Chavez, Cristobal Aguilar and Morris L. Goodman. Chavez and Aguilar resigned the following month, and Benjamin Wilson and his deputy county clerk Wilson Jones were elected to this first-year Common Council to fill the vacancies. The city attorney ruled that Wilson's position of county clerk presented "no incompatibility" to his serving on the Common Council as well.[37] In fact, dual positions in county and city government were common in that genesis era. The first mayor of Los Angeles, Dr. Alpheus Hodges, was the county coroner at the same time and Antonio F. Coronel simultaneously held positions as both city and county assessor. Cameron E. Thom was district attorney and city attorney simultaneously, and once defended each entity against the other in a land dispute.[38]

Wilson was sworn in as a member of the Common Council on September 13, 1850. By the end of the first council year, five of the original seven had resigned. In one case, Stephen C. Foster, the man appointed to oversee a fair election process, was himself elected to fill a vacancy.[39]

The council members decided not to accept pay for their service, although they did vote salaries for a secretary to the council ($7,200 a year), the mayor ($2,000 a year), the treasurer (two and a half percent "on all moneys which he may receive in the Treasury"),[40] and a school teacher.[41] Among the first matters to be taken up was the sale of public land to generate income for the new city government, a matter brought forward from the *ayuntamiento*. The first ordinance passed by the new Common Council was a seven-part law on the city's water supply.[42] It would seem that water was even more of a life-and-death issue to the early council members than the rampant crime. Standing committees were established for Police, Supplies and Finance. The council decided on the procedure for voting. If the vote was on the general terms of a proposition council members would stand, pronounce their names in a loud voice, and say "Aye" or "No." On routine matters those in favor would stand and those opposed would remain seated. If the governor of California announced himself while the council was in session, he was to be seated at the left of the council president.[43]

Despite all the crime in Los Angeles, the Police Committee widened its focus far beyond law enforcement "to attend to everything touching the comfort, health and adornment of the City."[44] For example, the Police Committee made recommendations on petitions for land, in the way a municipal planning commission might today.

The first criminal code of the City of Los Angeles was as follows:

> Art. 1st. The City's prisoners shall be formed in a chain-gang, and shall be put to work on public improvements.

> Art. 2d. The City's prisoners must be sentenced within two days.

> Art. 3d. When the City has no work in which to employ the chain-gang, the Recorder shall, by means of notices, conspicuously posted, notify the Public that such and such a number of prisoners will

be turned over to the highest bidder for private service, and in that manner they shall be disposed of for a sum which shall not be less than the amount of their fine and for double the time which they were to serve out as hard labor.

Art. 4th. The police shall gather in the vagrants of both sexes, putting them under arrest, and the Recorder shall assign them to serve private parties under proper and just conditions. Those who relapse into vagrancy shall be confined in the chain-gang until they produce a bondsman prepared to give a pecuniary security, at the Recorder's option, guaranteeing that the vagrant in question shall in the future be engaged in some useful occupation or leave the City limits. Such penal bonds shall, in due season, be vigorously enforced.

Art. 5th. In future no pits shall be dug in the City on premises that are not fenced in.

Art. 6th. On Saturdays every house-holder shall clean the front of his premises to the middle of the street, or for the space of at least eight *varas*.

Art. 7th. No filth shall be thrown into the *zanjas* carrying water for common use, nor into the streets of the City, nor shall any cattle be slaughtered in the same.

Art. 8th. Whosoever brings cattle into the City must have them tied to tame oxen and attended to by one or more conductors, so as to prevent the cattle doing any damage; should any be done, however, the conductor or conductors shall be held responsible for the same.

Art. 9th. Every owner of a shop or tavern, as well as everybody who lives in a house of two or more rooms, shall put a light in the door during the first two hours of every dark night.

Art, 10th. No spirituous liquors shall be sold after the hour of eight p.m. in winter and after nine p.m. in summer.

Art. 11th. Riding at a furious rate through the streets of the City is prohibited.

Arts. 12th. The washing of clothes in the *zanjas* which furnish water for common use, is prohibited.

Arts. 13th. Whosoever should walk the streets in a scandalous attire, or molest the neighbors with yells or in any other manner, shall be taken to jail if the hour be late for business, or the offender be intoxicated, and afterwards, at the proper hour, of when again sober, the Recorder shall impose a fine of not less than ten nor more than twentyfive (sic) dollars, which must be paid on the spot, otherwise the offender shall be sent to the chain-gang for a term of confinement not to exceed ten days. If he be an Indian, he shall pay a fine of three to five dollars or be imprisoned in the chain-gang for eight days.

Art. 14th. The same penalty shall be imposed for playing cards in the streets, regardless of the kind of game, likewise for playing any other game of the kind as is played in houses that are paying a tax for the privilege.

Art 15th. Infractions of articles 5, 6, 9, 10, 11 and 12 shall be punished with a fine of two dollars, and those of articles 7 and 8 with a fine of ten to twentyfive (sic) dollars, or with a term of arrest not to exceed ten days.

Art. 16th. The Recorder of the City shall enforce the penalties established by this Ordinance, and shall collect the fines from whosoever has to pay the same, turning over to the City Treasurer, every Saturday, the amount of such fines, of which he shall make proper entries; and inasmuch as he is a salaried officer he shall not charge any costs for performing the duties of his office.

Art. 17th. The Recorder shall, on the 1st or 2d of each month, produce a statement of all the prisoners of the City arrested during the preceding month, showing the amount of fine paid by each, the amount of indemnity received as per article 3, and a list of those who had served out their sentences in the chain-gang.

Art. 18th. Only those who have been arrested for infractions of the Regulations and Ordinances of the City shall be considered City prisoners.

Art. 19th. The marshal shall observe the fulfillment throughout the City of the provisions contained in these Regulations, and it shall be his duty to apprehend those who have made themselves liable to arrest, to report to the Recorder any important news that may transpire, and to furnish him the names of the persons who have violated the articles 6, 7, 9 and 10.[45]

The Police Committee's first draft had included laws against carrying or discharging firearms within the city limits but the council concluded that enforcement of this utopian fantasy in this Wild West town would be utterly impossible.

The following month, three additional articles were added:

All mixing with the Indians of California during their feasts or reunions within this City is prohibited.

Whosoever sells fruit or vegetables shall carry with him a paper proving his lawful acquisition thereof, except in the cases of direct producers.

The police shall have the power to apprehend and arrest the transgressors and bring them before the Recorder, who may impose a fine up to twenty dollars or ten days in the chain-gang for infractions of Article 1, and up to five dollars or two days in the chain-gang for violations of Article 2.[46]

Wilson was a member of the police committee of this original council at a time when police service was voluntary.[47] On October 9, the police committee suggested the formation of a Los Angeles Police Department, "consisting of a Captain and two roundsmen," but the council voted down the recommendation.[48]

Wilson was also in charge of a committee to find suitable quarters for the mayor and Common Council and was on a committee discussing the need for a hospital in view of the smallpox epidemic in the city.[49] Wilson was also a member of the council's school committee,[50] bridges committee,[51] and the sanitation committee.[52]

On November 6, 1850, the Common Council passed the first zoning code:

1st (On) lands . . . given away pursuant to the Municipal Ordinance of March 23d . . . the beneficiaries shall have the right to put up improvements, but a space of ten English feet must be left for a sidewalk or else the owner himself must put one down.

2d In future all those who wish to build on a line with the street shall first apply to the Council Committee having these matters in charge.

Among the taxes imposed by the council were:

Art. 3 "Sellers of intoxicating liquors . . . " $5/mo.

Art. 5 "Every billiard table or ten pin alley . . . " $5

Art. 6 "Every house where a game of chance or hazard is played
. . . " $100

Art. 10 "For every theatre, circus, or tightrope performance, caravan of animals, . . . " $5

Art. 16 ". . . tax on every piece of property . . . one quarter of one
per centum of its intrinsic value . . ."

The council also rejected proposed taxes on cockfights and bullfights.[53]

One of the most important officials in early Los Angeles government was the *zanjaria*, the man who looked after the water canals that chan-
neled water from the Los Angeles River into a network of troughs that in-
terlaced the city and the farmland nearby. So important was his job that he
was paid more than the mayor. Another key official was a court-appointed
commissioner of the salt ponds, who kept people and animals out of the
evaporation pools that kept the city supplied with salt.[54]

When Wilson reflected on his life years later, he remembered that
he had been the first mayor of the city. In those fluid early years of government in the tiny pueblo, with settlers and adventurers coming and going,
the legacy of Dr. Alpheus Hodges, who had apparently long since left the
area, was lost. Also, with so many offices to fill in those early days, so
many resignations, and so many men holding both county and city posts,
it was apparently easy to forget a little thing like who was the mayor of Los
Angeles. The City of Los Angeles had grown six-fold by the time Wilson
died, and there were few around in Wilson's later years who'd been there
almost three decades earlier, so almost no one was around who was able to
contradict his genesis stories. Wilson claimed he had been the first mayor,
and newspaper accounts of his death and funeral extolled Wilson as the
city's first mayor. But he wasn't.

The original minutes of the first years of government have been preserved and they are clear. They record the election of Dr. Alpheus Hodges as the first mayor of Los Angeles,[55] and they record Wilson's service on the first year's Common Council under Mayor Hodges. They also clearly record Wilson's election as the second mayor, on May 5, 1851.[56] Alas, history has not brought forward a photograph of Dr. Alpheus Hodges so we don't even know what the forgotten first mayor of Los Angeles looked like. Wilson was paid five hundred dollars for his year as mayor, plus fifty cents for every mayor's court decision that brought money to the city's treasury.[57]

The very first issue of the very first newspaper in Los Angeles printed Wilson's first report to the Common Council in which he began by talking about water and the need to build an aqueduct along the foothills west of the city. Again and again in those early records, the importance of water to the early settlers eclipsed all other concerns. In his report Mayor Wilson next suggested closing the public school since, in his opinion, its results were not worth the city's investment. He suggested using the education funds for a college instead. He urged a law against selling liquor to Indians and recommended a program of public labor for Indians and vagrants who'd been convicted of drunkenness. He also suggested that those arrested for breaking city laws not be fed during their first twenty-four hours in jail. Wilson, ever the fiscal conservative, also celebrated the fact that the new city had no debt.

Wilson appointed the first city marshal, Samuel Whiting.[58] In 1875 the title was officially changed from "marshal" to "chief of police." In addition to the marshal post, Wilson also convinced the Common Council to start a "police force," a volunteer organization headed by Dr. A.W. Hope, "to guard the security of the inhabitants and the conservation of peace in conformity with the laws of the state."[59] This law enforcement band was given Spanish lances and ribbons of authority reading "City of Los Angeles Police organized by the Common Council of Los Angeles, July 12, 1851."[60] When rumors flew that the Utes, who had so wantonly pillaged outlying ranchos, were planning to swoop down on the city itself, Wilson persuaded the Common Council to allocate fifty lances and a cannon to ward off any such attack. Maybe the Utes heard the news; there was no attack.[61]

Originally the civil affairs of Los Angeles County were overseen by the Court of Sessions, a three-man panel consisting of the county judge and two associate judges.[62] This same body oversaw the criminal justice system as well.

The original county judge was Augustin Olvera, who basically continued the role he was serving as "judge of the first instance," a post to which he'd been appointed by U.S. Military Governor Riley in 1849 to administer the existing Mexican law.[63] Judge Olvera assembled the township judges and they, in turn, selected two of their number to fill two posts of associate judges, or justices of the peace. They selected Jonathan R. Scott and Louis Robidoux. Robidoux, a former mountain man, had bought B.D. Wilson's Jurupa Ranch, the current City of Riverside. He lived so far away from Los Angeles that he was selected for his post before he even knew about the election.[64]

Later a Board of Supervisors was elected to govern the county's business. Wilson was elected to the Los Angeles County Board of Supervisors in 1853, its second year of existence. One of the pressing issues for this particular board was the pressure coming from Mormons in the San Bernardino Valley to win freedom from Los Angeles and form their own county. The other supervisors leaned heavily on Wilson because of his years of experience in that area. Wilson rode to his old neighborhood and interviewed the residents, finding those above the Santa Ana River in favor of a split and those below it opposed, but the state legislature drew the lines as requested by the new-county advocates.[65] Eight years later, in 1861, as the Civil War was beginning on the Eastern seaboard, Wilson was again elected to the Board of Supervisors, running as a Democrat. Of the fifteen contenders for the board he was the top vote-getter, amassing 573 votes.[66] He was elected again in 1862 and 1864.

Today's Board of Supervisors oversees a county workforce of over a hundred thousand employees and looks after the health, law enforcement, courts, flood control, water conservation and other services for a population of over ten million souls[67], but the business of the supervisors in early Los Angeles County, reflected in the minutes of its early meetings, was almost exclusively setting tax formulas. The value of all of the real estate in Los Angeles County in 1852 was $748,606. The value of land, improvements and personal property in Los Angeles County was $2,234,451.[68]

The original 1850 Los Angeles County was 4,340 square miles in size and contained only 3,530 people. It contained less than a fiftieth of the state's population, according to the 1852 census, but held a major part of the state's agricultural resources, with a fourth of its cattle and a fifth of its horses. One cultivated acre in twenty in California was in Los Angeles County.[69] Los Angeles County was enlarged before its first birthday to 34,520 square miles, stretching from the Pacific Ocean to the Colorado River. Over the years it gave up territory to present-day Kern, Riverside, San Bernardino, Orange and Ventura Counties.

While mayor, Wilson became one of the first members of the new Masonic Lodge No. 42, which held its first meeting on November 8, 1851.[70] The first Master of Los Angeles Lodge, Hillard P. Dorsey of Mississippi, was ignominiously kicked out of the Grand Lodge for fighting a duel, a violation of both Masonic and civil law.

NOTES FOR CHAPTER 13

1 Wilson ran for the State Assembly in 1851, losing to Andres Pico.

2 Newmark, Sixty Years in Southern California 1853-1913, 43.

3 Workman, The City That Grew, 173.

4 Newmark, Sixty Years in Southern California 1853-1913, 42.

5 Los Angeles Star, August 24, 1854.

6 Los Angeles Star, May 6, 1854.

7 Los Angeles Star, May 6, 1854.

8 Martinez, Facts About the City of Los Angeles, 2006.

9 Los Angeles Star, February 25, 1860,

10 Los Angeles Star, March 9, 1861.

11 City of Los Angeles Archives.

12 Guinn, A History of California, 293.

13 Starr, California: A History, 92.

14 Cameron, "Crime in the Early Pueblo Days," Los Angeles Times, B5.

15 Wolcott, Pioneer Notes From The Diaries of Judge Benjamin Hayes 1849-1875, 186.

16 Ibid.

17 Moroney, "Historical Background of Los Angeles County."

18 Guinn, A History of California, 285-286.

19 Robinson, Los Angeles From the Days of the Pueblo, 63.

20 Guinn, *Historical and Biographical Record of Los Angeles and Vicinity*, 147.

21 Wolcott, *Pioneer Notes From The Diaries of Judge Benjamin Hayes 1849-1875*, 186.

22 Kurutz, *Don Benito Wilson: A Pioneer In Transitional Southern California, 1841-1854*, 90.

23 *Los Angeles Star*, May 24, 1851.

24 *Los Angeles Star*, August 23, 1851.

25 The Democratic Party named Wilson inspector of election for San Gabriel. *Los Angeles Star*, October 14, 1856. Wilson was a Democrat from this point on.

26 Originally the post of county clerk was an elective office, serving as clerk to the county at large and the Superior Court. In 1852, with the establishment of the Board of Supervisors, the county clerk served that body as well. In 1913 the office of county clerk was changed from an elective office to an appointed office, and in 1958 it ceased to serve the Board of Supervisors. In 1991 the function of county clerk was assumed by the office of the County Registrar/Recorder, according to the *Guide to the Historical Records of Los Angeles County*, Los Angeles: Los Angeles County Task Force on Historical Records Preservation, 1991.

27 Wilson, "Observations."

28 Wolcott, *Pioneer Notes From The Diaries of Judge Benjamin Hayes 1849-1875*, 186.

29 Waldron, *Courthouses of Los Angeles County*, 214 and Layne, *Annals of Los Angeles*, 57, quoted in Kurutz, *Don Benito Wilson: A Pioneer in Transitional Southern California, 1841–1854*, 70.

30 Waldron, *Courthouses of Los Angeles County*, 351.

31 Hamilton "The Toughest Little Town," *Los Angeles Times*, H9.

32 Common Council minutes, July 5, 1850, City of Los Angeles archives.

33 Common Council minutes, July 6, 1850, City of Los Angeles archives.

34 Common Council minutes, July 13, 1850, City of Los Angeles archives.

35 Common Council minutes, August 3, 1850, City of Los Angeles archives.

36 The Common Council met on July 3, 5, 6, 8, 10, 13, 20, 27 and 31.

37 Common Council minutes, September 11, 1850, City of Los Angeles archives.

38 Newmark, *Sixty Years in Southern California 1853-1913*, 51-52.

39 Common Council minutes, January 4, 1851, City of Los Angeles archives.

40 Common Council minutes, July 10, 1850, City of Los Angeles archives.

41 Common Council minutes, July 31, 1850, City of Los Angeles archives. Hugh Overns to be paid fifty dollars a month to teach "English, French and Spanish . . . (for) six orphan boys or others whose parents are poor, and who shall be taught free of charge."

42 Common Council minutes, July 8, 1850.

43 Common Council minutes, July 27, 1850.

44 Common Council minutes, July 27, 1850.

45 Common Council minutes, August 7, 1850.

46 Common Council minutes, October 16, 1850.

47 Common Council minutes, September 26, 1850.

48 Common Council minutes, October 9, 1850.

49 Common Council minutes, March 12, 1850.

50 Common Council minutes, October 9, 1850.

51 Common Council minutes, November 20, 1850.

52 Common Council minutes, March 12, 1851.

53 Common Council minutes, November 14, 1850.

54 Cameron, "Crime in the Early Pueblo Days," *Los Angeles Times*, B5.

55 Dr. Alpheus Hodges was elected mayor on July 1, 1850, and served until May 7, 1851. Wilson was elected mayor on May 5, 1851, and served until May 4, 1852.

56 Common Council minutes undated, but bound chronologically at July 1, 1850.

57 Common Council minutes, May 21, 1851.

58 Crongeyer, *Six Gun Sound: The Early History of the Los Angeles County Sheriff's Department*, 25.

59 Common Council minutes, July 13, 1851.

60 Crongeyer, *Six Gun Sound: The Early History of the Los Angeles County Sheriff's Department*, 28.

61 Common Council minutes, November 27, 1851.

62 Cameron, "Crime in the Early Pueblo Days," *Los Angeles Times*, B5.

63 "Pioneer Courts and Lawyers of Los Angeles," 213-214.

64 Ibid., 214.

65 Letter from Stephen Foster to Wilson, February 27, 1853, and letter from Wilson to Foster, March 16, 1853, B.D. Wilson papers.

66 *Los Angeles Star*, August 24, 1861 and September 9, 1861.

67 Current figures taken from the Los Angeles County Web site, September 2007.

68 Guinn, *Historical and Biographical Record of Los Angeles and Vicinity*, 172-173,183.

69 Caughey, introduction to Wilson, B.D., *The Indians of Southern California in 1852*.

70 Spaulding, *History and Reminiscences: Los Angeles, City and County, California*, Vol. 1, 124.

CHAPTER 14

Sisters
of Charity

In January of 1856 Henry Rice Myles acted as Wilson's agent in selling the pueblo estate to the Sisters of Charity, which was shopping for a place for an orphanage and school in Los Angeles. Wilson played the hardheaded businessman to this Catholic group, asking for eight thousand dollars for the twelve acres or $4,500 down and another $4,500 in twelve months. The charity struggled with these terms, arguing that they'd been offered other properties on more advantageous terms. Myles insisted that Wilson would not lower his offer, and finally the Catholic Church accepted the deal,[1] figuring that revenue from Wilson's ten thousand-vine vineyard would help pay for running the place.[2] The deal closed on June 3, 1856.[3]

At the community level, it was the energy of Don Abel Stearns and John G. Downey, both Catholics,[4] who helped raise six thousand dollars and brought the new institution to a pueblo where public education had been a disappointment. Their ally in the Catholic hierarchy was Bishop Thaddeus Amat.[5] Bishop Amat, a Barcelona native, had come to the United States in 1838 and had served his Lazarist order in Louisiana, Philadelphia and Missouri before being consecrated as the second bishop of Monterey in 1854. With his diocese overwhelmed by the Gold Rush, he traveled to Europe for help. He brought back with him both Lazarists priests and Sisters of Charity.[6] Thus, the sisters who began their work on Wilson's old property came almost directly from Spain, and some spoke only Spanish.

The orphanage and school were overseen by Sister Scholastica, who had enrolled sixty-eight day students and admitted a number of orphans in her first month. Within a year the institution had grown to one hundred twenty, and the frame house of Don Benito Wilson had been replaced by an eleven-thousand-dollar brick structure. The school accepted tuition from parents able to pay their way, and provided free education to other girls.[7]

The Sisters of Charity continued their good work on the former estate of Benjamin Wilson for thirty-four years.[8]

NOTES FOR CHAPTER 14

1 Letter from Henry Rice Myles to Wilson, January 20, 1856; Power of Attorney for Mr. and Mrs. Wilson to Henry Rice Myles, January 28, 1856, B.D. Wilson papers.

2 Teiser, *Winemaking in California*, 66.

3 Letter from B.D. Wilson to his wife, June 4, 1856, B.D. Wilson papers.

4 Phelan, *The Gold Chain: A California Family Saga*, 189; and Wright, *A Yankee in Mexican California: Abel Stearns, 1798-1848*, 88-89.

5 Phelan, *The Gold Chain: A California Family Saga*, 189.

6 Catholic Encyclopedia.

7 de Packman, "Landmarks and Pioneers of Los Angeles," 73.

8 *Studies in the News*, 1856, California Research Bureau, California State Library.

B

CHAPTER 15

State Senate

In 1856[1] Wilson was elected to the state senate to represent the sparsely populated First District, and again in 1857 to represent Los Angeles County, which by then was its own senate district. At that time a single state senator represented all of Los Angeles, San Bernardino and San Diego Counties, everything from the Tulare County line to the Mexican border.[2] His district, one of the two largest in the senate, represented between a fourth and a third of California geography, among the most sparsely populated parts of the state. The senate contained thirty-four seats, each senator representing about 2,723 people,[3] a far smaller constituency than most City Council members represent in today's California.

California was wrested away from Mexico in a climate of desperate sectional jockeying in Washington, D.C., as the nation hardened more and more into slave vs. non-slave factions. Those divisions were transferred directly onto this incipient state as newcomers brought the prejudices of their former states to a frontier where a distinct California personality was yet to be forged. Most of the legislators had come to California within the past year and only two were native Californians.

California was not yet a state when the first state legislature convened on December 15, 1849, in what was to be the original state capital, *El Pueblo de San José*. The city had hurried to complete the meeting place for the legislature but had lost the race to time, a shortage of labor and rain. San Jose in 1849 was a few dozen abodes scattered about an empty plaza. Its population was about eight hundred fifty, which made it slightly smaller than the other pueblo in Alta California, Los Angeles.

Although the state was six years old by now, the legislature was meeting in its fourth capital city. The first two sessions met in San Jose, the second two in Vallejo and next in Benicia. In 1854 the capital was moved to Sacramento for the Sixth Session of the legislature. Wilson was elected to the following session, the second legislature to call Sacramento its capital.

This first legislature would be known in the future as "The Legislature of a Thousand Drinks," thanks to the famous shouts of Senator Thomas J. Green, "Well boys, let's go and take a drink, a thousand drinks!" The nickname of that first legislature belies a remarkable legacy. The representatives had borrowed from other states' constitutions, primarily those of New York and Iowa. The American military governors who had administered the state since it had come under American control had carefully left Mexican law and custom in place for the stability of the state. The first legislature swept aside that structure, leaving in place only such laws "as have been passed by the present Legislature." One concession to Mexican law was for registration of property by women, thus making California the first state in the union with a constitutional provision for married women's separate property. The legislature prohibited slavery, allowed free Blacks, (although without voting rights) and organized a militia, primarily to confront Indians. Of that first body of legislators some would wear blue and some would wear grey uniforms in the Civil War, two would die in duels (despite their votes for the law prohibiting such encounters), two would be committed to insane asylums, one would take his own life, and one would take the widow of another legislator as a lover, only to be murdered by her. Such was the work and future of "The Legislature of a Thousand Drinks."[4]

Wilson ran in 1856 as a Whig, but it was widely held that he went to the state capital as a Know-Nothing.[5] Since the Know-Nothings were a secret society, there are no records to confirm this connection, and Wilson himself made no public mention of such an affiliation in any record that has survived. A letter with the signatures of hundreds of local citizens vehemently denied that he was a Know-Nothing, indicating a very strong rumor to the contrary. The Sacramento *Democratic State Journal* listed Wilson's party affiliation as "Whig, but will be in opposition to the K.N.'s."[6]

Know-Nothings were at their peak political power in California in 1856, and most of the state offices were members of that party, including the governor, the speaker of the State Assembly, the president pro tem of the senate, the comptroller, treasurer and secretary of state.[7] But the Know-Nothings were soon to start down their steep path to oblivion in Sacramento and Wilson was to be a factor in their demise. The early important matter before the senate was the election of a U.S. Senator from California. United States Senators were not yet elected by popular vote, but were chosen by the state senate. Wilson was one of three Know-Nothings who switched to the Democratic side on the election of the U.S. senator, and he continued to vote with the Democratic Party, giving them a majority. Know-Nothing power in the Senate collapsed.[8]

Know-Nothings met in their secret society meetings to choose candidates, who would then run using their regular party labels. The candidates' names were often kept secret until just before an election to keep opponents off guard and to minimize political attacks. So powerful was this tactic that sometimes an entire local slate would be swept into office even though none of the winners had been announced publicly as candidates.[9]

The Know-Nothing Party came and went like a camera flash on the landscape of American political history. It was born of a sudden pang of native Americanism and a hostility to foreigners. It represented a reaction to the wave of German and Irish Roman Catholic immigrants of the mid-nineteenth century. It demanded that immigrants wait twenty-one years before becoming naturalized citizens, instead of the five required at the time, and thought that office holders should be native-born Americans. The party grew out of secret fraternal orders, like the 1849 Order of the Star Spangled Banner in New York, whose members answered questions about their organization with, "I know nothing." It spread like a prairie fire across the country, sweeping candidates into office at the local, state and federal level from 1854 to 1856. Candidates using the cover of both the Democratic and Whig Parties ran as camouflaged Know-Nothings. The Whig Party, crippled as it was by the slavery issue, was done in by the Know-Nothing movement. The Republican Party, while not a direct heir of the Know-Nothings, carried its mantle of nativism as late as the early twentieth century.[10]

Like a large group of teenagers who deny vehemently any use of illicit drugs, only to admit them smilingly in their more portly middle-age years much later, local politicians at the time protested with loud and righteous indignation that there were no secret meetings and that they were not connected with the Know-Nothing Party. A few years later, there was the shrug of, "Sure, everyone was doing it at the time."[11] In 1859 the Los Angeles Star, which had so loudly denounced the Know-Nothings only a few years earlier, defended a favored politician by saying, "There is scarcely a National Democrat of any prominence in the State or Union, who did not belong to that organization, and, in fact, the prominent members of every political party, were fascinated by its promises and seduced into its support. That organization died with the suddenness with which it was born, and those who survived its existence, marshaled themselves with the revived [Democratic Party], or united with the forces of antagonistic Republicanism."[12]

In 1868, a decade after his first service in the state senate, Wilson ran and won again.[13] The population of California had grown, so Wilson's prior district representing the entire southern part of the state had shrunk to the County of Los Angeles alone. The population of Los Angeles County in 1870 was 15,309, double what it had been in 1855 when he was in the senate before, despite the fact that the geographic size of the county was greatly reduced.[14] The number of senators had been increased from thirty-four to thirty-five.[15] Publicly he talked of simply responding to the tide of encouragement by his friends, but there was a darker, secret reason for seeking office in Sacramento again. Wilson was trying to occupy his mind with something other than his deep preoccupation with his son John's downward spiral of drinking and irresponsibility.

John had missed much school as a child growing up. Sometimes Benjamin Wilson kept the lad at home for help, and sometimes John simply refused to go to school until threatened with a whipping. When John was twenty-one years old, B.D. Wilson trusted his son with some responsibility in his company affairs in San Francisco to assist with his wine business, under the name B.D. Wilson & Son. John, however, was better at enjoying alcohol as an end user than marketing it as a middleman, and two years later, by 1868, Wilson had replaced his son with his new son-in-law, J. De Barth Shorb. Wilson not only cut John out of his business, but cut him out of his will as well.[16] John's behavior became a greater and greater public embarrassment to his father.

On December 8, 1869, the day Wilson was seated as a returning state senator he wrote to his wife: ". . . the Sadness of misfortunes over which I could not control weighed so heavy upon me . . . that unless I sought some way to throw off the melancolly (sic) and depression . . . I could not last many years . . . though I never said to you so before but I should never have entertained for one moment the idea of coming to the Legislature had it not been absolutely necessary for me at that time to enter into some excitement in order to divest my mind of sadness of heart to see the conduct of my poor unfortunate Son—but Enough of this—"[17]

J. De Barth Shorb had tried to console his father-in-law. "Your late years have certainly been most unhappy and made so from the same source which should now be giving that support and comfort so dear to the parents . . . Would to God!! I could spare or shield you from your troubles; but I hope you will allow me on my return to be as much a son to you as I would like, and in some small measure make up to you in love what pleasure you have lost and sorrows sustained. I am very sorry to hear of John's misconduct again, and his spending such a property as few young men ever have to enjoy. I really (think as you do that) his mind can not be settled or else he would try and lead a different life from the one now rushing him headlong on to ruin both temporal and Eternal. When I return . . . you had better leave time entirely for as long a time as possible as get away as far as you can from the constant . . . troubles. If you wish to do this I will live at the Vineyards as long as you are away."[18]

The following year, when John was twenty-five he was out drinking, as usual, and was offended by the insults of Charles E. Bean of the *Los Angeles News*, so John challenged him to a duel. Bean won the right to choose weapons and settled on rifles, with a distance of twenty paces. When John showed up on the field he had not practiced with the rifle and had not drilled himself on firing at the proper count. Somehow John's rifle misfired and the count was restarted. In the next round John was wounded in the left arm, although not seriously.[19]

Later that year Wilson wrote his wife from Washington, D.C., apprehensive that he had received no correspondence from home. "I feel as though something has gone wrong and you all are thinking it best to withhold the bad news from me." His paranoia was strengthened by a newspaper item he read in a California newspaper about the suicide of a "John Wilson." Could this be his John Wilson? With the mess his son had made of his life, it wouldn't surprise him, he wrote. Wilson's worst fears were true. Soon, correspondence from his wife reached him confirming that his son had taken his own life in the Bella Union Hotel, the Los Angeles landmark his father had once owned.[20] Wilson wrote back a tortured and anguished letter lamenting that this had been one of the saddest years of his life.

Wilson was not the strongest voice in the state capital, but he was elected by a sparsely-populated, agrarian section of the state against the gold-rich Northern Californians, who represented the overwhelming power in California at that time. Wilson helped bring railroads to Los Angeles and helped win government funding for a port at Wilmington. He took seriously the petitions he got on all sides of an issue. Some citizens of Anaheim petitioned him to revoke the charter of the city because of its "outrageous" plan to spend fifteen thousand dollars to bring a railroad there when such a debt could never be repaid. Other citizens lobbied him to support the city and its investment.[21] He was asked to promote bridges across the Los Angeles and San Gabriel Rivers.[22] But he sponsored little legislation and seldom made the Northern California newspapers. He was appointed to fewer committees in his second year than in his first, and in his second year he asked for, and was granted, a leave of absence from the senate for an indefinite period of time, not returning to the legislature during the rest of the session.[23] Why he left is not clear. Perhaps business matters back home were too pressing.

He got along well with the other elected representatives[24] and was probably respected for his business success in Southern California. He was lonesome for his family, finding the hotel accommodations in Sacramento "very common."[25]

A hint about Wilson's senate presence comes in the form of a speech he delivered in 1856 arguing against review of Mexican land titles by the new United States government. His speech reveals a self-deprecating style, an almost painful air of inferiority and a backwoods English that betrays his lack of formal education. But the senator representing all of Southern California showed a sophisticated grasp of parliamentary order[26] and a talent for weaving a persuasive argument. Wilson showed a clear idea of right and wrong, especially as it affected his own business affairs. Conflict of interest in that era didn't extend to promoting one's own affairs in the state legislature. This speech in Wilson's hand is characteristic of his writing and pubic speaking:

> . . . Now Mr. P[resident] with all due defference (sic) to the gentlemen who have proceeded me, whose superior acquirements in every respect I acknowledge, and I assure you that I feel much embarased (sic), to even attempt to raise my feeble voice here in opposition to so much intellect, but my duty in my mind demands it. . . . I am neither a Lawyer or Statesman but to defend the position that I take I think the Humblest citizen who has had the good fortune to be born and raised in the Land of Liberty knows his rights and he also knows the laws of his country will protect those rights.

He concluded with,

> that the world will not point to us and say with truth that the Ligislature (sic) of California in AD 1856 had the boldness and I might say the dishonesty to take from the weaker party and give to the stronger . . . why not call upon those rich bankers in the state and command them and tell them they must divide their money with those that have none.

Wilson's political career was almost capped by a seat in Congress.

His friend and former U.S. senator from California, William M. Gwinn, tried hard to win the Democratic Party's nomination for Wilson in 1875, but failed. Gwinn wrote to Wilson on July 13, 1875, saying, "All know now what I said time and again before the nomination was made. That you were the man the party and the country needed. My words were unheeded . . ." Thus, the California state senate was the highest office Wilson held.

Notes for Chapter 15

1 Election of September 5, 1855.

2 Hummelt, *California State Blue Book: Sesquicentennial Edition*.

3 Based on the United States Census numbers of 1850.

4 For a closer look at the first California legislature see Ignoffo, *Gold Rush Politics: California's First Legislature*.

5 Letter to Wilson signed by Jonathan R. Scott and thirty-two others, Feb. 5, 1856, endorsing his split from the Know-Nothings and his opposition to their candidate for the U.S. Senate, B.D. Wilson papers.

6 *Democratic State Journal*, January 7, 1856.

7 Hurt, "The Rise and Fall of the 'Know-Nothings' in California," No. 1, 16-49; 99-128. and *Democratic State Journal*, January 5 1856.

8 Guinn, *A History of California*, 47-48.

9 Hurt, "The Rise and Fall of the 'Know-Nothings' in California," 23-24.

10 Kutler, "Know-Nothing Party, or American Party."

11 The *Los Angeles Star* on August 24, 1854, had written that the body of Know-Nothing principles "surely strikes at the root of our glorious Constitution, which guarantees to every man the free expression of these principles, either political or religious." An editorial in the *Southern Californian* on May 2, 1855, denounced the alarmism of those railing against "Know-Nothings," claiming that there is no evidence of such a party except in the minds of politicians from "defunct partyism."

12 *Los Angeles Star*, August 21, 1859.

13 Election of November 3, 1868.

14 The population of Los Angeles County in 1855 is estimated to have been 7,430; the Census figure for 1870 was 15,309. See "Population Growth by Single Year: Los Angeles County, 1850-1998" at the Urban Education Partnership Web site (www.laep.org/target/science/population/table.html).

15 The number of senators in the first legislature in 1849 was 16. In 1852 it was increased to 28, increased again by 1854 to 34, in 1858 to 35 and by 1862 it was 40, and has remained at that number ever since.

16 Probate Court, Superior Court of Los Angeles County, #1030 Estate of B.D. Wilson.

17 Letter from Wilson to his wife, December 8, 1869, B.D. Wilson papers.

18 Letter from Shorb to Wilson, July 26, 1869, B.D. Wilson papers.

19 Letter from Shorb to Wilson, March 25, 1870, B.D. Wilson papers.

20 Charles Robinson Johnson wrote to Cave Johnson Couts "Johnny Wilson, old Don Benito Wilson son, committed suicide at the Bella Union yesterday. Case 'bad whiskey.'" Cave Couts papers, Huntington Library.

21 Petition from "the largest taxpayers" in Anaheim, January 6, 1871, B.D. Wilson papers; and petition of John Fischer and others, December 12, 1872.

22 Letter from S.W. Packard, January 12, 1872, B.D. Wilson papers.

23 *State Journal*, 1857, 623.

24 Benjamin D. Wilson letter from Sacramento to his wife, February 9, 1870, B.D. Wilson papers.

25 Benjamin D. Wilson letter from Sacramento to his wife, February 11, 1872, B.D. Wilson papers.

26 B.D. Wilson papers.

CHAPTER 16

Margaret Hereford

Perhaps no element of Wilson's life better represents his segue from the Don Benito of Mexican culture to the B.D. Wilson of the new American state than two marriages. In 1844, when Wilson was thirty-two and enjoying the life of a gentleman rancher in Mexican California, he had married Ramona Yorba, the fifteen-year-old daughter of the neighboring *ranchero*. They blessed their first born with a Spanish name, María de Jesús. Two years later, however, they gave their second child, John, an American first name, although his middle name, Bernardo, honored Ramona's father.

Wilson's Mexican wife, Ramona, died in 1849, and by the time Wilson remarried four years later, the world around him had changed dramatically. Los Angeles was a city under American administration and California was flying the American flag. Instead of the occasional American in Southern California the region was now teeming with them.

Wilson's second wife, Margaret Hereford, was an American pioneer, a woman with storied Wild West adventures of her own. Her Hereford family history was intertwined with one of the most legendary family names of the mountain-man epoch, the Sublettes. She had seen early Western history written in St. Louis, Santa Fe, Chihuahua, San Francisco,

San Jose and Los Angeles. Like Wilson, she had ventured far beyond the frontiers of the United States to make a life in Mexico only to have the red-white-and-blue tide overtake her.

Margaret was born in 1820 to a prominent Virginia family. When she was sixteen she received two letters from a suitor who signed his name in code. The suitor disappeared from her correspondence but she hauled his two letters through her various adventures the rest of her life. She was living in Pontotoc, Mississippi, when she began a courtship with her cousin, Thomas A. Hereford, who was living in Tuscumbia, Alabama. She married Dr. Hereford some time between 1840 and 1842 and the two took for granted the kind of physical comforts that their extended family had enjoyed. He had written, "I dislike to see this glorious harvest of physicians passing off without some of its benefits myself."[1] And she had written him in return, "I am truly delighted to hear that you have such flattering prospects for making some money for my dear Mother."[2]

The Sublette family was looking for someone to lease and run their ninety-acre resort and therapeutic springs in Sulfur Springs, Missouri. Andrew Sublette thought young Hereford would be ideal. He said that Dr. Hereford had "money and negroes" and "those who knew him spoke well of him," so older brother William Sublette leased him the resort and its therapeutic springs in 1842 along with rights to timber and coal beds. Hereford was to manage the property, profit from it, and pay rent to the elder Sublette.[3] While in Missouri their only child was born on October 27, 1843, a son they named Edward Sublette Hereford.[4]

It seemed that Dr. Hereford had fallen into a business arrangement that was sure to produce the wealth he so fervently craved, but his managerial skills were not up to the potential, and the resort failed. Having disgraced himself in the failed business in St. Louis, he banished himself to the frontier, where he could make a fortune and return to his relations with pockets full and head held high. Alas, the initial business failure was not a wild card of fate, but the symptom of a chronic lack of entrepreneurial common sense, or bad luck, or both. He would spend the rest of his life trying one scheme after another, in one frontier town after another, hauling his unhappy wife and family with him. The correspondences from

Margaret to her mother and sisters are litanies of chronically poor health and desperate loneliness. In one letter Margaret moans that she could hardly finish her letter because of her crying.

In 1848 Margaret and Dr. Hereford were in Santa Fe. Margaret found that she liked Mexico more than she thought she would, although she was wide-eyed at the shootings and the recent hanging of a horse thief. She socialized only with other Americans, avoiding social relations with the native Mexicans,[5] even though her five-year-old son now spoke Spanish "almost like a native of this country."[6] Dr. Hereford was in a business partnership with Solomon Sublette, the youngest of the five mountain men Sublette brothers.[7] Margaret's sister, Frances, was in Santa Fe, too. Frances had married William "Cut Face" Sublette, the oldest of the Sublette brothers, but he had died in 1845.[8] In May of 1848 Frances married Solomon. Dr. Hereford and Solomon were now engaged in trade, having spent "nine or ten thousand dollars" on goods.[9] The greatest wealth in that era was usually made by the merchants, for the simple reason that significant capital was needed to buy the goods in the first place and this set the bar out of the reach of all but those who already had capital or were able to raise it. But every such purchase was a gamble, pinned to the hope of customers to buy those very goods at a healthy markup. In the case of Sublette & Hereford, the gamble failed within a few months and the two would-be merchants had to spend more time unloading their goods than they had selling them at full markup. The unlucky Dr. Hereford lost "several thousand dollars," depriving him "of all the means I ever had."

Solomon Sublette packed up for a return to the United States, but Dr. Hereford wrote that "I have made up my mind not to return to the United States until I have made a desperate effort to regain my health & the money I have lost."[10] The "desperate effort" would be to give up merchandising and relocate deeper into Mexico, in Chihuahua, where he would take up the practice of medicine once again. He had been told that there was no physician in Chihuahua, and a doctor taking advantage of that void could make nine to ten thousand dollars a year.[11] Dr. Hereford wrote his mother-in-law, "I do not remain in this country . . . by choice . . . I am too poor to live respectably in the States & too proud (to) live otherwise . . ."[12]

Margaret reminded her mother that this dislocation to Mexico was necessary "as you would not always like to see me poor." She wrote, "Tell the Children that when the Dr. makes some money I intend sending them a pretty present."[13] In all of Margaret's letters she referred to her husband as "Dr. Hereford" or "the doctor," and never referred to him by his first name. She addressed her letters to Dr. Hereford, and later to Benjamin Wilson, as "Dear Husband."

As it turned out, there was no fortune waiting for Dr. Hereford in Chihuahua as a physician. He caught cholera and suffered miserably with chills and fever. Little Eddy was emaciated with the same chills and fever. Margaret avoided the cholera but suffered from her old (unnamed) malady. By late 1849 she was taking in boarders to make ends meet.[14] The couple talked of packing up and going home, but the Indian attacks on Americans in the country north of them had grown so severe that they dared not risk the journey.[15] Also, Dr. Hereford had a new prospect for making a lot of money.

He heard that mules were fetching a huge price in California, so he borrowed money and went from ranch to ranch buying mules, finally building a herd of two hundred. The arduous journey of two thousand miles would keep him in dangerous Indian country for three months, but he reckoned that he would make ten to fifteen thousand dollars from the venture. He would take twenty-five men with him who would make the trip for their expenses. He would also take his ailing kinsman, Rambler Hereford, who'd been injured by the Indian arrows. This would be a risky and miserable gamble, but with the extraordinary profit, Dr. Hereford said, "I think we will have enough to live on with our economy anywhere." Dr. Hereford wrote to a cousin, "nothing but poverty would, or could, make me undertake it, but my maxim is keep trying. And if desperate exertions will extricate me from my present condition I am resolved to do it."

The mule drive would be far too hazardous for Margaret, so she and little Eddy would ride mules with friends from Chihuahua over the Rocky Mountains to Mazatlan on the Pacific coast of Mexico, where they could catch a ship to California.[16] Once in California Margaret was to live anyplace in the state she deemed best and make decisions for her husband until he arrived. She was to write him in Los Angeles in about three months to let him know where she and Eddy were.[17]

In the spring of 1850 Margaret and little Eddy traveled with Dr. Hereford and his party to Durango, then the family sold their carriage and went their separate ways. Dr. Hereford gave Margaret all the money he had left, about a thousand dollars, for her to live on until he could meet her in California some months later. The injured Rambler Hereford continued on with Dr. Hereford. Margaret and Eddy spent fourteen days traveling the three hundred miles across the Sierra Madres. By her account she was almost the first American woman to cross those mountains. Steamship berths from Mazatlan were almost impossible to book, and would cost five hundred dollars even at that, so Margaret and her son took a sailing ship up the coast for the voyage to San Francisco.[18] Eddy recovered his health almost immediately aboard the ship as it struggled slowly north-ward, plagued by contrary winds or areas of calm the entire way.

Thirty-six or thirty-seven days later, in May of 1850, Margaret and her son arrived in San Francisco at the height of the Gold Rush. She found a larger city than she expected, with more than six hundred vessels in port with more constantly arriving from all parts of the world. Buildings were springing up "as if by magic" and prices were frighteningly high. She was desperately lonely and friendless in this "strange land with strange people so far from all who are near and dear to me."[19] She did not like San Francisco. "It is a great place for business, but I would not live in it for any consideration . . . on account of the climate." She wrote, "the winds blows continually and is cold enough to freeze you." Prophetically, she warned that fire would be the undoing of the city. "San Francisco . . . had two large fires . . . in a short time, houses go up as if by magic, but they will always be subject to those fires until they build their houses in a more substantial manner and make some provisions against them, property is not safe there." Margaret made contact with Andrew, one of the Sublette brothers, who agreed that she should leave San Francisco. He suggested San Jose, so Margaret and her little boy soon moved. "San Jose is the capi-tal of California and is considered the most desirable place for a residence in the country, on account of the health and mildness of the climate," she wrote.[20] While in San Jose she boarded with a Mrs. Branham, and was reduced to learning how to do her own washing and ironing.[21]

As the months went by, most of those who were aware of Dr. Hereford's perilous journey were convinced he had died or had fallen victim to a dreadful tragedy, and Margaret had just about given up hope of ever seeing him again. In September, though, he had finally made it to Los Angeles[22] after undergoing "almost every hardship and privation." He had managed to get most of the precious mules there but had lost many of his men to sickness, and, after the party reached California, had had to leave the suffering Rambler Hereford on the trail, where Dr. Hereford assumed that he had died. Once in Los Angeles the doctor left his mules there, and hurried to see his wife and son in San Jose, meeting up with them in October of 1850, six months after saying good-bye in Durango.[23] After all his troubles the doctor found the price of mules in Los Angeles the same as it was in Mexico and was forced to sell the animals for what he had paid for them.

Dr. Hereford and Margaret settled in Los Angeles where Dr. Hereford found the business conditions draconian. (This at a time when Wilson was doing very brisk business as a merchant and trader.) Despite the huge costs in transporting goods from the United States, the doctor judged retail prices to be no higher than in New York and hard currency was almost non-existent. Dr. Hereford involved himself in several different businesses in the port of San Pedro. He kept a tavern or inn, ran carriages and freight wagons from the port to Los Angeles and offered other services related to shipboard freight. W.T.B. Sanford was a partner in one of Dr. Hereford's business ventures, but Hereford bought out Sanford for $350. Dr. Hereford ruled out having more children since he had never been able to earn funds to educate them.[24]

In 1851, the Herefords were living in San Pedro.[25] He petitioned the court for title to 160 acres of land, writing that he intended to take possession of the plot on July 10, 1851, with his understanding that this shoreline property could be claimed "by first actual settlers." At this time they may have been running their inn, since the census survey shows nine laborers, Margaret's twenty-one-year-old brother Thomas S. Hereford and another man living with them. A year after that, however, they were living with the widower Benjamin Wilson, mayor of Los Angeles, in his pueblo house.[26] The wealthy Don Benito Wilson had no need for paid boarders, and there was no family connection to compel him to take the Herefords in, so it may be that Margaret was housekeeper or governess for the widower Wilson, or that Dr. Hereford was overseeing some part of Wilson's estate. While living there, less than a year and a half after arriving in Los Angeles, Dr. Hereford died on January 7, 1852.[27]

Edward Sublette Hereford, the eight-year-old son of Thomas and Margaret, was represented in the probate proceedings by Wilson's close friend, attorney Benjamin Hayes, who would later become a Superior Court judge. The judge in the probate hearing was Augustin Olvera, who is remembered today in Los Angeles' Olvera Street. Dr. Hereford's will, witnessed by B.D. Wilson, left everything to Margaret.[28]

A little over a year after Dr. Hereford's death, thirty-three-year-old Margaret Hereford married forty-one-year-old Benjamin Davis Wilson, on February 1, 1853.[29] Wilson wrote to Margaret's mother, ". . . you will say where you receive these few imperfect lines which strange things happened in this world. As strange as it will seem to you, yet to me it has appeared quite natural, that is natural that I should have loved your daughter, the only thing that has been strange in the whole event was that your daughter should have loved me."[30] The letter's eloquence and correct spelling and grammar hint that Margaret may well have helped pen this important announcement letter to her mother. And so, Margaret, who had been uprooted again and again and forced to live below her station while she followed her luckless husband throughout Mexico and the new state of California, married one of the wealthiest men in the growing pueblo of Los Angeles. She would never be uprooted again, never be poor again and would at last enjoy the station of a leading social figure.

NOTES FOR CHAPTER 16

1 Letter from Thomas Hereford to Margaret Hereford, May 23, 1840, B.D. Wilson papers.
2 Letter from Margaret Hereford to Thomas Hereford, June 21, 1840, B.D. Wilson papers.
3 Sunder, *Bill Sublette: Mountain Man*, 189.
4 Wilson-Patton Bible, B.D. Wilson papers..
5 Letter from Margaret Hereford to her mother, August 1848, B.D. Wilson papers.
6 Letter from Thomas A. Hereford to his aunt, Esther Sale Hereford, December 12, 1848, B.D. Wilson papers.
7 Articles of incorporation, Sublette & Hereford, March 31, 1848, B.D. Wilson papers.
8 Sunder, *Bill Sublette: Mountain Man*, 230.
9 Letter from Margaret Hereford to her mother, Elizabeth Sale Hereford, August 1848, B.D. Wilson papers.
10 Letter from Thomas Hereford to his aunt, Esther Sale Hereford, Margaret Hereford's mother, May 1849, B.D. Wilson papers.
11 Letter from Thomas Hereford to his aunt, Esther Sale Hereford, Margaret Hereford's mother, December 12, 1848, B.D. Wilson papers.
12 Letter from Thomas Hereford to his aunt, Esther Sale Hereford, Margaret Hereford's mother, May 1849, B.D. Wilson papers.
13 Letter from Margaret Hereford to her mother, Esther Sale Hereford, August 1848, B.D. Wilson papers.
14 Letter from Thomas A. Hereford to his aunt, Esther Sale Hereford, November 20, 1849, B.D. Wilson papers.
15 Margaret Hereford to her mother, Esther Sale Hereford, March 9, 1850, B.D. Wilson papers.
16 Letter from Thomas A. Hereford to his cousin, Thomas S. Hereford, April 15, 1850, B.D. Wilson papers.
17 Letter from Thomas A Hereford to Margaret Hereford, April 17, 1850, B.D. Wilson papers.
18 Letter from Margaret Hereford to her mother, Esther Sale Hereford, April 20, 1850, B.D. Wilson papers.
19 Letter from Margaret Hereford to her mother, Esther Sale Hereford, June 1, 1850, B.D. Wilson papers.
20 Letter from Margaret Hereford to her sister, Mary Catherine Cooper, August 25, 1850, B.D. Wilson papers.
21 Letter from Margaret Hereford to her mother, Esther Sale Hereford, October 13, 1850, B.D. Wilson papers.
22 Letter from Thomas A. Hereford to his aunt, Esther Sale Hereford, February 20, 1851, B.D. Wilson papers.
23 Letter from Margaret Hereford to her mother, Esther Sale Hereford, October 13, 1850, B.D. Wilson papers.
24 Letter from Thomas A. Hereford to his aunt, Esther Sale Hereford, February 20,1851, B.D. Wilson papers.

25 Petition to court for grant of public land.

26 Sworn probate statement of B.D. Wilson, January 24, 1852 ". . . and immediately before his death said Hereford resided at the house of witness . . . said Hereford departed this life on the 7th day of January, A.D. 1852, and died at the house of witness . . . said will was executed at the house of witness."

27 Wilson-Patton Bible, B.D. Wilson papers.

28 Probate of Thomas A. Hereford, Huntington Library collection.

29 Wilson-Patton Bible, B.D. Wilson papers.

30 Letter from B.D. Wilson to Esther Sale Hereford, March 28, 1853, B.D. Wilson papers.

CHAPTER 17

Civil War

The admission of California as a new American state was a hotly debated topic in Congress and it helped to cascade the Union into its eventual breakup and civil war. Slave and non-slave advocates in Congress had jealously watched the balance of proposed new states. California, by its geography, was a Southern state. Just as the states of the United States were divided north and south on the issue of slavery, so was California. Southerners formed a significant percentage of the Americans in Southern California and were prominent among its leading citizens. Wilson himself was a Southerner, having been born in Tennessee and having spent his entire life in Southern states prior to his sojourns as a fur trapper and his residence in the Mexican territories of New Mexico and California. Again and again Southern Californians tried to divide California into two states, and as a state senator Wilson participated in that drama. In the legislature immediately preceding Wilson's first service as a state senator, the Assembly passed a measure to divide California into three states, "Colorado" in the south, "Shasta" in the north, and "California" in central zone, including San Francisco. Pro-slavery forces dominated state politics, and a division into three states would increase West Coast pro-slavery votes in the U.S. Senate. The state senate failed to act on the Assembly's measure before the session ended, however. Wilson came to the state senate in the following session as Know-Nothings swept into power, and the Know-Nothings killed any chance of splitting the state for the time being.

In the legislature of 1858-59, long after Wilson had left, the issue of splitting the state arose again. Both the Assembly and state senate approved a measure to split off the six southern California counties as the state of "Colorado," and the measure was signed by the governor and endorsed by voters in Southern California 2,477 to 828. The measure died in Washington, D.C., however.[1] The federal government had enough on its hands trying to ward off a civil war without this added complication.

As the war clouds gathered in the states to the east, supporters and opponents of the Southern cause hardened their positions in Southern California. Years after the Civil War Benjamin Wilson would say, ". . . most of us (delegates to the state constitutional convention) Southern men, were positive that we wanted no slavery. We had enough of a variety of races, and the character of the country was not favorable to any but free labor." Although against slavery, he was opposed to forcing an end to the institution, "believing that gradual voluntary emancipation would be the only proper method of solving that problem."[2]

Both B.D. Wilson's family and that of his wife, Margaret, were rampant defenders of the Southern cause. Margaret's family back in Missouri owned slaves and during a visit back home in 1856 she wrote her husband, "I think it is very doubtful about my getting a good servant to take home with me, as it is hard to find one here, I have been thinking of buying one of Mother's women, but do not know what to do about it."[3] He responded, "I think it would be best to hire a white servant than to buy a black one as they (the black) would perhaps give you a great deal of trouble and the white or free one you can discharge when she gets impudent there is plenty of servants in the up country now I am told at fair wages . . ."[4] This may have been more the answer of a pragmatist than an opponent to slavery.

Margaret's son, Edward Hereford, was less ambiguous. In a virulent diatribe against President Abraham Lincoln early in the Civil War he said, "Jefferson Davis has few men compared to (Lincoln's), but they are fighting for their altars and their homes, and will conquer the North live, survive, or perish in the attempt."[5]

For the presidential election of 1860, the diminutive Republican Party nominated Abraham Lincoln as its candidate, and the Democratic Party, with its huge numerical advantage, had only to agree on a standard bearer and ride the high tide of their national majority to the White House. But the turbulence of the North-South debate split their ranks and their crippled leaders were forced to field two candidates. Stephen A. Douglas was a Democratic candidate acceptable to the Northern sentiment and John C. Breckenridge was the option more palatable to Southern emotions. B.D. Wilson was a member of the Democratic County Central Committee when the national choices were considered at the local level. The meeting of August 10, 1860, at the Montgomery Saloon began with a motion by General Drown to support the presidential candidate of the National Democratic Convention, Stephen A. Douglas. Wilson didn't agree, and he placed a counter motion before the committee in support of John C. Breckenridge, the candidate preferred by the South. Wilson's motion went on to resolve "That we believe in equality of States, and inscribing that motto upon our flag, we enter the presidential contest, with the assurance of the truth of our principles, and the righteousness of our cause."[6] His phrase, "equality of the states," was code for the Southern position, and clearly Wilson's fellow committee members were of a similar view. All committee members sided with Wilson except for General Drown, who said he "could have no further connection with this committee," and withdrew from its proceedings. The Democratic newspaper the *Los Angeles Star* endorsed Breckinridge, as did California's two U.S. Senators, its two Congressmen and most of its statewide officials.[7] Los Angeles County voters felt likewise, as well. In the 1860 election, Los Angeles voters cast 686 for Breckenridge and 494 for Douglas. Breckenridge got almost twice as many votes as Lincoln's 356.[8]

During the height of the Civil War the California Democratic Party hammered out its platform, and Wilson was present. That platform included this plank: ". . . we denounce and unqualifiedly condemn the Emancipation Proclamation of the President of the United States as tending to protract indefinitely civil war, incite servile insurrection, and inevitably close the door forever to a restoration of the union of these States."[9]

Among the ardent secessionists in Southern California was a well-known Black barber named Peter Biggs. Biggs was so outspoken in his enthusiasm for the Confederacy that he was arrested by the Army, shackled with a ball and chain and marched to the military brig at Drum Barracks. Even so, he yelled out on his trudge to jail for "three hearty cheers for Jeff Davis."[10]

As the war of words became a shooting war after Fort Sumter, South Carolina, on April 12 and 13, 1860, Benjamin Wilson's circle of friends began taking sides, most of them siding with the South. Wilson's friend and political ally, William McKendree Gwin, the U.S. Senator from California was an outspoken proponent of slavery and was actually thrown into prison by federal troops during the war. Some of the leaders of Los Angeles packed up and headed home to the South to stand with those they'd grown up with. Prominent local attorneys Cameron E. Thom and J. Lancaster Brent returned to the South. Thom came back after the war and figured in early Glendale history but Brent made his post-war home in New Orleans.[11]

After the war, Wilson continued to vent his Southern views. He helped raise funds for the Southern Relief Societies and was one of that agency's largest Los Angeles contributors.[12] He wrote to his good friend Brent after the war, "Last year the Legislature passed an act that no Lawyer should practice in the county who would not swear that he had never aided or assisted the rebellion of course the act will be repealed when good sense returns to the people but till then you would be embarrassed in practice . . ."[13] He actively opposed passage of the Fifteenth Amendment, granting the vote to citizens "regardless of race, color, or previous condition of servitude."[14] Many of his relatives were ruined by the Civil War. A cousin of Margaret wrote, "I have been forced from my home, made by honest toil in a honest profession, the accumulations of years swept away at one stroke & I fleeing for my life, because I would not and could not be an abolitionist & Negro equalitist."[15] Five years after the war ended Wilson traveled to see his brother in Mississippi, and wrote to Margaret, "I feel Somewhat disirous (sic) to see my brother leave this country on account of the Negro government they have here and the Terrible bad system of Labour here."[16]

So, Wilson had watched the Civil War from afar, had sympathized with his secessionist friends, had sat with the state Democrats as they voted to denounce the Emancipation Proclamation, and had continued to share many of the Rebels' feelings after the war. But he had remained in California and prospered during the conflict. And he had given land for a base which the Union Army could use to tamp down Southern activism in Southern California.

NOTES FOR CHAPTER 17

1 Guinn, "How California Escaped State Division," 226-228.

2 Los Angeles Star, September 18, 1869.

3 Letter from Margaret Hereford Wilson to B.D. Wilson, September 14, 1856, B.D. Wilson papers.

4 Letter from B.D. Wilson to Margaret Wilson, October 23, 1856, B.D. Wilson papers.

5 Essay titled "The War existing between the Northern and Southern States" by E.S. Hereford, written in an invoice book of Wilson & Packard, B.D. Wilson papers.

6 Los Angeles Star, August 11, 1860.

7 Ibid.

8 Los Angeles Star, November 10, 1860.

9 Los Angeles Star, July 25, 1863.

10 Newmark, Sixty Years in Southern California 1853-1913, 330-331.

11 Ibid., 294-296.

12 Los Angeles Semi-Weekly News, quoted in Aitken, "Benjamin Wilson, Southern California Pioneer."

13 Letter from B.D. Wilson to J. Lancaster Brent, September 21, 1865. Huntington Library collection.

14 Senate Journal, 1869-70, 149-152 and 430.

15 Letter to Margaret Wilson from Henry Foote Hereford, June 2, 1864, B.D. Wilson papers.

16 Letter from B.D. Wilson to Margaret Wilson, November 17, 1870, B.D. Wilson papers.

CHAPTER 18

San Pedro and Wilmington

L os Angeles was a small pueblo but still one of the more significant cities near the Pacific coastline and San Pedro was the port that served the pueblo twenty-five miles inland. Richard H. Dana, Jr., described his visit to San Pedro in the 1830s, writing in his *Two Years Before the Mast*, ". . . we let go our anchor at a distance of three or three and a half miles from shore . . . as far as the eye could see there was no sign of a town—not even a house to be seen. What brought us into such a place, we could not conceive." Hides were exported from this port and merchandise was received here for local merchants, but San Pedro was a lousy place for ships to call. There was no natural harbor and ships had to drop anchor three miles offshore,[1] even then staying ready to heave anchor at the first threat of a perilous sou'easter. Smaller boats ferried the freight to shore, and passengers would often have to climb into the water to free their boat from a sand bar, or worse, get tossed into the surf as their boat capsized. The only suitable beach for landing sat at the bottom of a sixty-foot bluff. Sailing vessels continued to carry most of the San Pedro trade even after the arrival of the first steamship there in 1849. Only highly perishable freight was shipped on the more expensive steamships and only wealthier passengers could afford the fifty-five dollar fare to San Francisco.

Banning controlled storehouses for hides, and for the temporary storage of goods received, invested in wagons and mules and competed with about five other firms for contracts to haul freight and passengers between the pueblo and the port. Banning bought five small steamboats for transferring freight and passengers to shore.

During the Mexican chapter of Los Angeles history, goods were hauled from the port to the pueblo in ox-drawn *carretas*. Passengers generally avoided the cumbersome, rough-riding *carretas* and rode to town on horseback. Americans brought four-wheeled stages to the route, pulled by mules or semi-wild horses. Disembarking passengers were immediately loaded into the competing stages for a fare of five dollars and the race to Los Angeles was on. Passengers and others placed bets on which stage would arrive first at Benjamin Wilson's Bella Union Hotel in the pueblo. The stages were fitted out with four seats, each seat holding four passengers, with the driver, often drunk, wedged between passengers on the front row. The drivers urged on their teams at reckless speed, through thousands of ground squirrels, over treacherous roads that were neither maintained nor inspected.[2] The trip normally took two to two-and-a-half hours. On October 6, 1855, the *Los Angeles Star* reported, "The Express Stage of A. W. Timms, Esq. came through from San Pedro to this city in the unprecedented short time of one hour and fifty-five minutes—distance twenty-five miles. This is the shortest time we believe on record."

Much of Benjamin Wilson's history in the port area was interwoven with that of Phineas Banning. Banning was born in Wilmington, Delaware, in 1830, and was thus nineteen years younger than Wilson. Banning worked in his brother's law firm in Philadelphia, then as a clerk in a retail store. He sailed to San Diego overseeing a shipment of crockery, and having finished that task, made his way to San Pedro, the port for the pueblo of Los Angeles. In San Pedro he worked in the shipping company of Captain W.T.B. Sanford, later marrying Sanford's sister, Rebecca. Banning then worked in the freight business of David Alexander and in 1853 became Alexander's partner, operating as Alexander & Banning until Alexander was elected sheriff of Los Angeles County and had to leave the partnership.[3] Banning and Wilson were both brash, competitive and ambitious and the two soon engaged in various forms of business together. Wilson relied on Banning's freighting business to receive and forward goods to his retail store in Los Angeles and his orchard and wine businesses in the San Gabriel Valley. Wilson and Banning operated briefly as "Banning & Wilson," forwarding and commission agents. Eventually Wilson and Banning began buying land together.[4]

Banning, along with Wilson, John G. Downey, J.L. Brent, H.R. Myles and W.T.B. Sanford[5] bought 2,400 acres from the *Rancho San José de Buenos Ayres* of Manuel Dominguez in 1854 for a little more than a dollar an acre.[6] In 1857 Banning and Wilson bought 777 acres from the larger partnership. Wilson owned 444 of these acres and Banning owned 333. With this land the two began to plan a new community, called at first New San Pedro or San Pedro New Town. The name was later changed to honor Banning's city of birth, Wilmington. As Banning opened his new city in 1858 a storm destroyed much of his facility at San Pedro, accelerating the move.[7] Wilmington offered great advantages over the anchorage off San Pedro. Wilmington presented a low coastline instead of a bluff, Wilmington was closer to potable water and was closer to Los Angeles. Banning and Wilson controlled this port leaving their competitors to make their best out of San Pedro with its shallow beach, tortuous bluff and absence of fresh water. Besides, Wilmington was six miles closer to Los Angeles. Still, the tides wiped away the effects of the constant dredging at Wilmington preventing large ships from entering the port. So, Wilson traveled to Washington, D.C., in 1871 at his own expense to testify before the House River and Harbor Committee[8] and lobby for a breakwater and elimination of the sand bar. Wilson's lobbying, and that of Banning after him, were instrumental in winning almost a half a million dollars for improving the new port. Congress voted two hundred thousand dollars for the Wilmington breakwater in 1871, another $150,000 in 1873 and thirty thousand dollars more in 1875.[9] A grateful population turned out to celebrate his success on his return to Wilmington. The townsfolk formed a procession to cheer him all the way to Los Angeles.[10]

Work parties of between one hundred and six hundred men built a mile-long three-part breakwater, using a million square feet of lumber, to deepen the ship lane from wading depth to fourteen to seventeen feet.[11] The breakwater was detailed in a report from Brevet Brigadier-General B.S. Alexander, Chief of the U.S. Army Engineering Corps on the Pacific coast, running from Deadman's Island to Rattlesnake Island (later renamed Terminal Island). The wooden breakwater was designed to collect a sand-bank along its seaward side, which would form solid land before the wood-en structure rotted. The engineering effort worked as planned, and the wave action did carry the sand from the harbor mouth to build up on Rattlesnake Island.[12] (Deadman's Island itself was cleared away and added to the newly re-named Terminal Island in 1929 to widen the ship channel.[13])

In those swashbuckling frontier days, conflict of interest had a much more flexible meaning than it does today. While Wilson was a state senator he sponsored a legislative resolution urging Congress to appropriate $350,000 for the construction of a breakwater that would directly benefit his financial interests in Wilmington, giving to close friends and his own son-in-law J. De Barth Shorb the exclusive right to construct and maintain a breakwater and wharves in the Bay of San Pedro. These Wilson associ-ates were also named to widen the San Pedro channel entrance, and given ownership of up to 320 acres of state land. They were handed eminent domain rights to build streets and wharves on the private land of others and granted the rights to collect tolls and wharfage. Wilson wrote in notes for a speech or article, "During my senatorial service I took Wilmington as my Especial hobby . . . believing then as I do now that the development of Wilmington of the most important interest to any county & section."[14]

The year 1858 turned out to be significant for transportation in other regards, too. In that year Secretary of War Jefferson Davis introduced camels into the Far West as beasts of burden. The camels were a frequent sight in the frontier pueblo of Los Angeles. Also in that year the Butterfield Stage Line opened service from St. Louis to Los Angeles and on to San Francisco, a route of 2,800 miles.[15]

Wilson and some of his family members were on the small trans-fer steamer, *Ada Hancock*, on April 27, 1863, making their way to the steam-ship *Senator* when the boiler of the forty-two-ton boat exploded. Phineas Banning was thrown from the ship and his wife, Rebecca, was among those injured. The explosion killed twenty-six of the fifty-three aboard including Thomas W. Seeley, the captain of the *Senator*.[16] Wilson's daughter, Sue, was injured but survived. Dr. Henry Rice Myles, a part owner of Wilmington and fiancé of Margaret's sister, Medora Hereford, died in the explosion and Medora herself was so severely injured that she died almost three months later.[17] Mrs. Albert Sidney Johnson, who had just lost her husband, the Confederate general in the Battle of Siloh, lost her son, Albert Sidney Johnson, Jr., in the *Ada Hancock* disaster. Other prominent figures killed in the explosion included both Thomas H. Workman, a nephew of William Workman of the Roland-Workman party and W.T.B. Sanford.

After Myles was killed on *Ada Hancock*, dying without heirs, Banning sought his 200 acres of Wilmington property from the administrator of his estate, Benjamin Wilson. Wilson estimated the value of the land to be about two thousand dollars. Banning offered a thousand dollars in gold coin,[18] but ended up paying more.

Wilson was more and more engaged in Wilmington in his later years and less and less engaged in the business affairs of Lake Vineyard, which he had turned over to his son-in-law Shorb. According to the president of Wilson College "he was looking forward to the time when he could separate himself from the large business at San Gabriel and return to Wilmington, to spend his last days at the beautiful homestead adjoining the college."[19] Wilson claimed one of the officers quarters of Drum Barracks as a second home, naming the new estate Wilson Park.[20] His home was probably on the far western edge of the Army base and may have been the building that is now the Drum Barracks Civil War Museum on Banning Boulevard in Wilmington. Wilson turned the former government structure into a prestigious residence, but with the demise of Wilson College, he moved back to Lake Vineyard.[21] The last written words of Benjamin Wilson that have come down to us are notes for a speech or article spelling out his concern about pending state legislation regarding Wilmington, and stressing that Wilmington and the port had been his top priority when he served in the legislature.[22] The early development of the port for Los Angeles owes more to Benjamin Wilson than to any individual other than Phineas Banning.

NOTES FOR CHAPTER 18

1 American Law Register, November 1865, California Supreme Court decision George F. Hooper v. Wells, Fargo & Co., 17.

2 Newmark, *Sixty Years in Southern California 1853-1913*, 24.

3 Barsness, "Los Angeles' Quest for Transportation, 1846-1861," 297.

4 Yoch, *On the Golden Shore: Phineas Banning in Southern California*, 14-20.

5 Deed from William T.B. Sanford to Wilson, September 27, 1855, B.D. Wilson papers.

6 Fink, *Palos Verdes Peninsula: Time and the Terraced Land*. Also, Barsness, "Los Angeles' Quest for Transportation, 1846-1861," 297. In a deed in which W.T.B. Sanford pledged a large number of his real-estate parcels to Wilson as surety for a 10-month bank loan, reference is made to an earlier purchase of *Rancho Buenos Ayres* land of Manuel Dominguez made by Wilson and John G. Downey, J.L. Brent, H.R. Myles and W T B Sanford, "known as the site of the new town of San Pedro," with no mention of Banning.

7 Newmark, *Sixty Years in Southern California 1853-1913*, 236.

8 O'Flaherty, *An End and a Beginning:The South Coast and Los Angeles 1850-1887*, 169.

9 Act of March 3, 1871, ch. 118, 16 Stat. 538; Act of June 10, 1872, ch. 416, 17 Stat. 370; Act of March 3, 1873, ch. 233, 17 Stat. 560; Act of March 3, 1875, ch. 134, 18 Stat. 456.

10 *Los Angeles Star*, March 21, 1871.

11 Yoch, *On the Golden Shore: Phineas Banning in Southern California*, 66.

12 O'Flaherty, *An End and a Beginning: The South Coast and Los Angeles 1850-1887*, 169-170.

13 Sato, *San Pedro Bay Area Headlines in History*, 47.

14 Draft of article or speech c. March 4 1878. This is the last document in the papers of B.D. Wilson in his own hand.

15 Barsness, "Los Angeles' Quest for Transportation, 1846-1861," 303.

16 *The Journal of San Diego History*, San Diego Historical Society Quarterly, July 1957, Vol. 3, No. 3.

17 Letter from B.D. Wilson to J. Lancaster Brent, October 4, 1864, Huntington Library Collection. Medora died on July 13, 1863 (see Letter from Anna Ogier to Margaret Wilson, B.D. Wilson papers).

18 Letters from P. Banning to Wilson February 21, 1864 and March 1, 1864, B.D. Wilson papers; and Probate Court Case No. 238, Estate of Henry R. Myles, Petition of Benjamin D. Wilson.

19 *Los Angeles Evening Express*, March 14, 1878.

20 *Los Angeles Star*, August 5, 1873.

21 McDowell, *The Beat of the Drum*, 56.

22 Draft of article or speech on control of Wilmington Harbor, B.D. Wilson papers.

CHAPTER 19

Drum Barracks and Wilson College

Southern California represented a strategic problem to Abraham Lincoln and the U.S. in the nation's war against its Southern adversary, since the Los Angeles area was populated by Americans who were mostly from the South and whose sympathies were with their homeland confederates. When hostilities began, the first U.S. Army contingent established themselves in a post they called Camp Fitzgerald in the heart of the pueblo, at Third and Main Streets, causing much interest because of the camels the soldiers used for transport. Problems with the noise and odor of the animals, and the need to bring water from great distances, however, caused them to move to a site in present-day Culver City, where Overland Avenue passes over Ballona Creek, which they called Camp Latham. Confederate forces made inroads into New Mexico and Arizona in the first year of the war, causing the U.S. Army to take the defense of the West very seriously, indeed.

U.S. Army troops had camped in tents near the wharf in Wilmington while waiting for ships to take them to the East Coast to fight the rebellion and other troops had guarded the supplies coming into the port. By the first day of 1862 this base of troops was given a formal name, Camp Drum, named for Lieutenant Colonel Coulter Drum, the assistant adjutant general of the Army of the Pacific.[1]

So, the federal government sought a site for an Army base where the large military presence would keep Southern California loyal. Phineas Banning offered the Army all the land it wanted in his new port city of Wilmington, where it would be close to its supply point. On October 31, 1863, he deeded a huge site to the national government, and followed it up with another donation. On February 12 of the following year, his major Wilmington partner, Benjamin Wilson, donated a huge tract of his own to the U.S. Government[2] for use as a watchdog on Southerners in Southern California.

It's easy to understand why Banning, the staunch abolitionist Republican, made his gift.[3] He was outspoken in his support for the Northern cause and his port structure would benefit from the huge federal government supply chain. But Wilson was an unflinching Southerner who'd worked hard within the Democratic Party to impede what Lincoln stood for. It had been Wilson who steered the local Democratic Party's support away from the Northern Democratic candidate, Stephen A. Douglas, and to the candidate favored by Southern Democrats, John C. Breckenridge. If Wilson was sympathetic to the Rebel cause why did he give up so much of his land for an occupying, anti-Southern army? Was he steamrollered by the dominant voice of his younger business partner? Not likely, since Wilson was anything but a milquetoast. Did Wilson put business interest above political principle? Wilson and Banning certainly benefited from this "gift" since they may have been paid to build all of the buildings and to construct a canal from the San Gabriel River for the base's water supply.[4] And the presence of thousands of salaried soldiers also benefited the business interests in Wilson's adjacent lands. [5] Did he welcome this major military interest as an antidote to the frontier anarchy that had overwhelmed this remote corner of the Wild West? Was it a sense of partisanship by a former U.S. Army Captain? Alas, the correspondence that has come down to us does not hold the answers.

When Banning offered the Army of the West all the land it would need, the Army plotted sixty acres, and an Army quartermaster facility was built in 1862 in Wilmington instead of San Pedro. Some of the land was solely owned by Banning and some was jointly owned by Banning and Wilson. The jointly owned land was sold to the Army late in the war for one hundred dollars.[6] Drum Barracks garrisoned as many as seven thousand Union troops. These troops kept the Southern California of Benjamin Wilson and his fellow Southerners firmly in the Union. According to the Northern California newspaper, *Alta Californian*, "It has been established beyond question that the Secessionists in the lower part of the State were plotting for the overthrow of the Government."[7] The Democratic and pro-South newspaper, *Los Angeles Star* complained bitterly about the high profile presence of Army troops at election posts, a military band parading conspicuously on election day, and the fact that the Union soldiers were being allowed to vote in local elections.[8]

After the Civil War the army had no further use for the facility and it was deeded back to Banning and Wilson, although the two paid cash for the buildings that the government had built on the land.[9] The Army had spent over a million dollars to build the Drum Barracks structures; and Wilson and Banning, with P.H. Downing, were able to buy these for $3,627 when the government gave up the base.[10]

Drum Barracks is sometimes confused with Fort MacArthur, but the two were different bases. Fort MacArthur, named for Lieutenant General Arthur MacArthur, father of General Douglas MacArthur of World War II fame, was started with the 1888 dedication of a strip of land next to the newly incorporated City of San Pedro by President Grover Cleveland.[11]

Wilson College

After the federal government abandoned Camp Drum and returned his land in the Wilmington area, Wilson donated the land for use as a co-educational, non-sectarian[12] college bearing his name.[13] Wilson, ever the ardent Protestant, donated ten acres of land to the Methodist Episcopal Church, South, for use as a "Literary College of high grade school" named Wilson College. The first college in Southern California, St. Vincent's College, had been established between Sixth and Seventh Streets, Broadway and Hill in downtown Los Angeles, by the Fathers of the St. Vincent de Paul Mission in 1867,[14] and Wilson was eager to offer a Protestant alternative. The deed was to be transferred to the college after the school's other trustees (Wilson himself was on the board) had raised an endowment fund of five thousand dollars. Wilson included the former hospital and twelve-room building that had been the residence of the post commander in the campus gift.[15] The upper floor of the main college building, the former hospital, contained a "chapel and exhibition room" and a "recitation room" on the first floor and "a large library and philosophical apparatus" on the second. The former residence contained sixteen "well furnished" dorm rooms, rented to students for four dollars per week. The church's conference named Rev. A.M. Campbell, a graduate of Emery College in Oxford, Mississippi, as its president.[16] The Wilsons enrolled their two daughters, Ruth and Annie, at Wilson College, and the Bannings enrolled their sons, Hancock and Joseph. By the second school year the enrollment was up to seventy-five.

The church officials, though grateful, soon came back with hat in hand saying that their members were unable to fund even the bare upkeep of the property and were unwilling to volunteer even to plant shrubbery and care for the buildings. Wilson's famous temper exploded. If the church was too poor to care for the property, then it was too poor to own it, he wrote. And if it was too poor to own it, then the property should be placed in the hands "of a few friends" who were able to look after their investment. "Let me [be] distinctly and clearly [understood]," he wrote. ". . . not to be too long and wordy I will repeat unless the church can do Something other than disagree over the property they must abandon it." He ended his letter to the church by saying, "And in conclusion I must insist and shall insist that unless the above points so far as the church is concerned are answered satisfactorily that I must be allowed to make the deed to those that will promise harmony and success."[17]

The struggling Methodist organization, which had not been able to meet expenses even with free land and buildings, was done in by the financial panic of 1875. Also, the attention and energy of the Methodist officials were diverted by the offer of a much larger campus, much closer to

Los Angeles. Civic leaders I.W. Hellman, O.W. Childs and former governor John G. Downey each donated land and other citizens gave money to form their own Methodist college, an institution which would survive and claim the mantle of the area's legendary Methodist university. Wilson College, then, was the predecessor to the new University of Southern California, which opened its doors in 1880, two years after Wilson's death.

NOTES FOR CHAPTER 19

1 McDowell, The Beat of the Drum, 29. Much of the information on Wilson College in this chapter is drawn from this book.
2 "An Act to restore certain Property to Phineas Banning and Benjamin D. Wilson," U.S. Congress, February 25, 1873.
3 Newmark, Sixty Years in Southern California 1853-1913, 296.
4 Sato, San Pedro Bay Area, 19.
5 Newmark, Sixty Years in Southern California 1853-1913, 311.
6 Handwritten accounting of Drum Barracks property, B.D. Wilson papers.
7 Quoted in the Los Angeles Star, September 28, 1861.
8 Los Angeles Star, September 5, 1863.
9 Handwritten accounting of Drum Barracks property, B.D. Wilson papers.
10 Yoch, On the Golden Shore: Phineas Banning in Southern California, 72; Letter from Phineas Banning to Wilson, August 3, 1873, B.D. Wilson papers.
11 Vickery, Harbor Heritage: Tales of the Harbor Area of Los Angeles, California, 56.
12 Draft in Wilson's handwriting of deed from Wilson to the Southern Methodist Conference for Wilson College, 1872, B.D. Wilson papers.
13 Deed to W.A. Spurlock to land donated by B.D. Wilson, August 29, 1873. Also, Wilson's handwritten draft for deed, B.D. Wilson papers.
14 Guinn, Historical and Biographical Record of Los Angeles and Vicinity, 172-173.
15 For a more extensive discussion of Wilson College see McDowell, The Beat of the Drum: The History, Events and People of Drum Barracks.
16 Truman, Semi-Tropical California, 172.
17 Letter from Wilson to Rev. A.M. Campbell, President of Wilson College, October 24, 1874, B.D. Wilson papers.

CHAPTER 20

Indian Agent

A t the end of his life, Benjamin Davis Wilson looked back over a cornucopia of lives. He'd lived by the gun, held many elected offices, succeeded in any number of businesses, and added to the early history of religion, education, law enforcement, agriculture and trade in the region. Yet the part of his life that he was most proud of was the fact that he had been Indian Agent and done what he could for the Indians. He was very much a product of his time, and although his views were not entirely enlightened by today's thinking, he was known by his contemporary Whites, and by contemporary Indian leaders, as a friend of the Indians. He had lived in Indian country before the white settlers came West and Indians had saved his life on three occasions.

Congress set up an office of Superintendent of Indian Affairs for California on March 3, 1852, and the next day installed Lieutenant Edward Fitzgerald Beale in the position. Beale was born in 1822, was appointed to the Naval Academy by President Andrew Jackson and was aboard USS *Congress* off the California coast during the Mexican War. Beale, Kit Carson and a Delaware Indian played a historic role in that war by sneaking through lines of the *Californios* to alert Commodore Stockton in San Diego of the desperate situation of General Stephen Kearney at San Pasqual.

Beale acted as a messenger between the U.S. forces on the Pacific Coast and Washington, D.C., crossing the country six times. In one such trip he carried the evidence of the discovery of gold at Sutter's Fort, thus, in effect, starting the Gold Rush of 1849.[1]

It took Beale over six months to get from the East Coast down to Panama, across the isthmus and up the Pacific Coast to San Francisco.[2] By the time he arrived, B.D. Wilson had already been appointed by President Millard Filmore and his Secretary of State, Dan Webster, as the Indian Agent for Southern California.[3] Wilson did not seek the office and didn't even know he was being considered for the post until his commission arrived.[4]

When Europeans first arrived in North America there were perhaps 133,000 Indians in what is presently California. By the time Wilson became the first Indian Agent for Southern California, the number of Indians in the state had shrunk to fewer than eighty thousand because of the white man's disease and because of the white man's reckless slaughter of their competitors for the land, game and resources.[5] Indians were the majority group in Los Angeles County, according to the 1852 census.

The *Los Angeles Star* praised the appointment: "The universal expression of satisfaction at the appointment of Mr. Benj. D. Wilson to the office of Indian Commissioner, is the surest evidence that the appointment is a good and proper one. Mr. Wilson is thoroughly acquainted with the Indian character, and has visited most if not all, the tribes within one hundred miles of this point. In occasions of difficulty between themselves he is always looked to as a mediator, and scarcely a week passes that does not bring some of the chiefs to his residence invoking his aid and protection. Mr. Wilson accepts the office as much from a desire to secure peace and justice to the Indians, as from a disposition to render to the government of the United States whatsoever service may be in his power. We regard the appointment as securing permanent peace with all those tribes which have, in times past, been so troublesome to this country."[6]

Another article in the same newspaper said, "Two of the chiefs of the Tulare Indians have been in town this week. Endeavoring to seek redress for some alleged aggressions committed by their white neighbors. They say that some white people have encroached upon their grounds near the Four Creeks, and have taken prisoners several of their children. Mr. Wilson, to whom their complaints were made, dismissed them with the promise that he would look into the matter, and would use his endeavors to see them righted."

Wilson's job was to look after the welfare of Native Americans who had been wrenched from the habitat that had sustained them for millennia and herded onto confined plots of land without natural resources for survival or the economic skills to make them competitive in their new White environment. He used government money to buy them shovels, axes, hoes, blankets, shoes, flour, sugar and other basic necessities.[7] Using the federal government's money he bought supplies from his friends and relatives, including Margaret's cousin, Thomas S. Hereford. One receipt was noted by Wilson's kinsman and largest supplier, "I the undersigned being a disinterested person hereby certify that I saw B.D. Wilson give the Coyote Indians . . ." Disinterested, indeed.[8] But in a small community most of the people in important positions would have been Wilson's friends or kinsmen.

Wilson engaged a distant relative of Margaret's, Andrew Sublette, of the most famous of all mountain men families, to kill game to help feed his Indians. Andrew Sublette, after surviving the untold hardships and close calls of a life in the perilous mountain man work throughout the untamed West, met his end with the fate that killed other mountain men, a grizzly bear attack, while on a hunting foray to help Wilson feed his Indian charges. Andrew had wounded the bear and was following the animal's tracks when the beast charged him from a thicket. While waiting for the perfect, last minute shot, Andrew stumbled, lost his rifle, was mauled by the bear, and later died of his wounds. Those familiar with Southern California today will be surprised to learn that the site of this Wild West wilderness spectacle was a locale known today more for wild parties than wild animals: Malibu Canyon.[9]

Wilson railed against a bureaucracy that had no understanding of the Indians' desperate needs. What they needed most was something to eat and wear, he protested in one letter to Beale, suggesting that the shipment of goods meant as "presents" to the Southern California Indians might as well be left in San Francisco since most of the shipment was useless to the suffering community it was bound for.[10] But Wilson also used his contacts with the Indian leaders to locate and punish Indian fugitives from White justice. In one such instance he wrote a letter to the *Los Angeles Star* to let the White public know how firmly he was dealing with the pursuit of Tejon Indians who were stealing horses with impunity. He described the intelligence he had gathered from Indian leaders on the renegades' camp location from Indian leaders and their methods for evading capture and wrote, "I am . . . satisfied that any treaty made with these Indians without their first feeling our power would be of no avail—How easy [it would be] for those interested to make up a party and pay them a visit and convince them that they can no longer steal with impunity."[11]

Wilson prioritized the Indians in terms of their importance for government help. Of the greatest importance, he said, were "Indians of the four creeks," of the San Joaquin Valley who occupied "a central position in the Southern district of this State & consequently they exercise a great influence over the other detached tribes living more immediately upon our frontiers." Wilson felt that the "Cauhilla and San Luis Indians" of the desert and mountain areas around present-day Palm Springs, though "large in number" were "easily managed" because they had had "great intercourse" with the White population and were "more disposed to be friendly." The five thousand or so[12] Indians living far to the east of Los Angeles, along the Colorado River, were of lesser importance since they did "little or no mischief in our State," even though they were "a great annoyance" to White travelers and settlers bound for Southern California.[13]

Wilson addressed the former Mission Indians of Los Angeles in a special way. Their poverty and drunkenness were major nuisances to the White community, but they were individual unfortunates and no longer organized as independent nations. Their means of independent life had long since been forced from them by Spanish conquerors and they had lived for generations as vassals of the San Gabriel Mission. When the Missions were secularized, these dependent natives were again robbed of their means of economic survival. By the 1850s these Indians were relegated to a system of slavery, which Wilson oversaw as mayor of the city. The pueblo's Indians served in the most menial of day labor jobs, getting paid for their week's work on Sunday. They were paid in either booze or in cash (which too often was exchanged for alcohol) and by Sunday night a large number of them were dead drunk, contributing to Los Angeles' status as the most crime-ridden city in the country. By the wee hours of the night the city marshal had thrown a number of the unruly Indians into the jail. On Monday morning fines were levied on the Indians arrested for disturbing the peace, and those not able pay (most of them) were auctioned off to those needing casual laborers. Whites arrested for the same crime were not subjected to the auction system. The indentured Indians then worked for a week, got paid, got drunk, got thrown in jail and got auctioned off the following Sunday night, in a constant cycle.

Wilson wrote, "That they are corrupt, and becoming more so every day, no candid man can dispute. They do not always find better examples to imitate now than they saw in the past generation of Whites; for the latter have not improved in the social virtues as fast as the Indians have declined." Indians, he claimed, "must have [ardent spirits] on Saturday night and Sunday. Very little of the money earned during the week goes for meat and bread—their chief want with it is for drink and cards. They are universal gamblers, and inveterately addicted to the vice."[14] Despite what he viewed to be their genetic flaws, he observed that the Indians were indispensable to the local economy. "They are almost the only house or farm servants we have," he wrote.

Despite their majority in the local population, Wilson estimated that fewer than fifty owned land. A fundamental problem was their low pay, which was less than half of what white men made. And yet, they could certainly learn job skills. He pointed out that under the missions' supervision they had "filled all the laborious occupations known to civilized society," noting that they had once been "masons, carpenters, plasterers, soap-makers, tanners, shoemakers, blacksmiths, millers, bakers, cooks, brickmakers, carters and cart-makers, weavers and spinners, saddlers, shepherds, agriculturists, horticulturists, *viñeros* [and] *vaqueros*." Indians made only eight to ten dollars as farm hands and no more than a dollar a day for wages in the pueblo. But even with fair wages for their labor, Wilson was convinced that the Indian "would only pursue his evil tastes to greater excess."

Indians were not citizens, and hence, had no say in the governance that so mistreated them. And they usually could not seek redress under the law for the simple reason that Indians, by law, could not be witnesses in court, except for and against each other.

Wilson composed a long report to the federal government on promoting the welfare of the Indians, a report that was published in the *Los Angeles Star,* and ultimately, one hundred years later, as a book, *The Indians of Southern California in 1852.* The prose of that treatise is much more polished than Wilson's usual rough English. The real author seems to have been Wilson's close friend Judge Benjamin Hayes. Hayes wrote in his diary, "This report is of date December 26, 1852, prepared by me, at his instance."[15]

The thrust of the long essay was a suggestion to huddle Indians together on reservations by tribal group where compulsory labor would be overseen by benign caretakers, establishing the Indians as farmers and ranchers. That philosophy of enforced segregation is much maligned today, but in their time the solution that Hayes and Wilson advocated was humane and honorable compared to the common sentiment that "the only good Indian is a dead Indian." California had engaged in a number of "Indian wars," which were little more than butchery and genocide, whose goals had been to wipe out entire Indian populations.[16] The Hayes-Wilson system was never implemented "because the U.S. Senate refused to ratify treaties that would have reserved lands for Indians," according to Albert L. Hurtado, who added his own introduction to a reprint of Wilson's book. The proposal applied to three temporary local Indian reservations, Tejon, Fresno River and Kings River, all three of which were scrapped in the 1860s.[17] By that time the Indian population had fallen from a pre-Columbian figure of perhaps three hundred thousand to about thirty thousand state-wide.

In his treatise, Wilson argued that Indians hated war, wanted peace with the Whites, were "docile and tractable . . . accustomed to subjection," and were willing enough to work when treated with respect and paid fair wages. He wrote, "I have no sympathy for the white man who would violate a single right of the simple Indian; and the laws should be so framed as to mete out to him, in all such cases, exemplary punishment." The white man who abducted an Indian from his home, or compelled him to work against his will or who furnished an Indian intoxicating beverages, should be imprisoned for at least five days. Indians should be disciplined as much as possible by officers of Indian descent, and crimes of theft and trespassing should be punished on the spot by Indian "justices of the peace," he wrote.

More than a year after being appointed Indian Agent for Southern California, Wilson named Capt. Cave Johnson Couts as Sub Indian Agent for San Diego County.[14] At the time there were an estimated 3,500 Indians living independently in San Diego County.[15] Couts showed the same humanitarian concern for the Indians that Wilson himself displayed, seeking permission at one time to house a number of elderly Indians in government quarters in bad weather.[16] Couts was fired after a year on the job because of an old controversy unrelated to his Indian Agent duties.[17]

Other Whites who were sickened by the treatment of Indians turned to Wilson for redress. Lewis A. Franklin, a San Diego justice of the peace, sought Wilson's help in bringing to justice a group from the Los Angeles area who had committed a "gross outrage" against Indians in San Diego area.[18]

Both Wilson and his boss, California Superintendent of Indian Affairs Beale, had one major concern regarding the Southern California Indians: The establishment of a reservation at Ft. Tejon for the independent Indians of the lower San Joaquin Valley. The two fought tenaciously for this reservation and for the independent welfare of the Indians quartered there. The reservation was closed down a few years later because of a variety of problems.[19] The Army post at Tejon was shut down on September 11, 1864.[20]

Beale envisioned reservations with military posts for the protection, discipline and instruction of the Indians, to be paid for by "surplus produce of Indian labor."[21] The protection the Indians needed was, of course, from the White population.

In the summer of 1854 Beale was fired by President Franklin Pierce from his post as California's Indian Agent, following rumors of fiscal irregularities which were not proved.[22] The cause of the Indians in California was doomed, and none of Beale's successors championed the Indian cause with the same vigor. Wilson, by then was fed up with the insensitivity of the government under Beale's successors and his inability to bring real help to the Indians, so he quit his post soon afterwards.

Wilson's legacy was continued by an unlikely source. Helen Hunt Jackson, while preparing her novel to glorify the Indians, drew from Wilson's descriptions of expeditions against Indians.[23] In a visit to Wilson's daughter, Sue Shorb, Jackson was introduced to Sue's daughter, Ramona, who was named for Wilson's first wife. Jackson was taken by the name, and used it for her protagonist and the title of her famous work.

NOTES FOR CHAPTER 20

1 Starr, Inventing the Dream, 22.
2 Nunis, Andrew Sublette: Rocky Mountain Prince, 110.
3 Appointment by President Millard Fillmore and Secretary of State Dan Webster of Benjamin D. Wilson as Agent for the Indians in California for four years. September 1, 1852, B.D. Wilson papers.
4 Letter from E.F. Beale to George W. Manypenny, Commissioner of Indian Affairs, August 22, 1853.
5 Kroeber, Handbook of the Indians of California, 891 and 894.
6 Los Angeles Star, October 16, 1852.
7 Voucher for supplies furnished to Indians, April 9, 1853, B.D. Wilson papers.
8 B.D. Wilson papers.
9 Los Angeles Star, May 28, 1853.
10 Letter from Wilson to Beale, November 11, 1852, B.D. Wilson papers.
11 Los Angeles Star, May 7, 1853.
12 Letter from Cave J. Couts to Wilson, August 15, 1853, B.D. Wilson papers.
13 Letter from Wilson to Beale, November 22, 1852, B.D. Wilson papers.
14 Letter from Wilson appointing Capt. C.J. Couts as Sub Indian Agent for San Diego County, June 13, 1853, B.D. Wilson papers.
15 Quoted by Wolcott, Pioneer Notes From The Diaries of Judge Benjamin Hayes 1849-1875, 94.
16 Caughey, Introduction to Wilson, B.D., The Indians of Southern California in 1852.
17 Introduction to the Bison Books Edition by Albert L. Hurtado to Wilson, The Indians of Southern California in 1852.
18 Letter from Cave J. Couts to Wilson, August 15, 1853, B.D. Wilson papers.
19 Ibid.
20 Letter from Cave J. Couts to Wilson, June 5, 1854, B.D. Wilson papers.
21 Letter from Lewis A. Franklin to Wilson, August 5, 1853, B.D. Wilson papers.

22 Carpenter, "Benito Wilson: Yankee to California," 31-43.

23 Newmark, *Sixty Years in Southern California 1853-1913*, 249.

24 Extract of letter from Edward F. Beale to Department of the Superintendent of Indian Affairs, October 29 1852, B.D. Wilson papers.

25 *Southern Californian*, June 13, 1855.

26 James, *Through Ramona's Country*, 60-61.

In 1857, B.D. Wilson built his house on a hill overlooking a natural lake, and called his estate Lake Vineyard. At various times the lake was known as Lake Vineyard, Mission Lake, Wilson's Lake, and Kewen Lake. As development choked off the stream that fed it, the lake dried up and eventually its depression was filled to form a nine-hole golf course for the nearby Huntington Hotel. Later the City of San Marino bought the property and turned it into a public park now called Lacy Park. The road Wilson had created from his estate north through Pasadena was once called Lake Vineyard Avenue, but today is simply called Lake Avenue. The decorative letterhead of B.D. Wilson & Co. Wine carried the names of Wilson and his son-in-law J. De Barth Shorb.

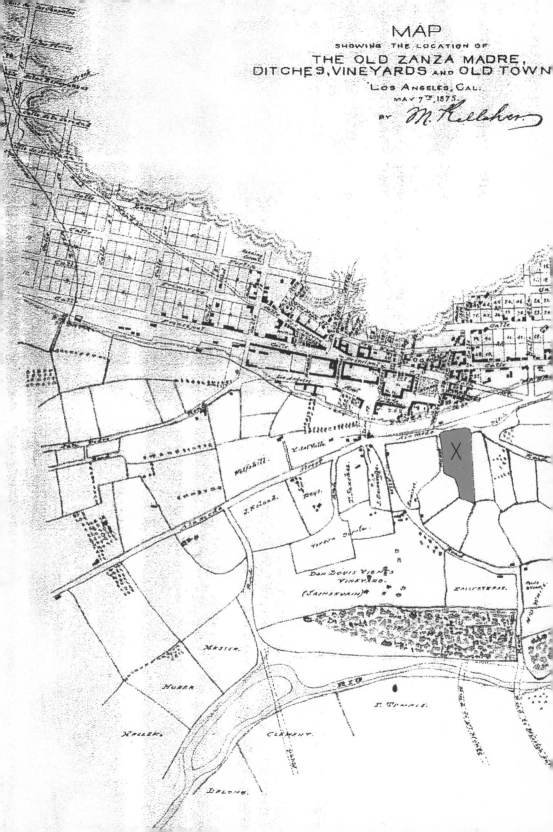

MAP
SHOWING THE LOCATION OF
THE OLD ZANZA MADRE,
DITCHES, VINEYARDS AND OLD TOWN
LOS ANGELES, CAL.
MAY 7TH 1875.
BY M. Kelleher

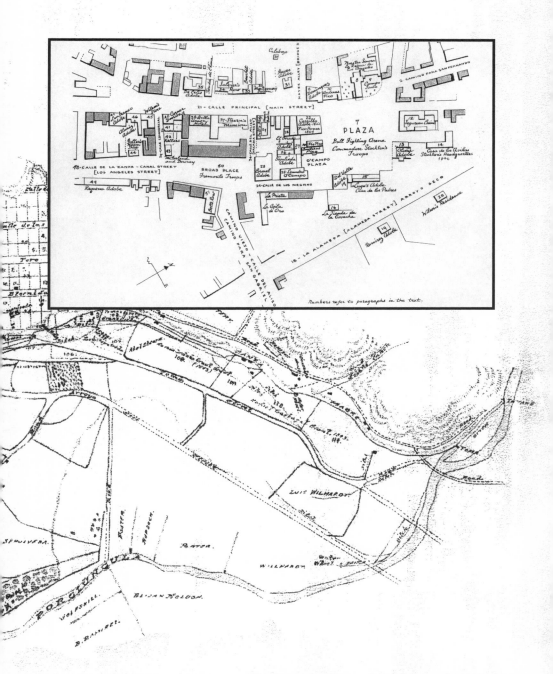

This 1875 map of downtown Los Angeles shows the layout of the town, with an X marking the location of Wilson's property. Inserted is a close-up of the Plaza area, which indicates Wilson's residence across La Alameda from the Plaza.

In 1852, President Millard Fillmore appointed Benjamin Davis Wilson to be the first Indian Agent in California.

The Lake Vineyard residence of Benjamin Davis Wilson, an image created after his death.

The interior of Wilson's Lake Vineyard home.

The Church of Our Savior in San Gabriel stands near the cemetery where B.D. Wilson was laid to rest. Stained-glass windows dramatize the Wilson family and how important the clan was to the formation of the church.

Benjamin Wilson and Phineas Banning owned the Los Angeles and San Pedro
Railroad, a misnomer for a line that actually connected Los Angeles to Wilmington.

Reproduced by permission of The Huntington Library, San Marino, California.

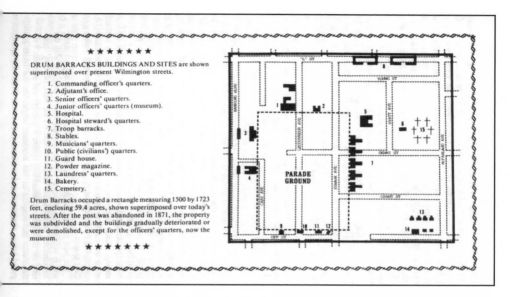

★ ★ ★ ★ ★ ★ ★

DRUM BARRACKS BUILDINGS AND SITES are shown
superimposed over present Wilmington streets.

1. Commanding officer's quarters.
2. Adjutant's office.
3. Senior officers' quarters.
4. Junior officers' quarters (museum).
5. Hospital.
6. Hospital steward's quarters.
7. Troop barracks.
8. Stables.
9. Musicians' quarters.
10. Public (civilians') quarters.
11. Guard house.
12. Powder magazine.
13. Laundress' quarters.
14. Bakery.
15. Cemetery.

Drum Barracks occupied a rectangle measuring 1500 by 1723
feet, enclosing 59.4 acres, shown superimposed over today's
streets. After the post was abandoned in 1871, the property
was subdivided and the buildings gradually deteriorated or
were demolished, except for the officers' quarters, now the
museum.

★ ★ ★ ★ ★ ★ ★

Drum Barracks, a military facility built on land owned jointly by B.D. Wilson and
Phineas Banning and donated to the U.S. Government during the Civil War, once
garrisoned as many as seven thousand Union troops. After the war, the Army
deeded the land back to Banning and Wilson.

From *The Beat of the Drum,* by Don McDowell; used by permission.

The historic cannon at corner of Main and Commercial
streets.—Photo 1895.

Downtown, B.D. Wilson buried two cannons in the street to keep cart drivers from
cutting the corner in front of his general merchandise store.

Reproduced by permission of The Huntington Library, San Marino, California.

At the end of Don Benito Wilson's life, Los Angeles was beginning to take shape as a modern city complete with streetcar tracks and light posts, a far cry from the pueblo he found when he first came west.

J. De Barth and Sue Wilson Shorb's home, called San Marino, overlooks Lake Vineyard estate.

The property at the corner of what is now Colorado Boulevard and Fair Oaks
Avenue in Pasadena was originally donated to the city by Don Benito Wilson for
use as a schoolhouse and community center. After Wilson's death, that intersection
became the center of Pasadena and was much too valuable to be used as a public
school, so the parcel was sold at public auction.

To commemorate a life well lived, an American merchant Liberty Ship was named
S.S. *Benjamin D. Wilson* and launched on April 30, 1943.

From the collection of William F. Hultgren.

CHAPTER 21

The Cities
of Don Benito

Benjamin D. Wilson was involved in many businesses and was one of the wealthiest men in Southern California. He made a great deal of money through merchandising and trading and a lot more by supplying Southern California cattle and sheep to the eager Northern California markets, and through real estate. It wasn't just that he arrived early and rode the market up as land values increased. Many Americans were here earlier and many others were buying and selling at the same time. His sensitivity to real-estate opportunities was what sanded fingertips are to a safecracker. Wilson made the first real-estate transaction recorded in the new County of Los Angeles in the new State of California, and proceeds through 138 recordings in his lifetime.[1]

Wilson's real-estate dealings straddled the Mexican and American administrations. The United States, not trusting the Mexican system of determining ownership established a Land Commission to make an American determination of ownership on all property. In the days when a few people enjoyed immense property grants from the government, the boundaries had not always been precise, and even the measurements used in the Mexican system were sometimes vague. Also, the United States questioned the authority of some of the governors who had made the original grants. Wilson and other *yanqui* dons opposed this revalidation believing that the old system's flaws were minor and did not need to be thrown out altogether.

As one of Southern California's major landowners, he dreaded the expense and exasperation of reproving his many land titles. But Congress established its U.S. Land Commission over the objections of Southern California, and as the landowners feared, the process bogged down in a quarter-century process that was expensive, sometimes unjust, and dragged on till many of the owners were broke or dead.[2]

At one time or another Wilson owned various parts of downtown Los Angeles, including the twelve-acre tract on today's Union Station site. He owned what is now the City of Riverside. He owned the Greater Pasadena area, from the mountains down to the San Bernardino Freeway, including what is today Altadena, Pasadena, South Pasadena, San Marino, Alhambra. He owned what is now Beverly Hills, UCLA, Culver City and large parts of Wilmington. Through his wife he controlled a large part of *Rancho Santa Ana*.[3] The early real-estate records of the County of Los Angeles are crisscrossed with his purchases and sales. His first purchase was the *Rancho Jurupa*, today the City of Riverside. He was not eligible for a land grant since he refused to become a Mexican citizen, so he bought the land. He may have gotten the money for that purchase from a comfortable bankroll he brought with him from Santa Fe. That money could have come from the legal trading business he sold there and from his smuggling activities, perhaps in the illicit brandy trade. Whatever the source of capital for his first real-estate investment in Southern California, he was never without land again.

Pueblo de Los Angeles
Downtown Los Angeles

O ver the years Wilson owned a sizable part of downtown Los Angeles. He was part of over thirty land transactions in a space of four years.[4] His home was on twelve acres where Union Station is today,[5] and he took ownership of five acres of nearby land on Aliso Street from Juan Ramirez to satisfy a debt of $422.93 plus $95.69 interest.[6] (Ramirez Street in the Union Station area today recalls the name.) He bought a lot thirty-one feet by eighty-four feet on Main Street for six hundred dollars.[7] He owned the corner property at Commercial Street and Requena Street, at $4,500.[8] He owned a lot on the northern side of Commercial Street, eighteen feet six inches by fifty-three feet seven inches.[9] He owned one hundred and five acres on San Pedro Street.[10] He owned five acres on the Los Angeles to San Pedro public road.[11] He owned a lot with one hundred twenty feet of frontage on Fort Street between Third and Fourth Streets.[12] He owned property fronted on Main Street of eighty-two feet, more or less.[13] In 1849 he bought thirteen city lots for fifty-six dollars apiece.[14]

He owned the Bella Union Hotel, the Ritz-Carlton of its day. Its walls were adobe and its floors were dirt, and yet, crude as it was by the standards of hotels in Eastern cities, it was by far the best of the pueblo, the only hotel in town to serve meals, for example. Wilson bought it from Isaac Williams, the man whose ranch was the site of his POW imprisonment three years earlier, for the incredible sum of eight thousand dollars.[15] The Bella Union was perhaps the most significant building in town. Governor Pío Pico used it as his governor's mansion during his time in office, it served as the U.S. headquarters during the Mexican War and as Los Angeles County's first courthouse. Passengers hauled from the port of San Pedro were delivered here and its billiard room served as the upscale drinking emporium of the city.

Rancho San José de Buenos Ayres
UCLA and Westwood

On January 7, 1852, while he was mayor of Los Angeles, Wilson became half owner of *Rancho San José Buenos Ayres* (St. Joseph of the Good Air), which today is roughly the UCLA campus and Westwood. He turned it from a land of the occasional bruin to a land of cattle,[16] and built wealth by driving these cattle to the gold mine country. This rancho was a parcel of about 4,428 acres bounded on the south by Rancho La Ballona, on the north by the Santa Monica Mountains, on the west by lands of Francisco Sepúlveda and on the east by lands of Ricardo Vigar. The land had been granted originally by Mexican Governor Micheltorena on February 24, 1843, to Maximo Alanis.[17] After Alanis died, his family sold the rancho to Wilson W. Jones (the man Wilson had engaged to do the real work as the original Los Angeles county clerk) and W.T.B. Sanford on November 1, 1851 for $1,600.[18] Jones conveyed his half to Wilson on January 7, 1852, for $662.75.[19] Wilson and Sanford defended their ownership of this land before the California Land Commission in September 30, 1852, and the Commission affirmed their ownership on February 20, 1855.[20] On July 23, 1858, Sanford conveyed his undivided half interest to Wilson for $1,600,[21] so that Wilson now owned the entire Rancho San José de Buenos Ayres. On November 26, 1859, Wilson sold a half interest in the rancho to Cyrus Sanford for $2,500,[22] and on June 8, 1861, Wilson and his wife sold the other half to Samuel K. Holman for $1,750.[23]

Rodeo de los Aguas
Beverly Hills

In 1854 Benjamin Wilson and Major Henry Hancock offered María Rita Valdez four thousand dollars for what is now Beverly Hills. María Rita had settled there on 4,539 acres around 1822 with her army husband, José Ramon Valdez, a corporal in the Santa Barbara company, but her husband died in 1835, leaving the widow with a challenging piece of property and eight children. She had been granted the rancho by Governor Alvarado after she had lived on the land for a few years. Her ranch was bounded on the east by Rancho La Brea (tar), on the west by Rancho San José de Buenos Ayres by mountains on the north, and on the south by Rancho de la Cienega (Swamp), Rincon de los Bueyes (The Corner of the Oxen) and Rancho La Ballona. Her ranch was the present City of Beverly Hills, more or less, but with its southern boundary about a few blocks south of Pico Boulevard and extending a few blocks beyond Fairfax Avenue to the east. Her rancho house was near what today is the northwest corner of Sunset Boulevard and Alpine Drive. She called her rancho *Rodeo de los Aguas*, meaning "gathering place of the waters" because of the seasonal rivers that flowed down two local canyons, *Cañada de las Aguas Frias* (Canyon of the Cold Waters, or Coldwater Canyon) and *Cañada de los Encinos* (Canyon of the Live Oaks, today known as Benedict Canyon). The waters flattened onto the plain below in a series of *cienegas*. María Rita also had a town house in the pueblo at what is now Temple and Main Streets.

In 1831, her rancho was recorded under its historic name, *San Antonio*, jointly in her name and that of a relative, Luciano Valdez. The property was a monumental headache to the unlucky María Rita. She farmed a small garden and stocked her ranch with cattle and horses, allowing them to roam free, which was the custom of the time. Her kinsman and fellow title holder, Luciano Valdez, gave her immense grief.[24] She complained that he'd built his house too close to hers, and in retaliation Luciano denied her cattle access to the only watering hole on the property. This forced her cattle onto the land of neighbors, causing further strife. She submitted her dispute with Luciano to the Los Angeles Common Council, which took her side and evicted Luciano. María Rita had to pay Luciano for the improvements to the land, which included his house ($15), a peach tree ($2), and "two poles for farming purposes" ($.50). On August 11, 1844, María Rita dutifully paid Luciano the $17.50 of his appraised value of his large part of Beverly Hills.

Luciano was not her only problem, though. American soldiers looted María Rita's home of the trunk containing her land grant, leading her to three frustrating years before the U.S. Board of Land Commissioners to prove her ownership. Then there were those pesky Indian attacks. Chief Walker and his Utah band and other Indians raided her rancho. In one attack in 1852 she was able to hold off three Indians and their bows and arrows for several hours, till the family's musket ammunition began to run out, so she dispatched a nine-year-old Mexican boy to sneak around the attacking Indians to fetch help from the nearby town of Sherman (now West Hollywood). The youngster was able to dash from the front door unseen, crawl in a low ditch for half a mile to keep out of the sight, then ran the rest of the way. Ranchers arrived on horseback and chased the Indians down to a stand of walnut trees near present-day Chevy Chase Drive and

Benedict Canyon Drive, where the Indians were shot and buried.

By the time Benjamin Wilson and Major Henry Hancock[25] showed up with money in hand to buy her out, the exasperated María Rita was ready to sell. The two men offered her four thousand dollars, with five hundred dollars to be paid in cash and five hundred dollars in notes, with the remainder to be paid after the U.S. government certified her title, applied for under the new American government in 1852. María Rita's frustration with this unlucky piece of property lumbered on as legal entanglements delayed the final certification of ownership for years. Sadly, her problems with the U.S. government proving her land title had been caused by that government's own soldiers, who had looted her trunk of her precious title. President Andrew Johnson signed a confirmation of the ownership of the rancho to Wilson and William T.B. Sanford on July 25, 1866.[26]

Wilson and Major Henry Hancock bought the land as a wheat farm. Hancock almost immediately sold his interest to William Workman, the co-leader of the Roland-Workman party that Wilson had come west with in 1841.[27] Hancock kept his ownership of the next-door *Rancho La Brea*, which became Hancock Park. To start a wheat venture of the scale Wilson and Workman envisioned would require a vast amount of money. Cattle roamed the countryside so the entire project would need to be fenced. The owners built a four-board fence around the three exposed sides of their acreage. (The north side was bounded by hills.) So, Beverly Hills in the early 1860s was a gated community. Wilson and Workman built an elongated, three-room headquarters on their land and planted two thousand acres of wheat within their expensive fence. (Wags note that the area once known for its wheat is now known for its bread.)

But the land seemed to be cursed and Wilson and Workman suffered the same rotten luck that had plagued the hapless María Rita. Their expensive fence in this remote area was an inviting target for nearby ranchers who needed lumber for buildings. Neighboring ranch hands invited their herds into the feeding fields and squatters made the future Beverly Hills their new address. A devastating drought gripped Southern California in the late 1850s and early 1860s, closing banks and ruining the economy. According to J.M. Guinn, who chronicled Los Angeles history in 1901, it was "the greatest depression the county has ever known."[28] When the long-sought rains finally arrived, they turned the former swampland into one vast lake. Even the vast resources of Benjamin Wilson were not enough to keep the wheat venture going, and Wilson and Workman began selling off the land.

They offered the entire parcel to Edson A. Benedict for twelve thousand dollars, who declined the offer. When Benedict declined, they sold 160 acres for five hundred dollars to two Basques, Domingo Amestoy and Bernhart Domaleche, who got rich herding thirty thousand head of sheep. Wilson and Workman sold 125 acres between today's Robertson Boulevard and La Cienega Boulevard north of Pico Boulevard for $1,150. In 1868 storekeeper Benedict who had found the entire parcel to be too much, bought part of it, along with his son, Pierce to plant walnut trees and vegetables and raise bees. A German pharmacist, Dr. Edward A. Preuss bought the last 3,608 acres for $10,775.

During the time Wilson was selling off Beverly Hills, oil fever swept the area. Pioneer Oil Company, with Wilson on its board, gobbled up the mineral rights to the *Rodeo de los Aguas* ranch because of its proximity to the tar pits. Although oil was there, the company didn't find much because its wells were drilled in the wrong places or were not deep enough.

In 1874, although he'd sold off the "Beverly Hills" portion of his holdings, he and his co-owners still held onto 4,438.69 acres of "UCLA" land to the west in *Rancho San José de Buenos Ayres*.[29]

Benjamin Wilson owned Beverly Hills, Bel-Air and San Marino, which today are three of the most tony neighborhoods in the U.S.

Culver City

Wilson became a part owner of *Rancho La Ballona*, a plot of land which became Culver City, in 1855 because the land had been security for a loan Wilson made to Tomas Talamantes. Talamantes had needed money and had borrowed $1,500 from Wilson and W.T.B. Sanford on June 14, 1854. The loan was to be repaid in six months with five percent interest per month. Talamantes had used his undivided fourth part of *Rancho La Ballona* as security, and by the time a writ of execution for the repayment was issued on December 5, 1855, the interest had ballooned to $1,690.28, meaning that he now owed $3,190.28. Borrowing at such high interest rates is a dangerous game, and one must repay quickly to keep from being swallowed by the interest. Talamantes couldn't come up with the cash so his property was sold by Sheriff Alexander in front of the courthouse to satisfy the debt. Wilson himself was the highest bidder, buying the ownership share for two thousand dollars, thus becoming the first American owner of *Rancho La Ballona*. Talamantes' litigation to get his land back stretched on for years, but Wilson's legal position was solid, and he held onto the land.[30]

This was a story replayed across Southern California. *Californio rancheros* owned vast amounts of land but were cash poor. In some cases they needed the cash just to hire attorneys and defend their ownership before the U.S. Land Commission. They borrowed, at steep rates of interest, from the *yanquis* who had the cash, pledging the lands granted to them or their families. With interest inflating their repayment amounts their financial holes got deeper by the day. The quiltwork rancho map with its Spanish names began to change almost overnight as ranch after ranch was lost to *yanqui* lenders.

Wilson would be criticized in years to come for seizing the land of a family which had lived on it and held title for a generation or more, demanding interest rates which are grossly illegal today. After all, he bled Talamantes for sixty percent per annum, when today charging anything over 10.25 percent per annum in California would be unlawful.[31]

But he may not deserve the rap. When Wilson himself needed money he had borrowed at up to the same rate of five percent per month.[32] Wilson loaned money to many who needed cash, *yanquis* as well as *Californios*, and land was the common security then, as now, for loans. By karma or coincidence, Wilson's real-estate empire would one day be lost by his heirs because it had been pledged for loans which could not be repaid.

Augustin and Ygnacio Machado and Felipe and Tomas Talamantes had moved onto the land, then known as *Paso de las Carretas* (Pass of the

Oxcarts), around 1819 under a cattle-grazing permit issued by military commander José de la Guerra y Noriega over the protest of the church authorities. The Machados had been too young at the time to qualify on their own for a government land grant, but with the older Talamantes brothers in the mix, the permit fell within the customary bounds. On November 27, 1839, their legal claim of the four relatives to the rancho was confirmed by Governor Alvarado. In October of 1852, the Machado and Talamantes families petitioned the U.S. Land Commission for confirmation of their title, and their title to the fourteen thousand acres was approved by the Commission in 1854 and upheld by the U.S. District Court.[33] The four owners, all illiterate, raised cattle and tilled the soil.

History has forgotten why the rancho came to be called *La Ballona*. Perhaps it was a corruption of the Spanish word *ballena*, or "whale," or maybe it was a "Spanglish" word for "bay." Augustin Machado married Francisco Sepúlveda's daughter, and Ygnacio Machado had married Estefana Palomares. As on other ranchos, Indians provided the labor.

Wilson held onto his undivided fourth interest until 1859, when he sold it for $5,500 to John Sanford, James T. Young and John D. Young. These three, in turn asked the District Court[34] for permission to partition the rancho. In 1864 the court granted the request and *Rancho La Ballona* was divided up among twenty-three individuals, each of whom got a slice of the rancho that included beach frontage, "pasture" land and "irrigable" land. To guarantee each owner a piece of the beach, some lots were two and a half miles deep, yet only as wide as a city lot.[35]

Pasadena Area

Wilson eventually owned most of the West San Gabriel Valley, from Altadena and the San Gabriel Mountains to the Union Pacific tracks just above today's I-10 Freeway, an area containing parts of Pasadena, Altadena, South Pasadena, San Marino, Alhambra and Monterey Park. He came to own most of the lands that had been part of the San Gabriel Mission. He first bought the 128-acre *Huerta de Cuati* in 1854 where he built his Lake Vineyard home. He then bought other nearby land, the "Orizaba" and "Prospero" tracts, which had also been granted to Indians.[36] In 1859 he bought *Rancho San Pasqual*, which became Pasadena and Altadena. When the State of California began selling land to raise money for education Wilson bought up other nearby parcels to the south and west of Lake Vineyard.[37]

Alhambra

In 1873,[38] Wilson and Shorb subdivided a portion of the acreage Wilson had bought from the state into a new community.[39] The community was not a city, but parcels of five to ten acres each, suitable for farms or orchards with or without a residence on the site.[40] It was bounded by what is today the boundary with the City of San Gabriel on the east, the *Arroyo de San Pasqual* (Story Park) to the west, Alhambra Road to the north and the Union Pacific Railroad to the south. To get water to the new tract Shorb tried something new: iron pipes instead of the traditional *zanjas* (open water ditches) or wooden pipes. He piped the water from Lake Vineyard to two reservoirs, one at Almansor Avenue and Alhambra Road and the other at Granada Avenue and Alhambra Road.[41] Thus, Wilson and Shorb made history by creating the first subdivision in California, and perhaps the world, to be served by water piped onto the property.[42] Lots went up for sale in April of 1875. When the parcels sold out in two years Wilson and Shorb bought another 2,500 acres to the west, calling this the Alhambra Addition Tract, bringing the community west to today's Marengo Avenue. Alhambra was settled by families of comfortable means, often from the East, who bought the property to live on and farm, not as an investment.

Wilson's name for the community was the not-very-melodic Lake Vineyard Extension. His daughters, Annie and Ruth, thirteen and sixteen years old at the time, were reading Washington Irving's *The Alhambra*, and suggested the book's romantic title for the new tract.[43] Streets in the division were given names like Alhambra, Granada, Almansor and Vega. Another street was named Boabdil, for the last Moorish ruler of Granada, but in 1902 it was changed to something easier to spell: Main Street.[44]

Other holdings

He also owned the southern half of the Rancho Rincon and the Rancho Cajon de Santa Ana or Rancho de San Antonio in San Bernardino and Orange Counties, including present day Yorba Linda, parts of Anaheim and Placentia.[45]

NOTES FOR CHAPTER 21

1 Los Angeles County property recordings.

2 Newmark, Sixty Years in Southern California 1853-1913, 509.

3 Dumke, The Boom of the Eighties in Southern California, 213-214.

4 Kurutz, Don Benito Wilson: A Pioneer In Transitional Southern California, 69.

5 Plat of a lot on Alameda Street; Deed to 11.97 acres of land on Alameda Street in City of Los Angeles from Albert Packard and wife Manuela to Wilson. Quitclaimed by Packard for $1 in 1856, B.D. Wilson papers.

6 Los Angeles Superior Court, First District, Civil Case #230, July 17, 1855.

7 Mortgage deed, B.D. Wilson papers.

8 Property deed, B.D. Wilson papers.

9 Mortgage deed, B.D. Wilson papers.

10 Mortgage deed, B.D. Wilson papers.

11 Mortgage deed, B.D. Wilson papers.

12 Letter from the firm of Glassell, Chapman & Smith to Wilson, November 11, 1875, B.D. Wilson papers.

13 "The View of Los Angeles," October 2, 1857. Wolcott, Pioneer Notes from the Diaries of Judge Benjamin Hayes 1849-1875, 174-175.

14 Kurutz, Don Benito Wilson: A Pioneer In Transitional Southern California, 1841-1845, 470.

15 Deed Book A, Title Insurance and Trust Company, December 11, 1849, 817.

16 Workman, The City That Grew, 17.

17 Probate of the estate of Maximo Alanis, Probate Court, County of Los Angeles, California, Case No. 49, commenced October 20, 1851.

18 Deed of sale of Rancho by Concepcion Alanis, Josefa Alanis, Susanna Alanis married to Francisco Correa, and Marcos Alanis to Wilson Jones and W.J.B. Sanford, November 1, 1851, Book 1, Page 66 of Deeds.

19 Deed for sale by Wilson W. Jones to Benj. D. Wilson, recorded in Book 1 page 108 of Deeds, January 7, 1852. This and other legal actions regarding Rancho San José de Buenos Ayres, available on Web site of Calisphere, University of California.

20 Affirmation of the U.S. of the 1852 title of Wilson and Sanford, July 25, 1866.

21 Deed for sale by William J.B. Sanford to Benjamin D. Wilson, recorded in Book 4, page 189 of Deeds, July 23, 1858.

22 Deed of sale of Rancho by Benjamin D. Wilson and Margaret his wife to Cyrus Sanford, Book 4, page 575, November 26, 1859.

23 Deed of sale of Rancho by Benjamin D. Wilson and Margaret his wife to Samuel K. Holman, Book 5 page 331, June 8, 1861.

24 Benedict, *History of Beverly Hills*; Wagner, *Beverly Hills: Inside the Golden Ghetto*, 13-14.

25 Deed to 1,600-acre portion of *Rancho Rodeo de Las Aguas* or *San Antonio*, north side of road leading from Los Angeles to the *Rancho San José Buenos Ayres* and Wilson's house, Henry Hancock to Wilson, December 18, 1856, B.D. Wilson papers.

26 Recorded in Book 3 page 291. of U.S. Patents. *Los Angeles Star*, March 1, 1855 reported on U.S. Land Commission Case No. 368 of February 20, 1855, in which Benj. D. Wilson, et al. sought title to "*San José, Buenos Ayres*, one square league in Los Angeles County, claiming from Micheltorena, 1843." The *Los Angeles Star* reported on May 1, 1858, that appeals against Wilson for the *Buenos Ayres* ownership had been dismissed.

27 Wilson quitclaim to Henry Hancock, October 21, 1856 and deed to *Rancho San Antonio* or *Rancho de los Aguas* from Wilson to John Hancock, for sum of one dollar, February 11, 1868, B.D. Wilson papers.

28 Guinn, *Historical and Biographical Record of Los Angeles and Vicinity*, 182.

29 Truman, *Semi-Tropical California*, 172.

30 Los Angeles Superior Court, First District, Civil Case #604.

31 As of September 18, 2007.

32 Wilson borrowed at five percent per month in 1853 on his $600 purchase of pueblo property on Main Street. Mortgage deed, B.D. Wilson papers.

33 United States District Court for the Southern District of California #123, August 6, 1859.

34 Ibid., Case #965.

35 This history of *Rancho La Ballona* and Culver City draws heavily upon historian W.W. Robinson's 1939 essay, "Culver City Calendar of Events."

36 Receipt for $150 for survey from U.S. Surveyor General's Office, January 21, 1869, B.D. Wilson papers.

37 Carpenter, "Benito Wilson: Yankee to California," 36.

38 Newmark, *Sixty Years in Southern California 1853-1913*, 445.

39 Carpenter, "Benito Wilson: Yankee to California," 36.

40 Ibid., 39.

41 Risher, *Alhambra: 100 Years in Words and Pictures*, 12.

42 Carpenter, "Benito Wilson: Yankee to California," 39.

43 Ibid.

44 Risher, *Alhambra: 100 Years in Words and Pictures*, 13.

45 Bounty Land Division, California 18th District Court, January 8, 1873. Plaintiffs Andrea E. de Davila et al. Defendants included Wilson, María Susan Shorb and J. De Barth Shorb. The plaintiffs, who were tenants in common with the defendants, asked for a partition of this property along the Santa Ana River, B.D. Wilson papers.

CHAPTER 22

Pasadena

Don Benito Wilson is perhaps most remembered today in Pasadena, where Don Benito School and Wilson Avenue live in the broad lap of Mount Wilson above. Pasadena today thrives on former Wilson land. Its grid radiates out from Colorado Boulevard and Fair Oaks Avenue where Don Benito gave land for the town's community center and school. Pasadena's major north-south commercial street, Lake Avenue, is the vestigial remainder of the road that connected Wilson's Lake with Wilson's Trail and Mount Wilson.[1]

Wilson's first purchase in the San Gabriel Valley was *Huerta de Cuati* in 1854, the turf that became, roughly, San Marino. He had moved onto the land that had long been associated with the San Gabriel Mission. The secularization of Mexico had prompted the sale of the former church lands a generation before Wilson bought *Huerta de Cuati* from a widowed Indian who had faithfully served the mission and, with her husband, had been rewarded with part of the former mission land. Wilson bought other smaller parcels of land that had been granted to Indians and bought larger parcels as well, until he owned most of the land that had once been San Gabriel Mission. In 1858 he added *Rancho Cañada de San Pasqual*, or *San Pasqualito*, a seven-hundred-acre parcel next to Lake Vineyard, and the following year bought 13,500 acres of the *Rancho San Pasqual* from Don Manuel Garfias, land that was to become Pasadena.[2] Wilson's good friend, Dr. John Strother Griffin, executed the deal on his behalf, closing on January 15, 1859, at a price of $1,800.[3]

    The story of Wilson's role in the founding of Pasadena cannot be told without mention of his close friend and business partner, Dr. John Griffin. Dr. Griffin was born in Virginia in 1816 and studied medicine at the University of Pennsylvania. He came to Los Angeles as the senior surgeon on the staff of the conquering American Army. After the American victory he resigned from the service and settled in Los Angeles. In 1871 he served as the first president of the Los Angeles County Medical Society.[4] He became very interested in a landmark case being decided by his brother-in-law, Judge Benjamin Hayes, as to whether a slave holder who'd bought his slaves in a slave state and brought them to Los Angeles, could continue to claim them as property in Los Angeles and transport them to another slave state where he could sell them. Judge Hayes, a Southerner, ruled that the slaves were free. One of the defendants in the trial was a young midwife named Biddie, who, upon gaining freedom added a last name of Mason. Dr. Griffin hired the recently freed slave woman, helping her on a path of independence and success that ultimately led her to wealth through real-estate purchases, position and lasting local historical fame.[5]

    Like his good friend Don Benito, Griffin had a famous temper. He once flew into a rage over a railroad issue and struck the head of banker Isaias Hellman with his cane with such force that the banker walked home with blood flowing from the gash. Once home Hellman summoned his doctor, who came immediately to tend his wound. The doctor was John Griffin, temper now cooled. Their friendship survived.

    Dr. Griffin was tending to an illness at the home of merchant Harris Newmark when news of Lincoln's assassination was shouted from the street. Griffin, a fanatical Southern partisan, began cheering and rushed for the street to celebrate the news. Newmark restrained him till he had calmed down, a case of the patient saving the doctor's life

    The *Rancho San Pasqual* that Wilson and Griffin bought was originally granted to Eulalia Perez de Guillen, the keeper of the keys of the San

Gabriel Mission in 1826. Eulalia, though, was in a bad marriage, and to get out of it she ceded Pasadena, South Pasadena, Altadena and a part of San Marino to her husband in exchange for her freedom. (Some marriages are that bad.) Her husband turned it over to his son, who sold Pasadena, South Pasadena, Altadena and a part of San Marino to violinist Juan Perez for six horses and ten head of cattle. After Perez abandoned the rancho, Governor Manuel Micheltorena granted the land to his good friend, Lieutenant Colonel Manuel Garfias as a wedding gift. Garfias was socially prominent in the pueblo, but the ruling class of the day had both townhouses and vast cattle ranches, and now he had his rancho. He built a grand estate, lived the good life, lost a lot of money trying to raise cattle on land entirely unsuited for that purpose, and was soon in need of cash. Griffin obliged him with a loan of eight thousand dollars at a rate of four percent per month (forty-eight percent per annum), and almost a year later the interest was over a thousand dollars. Garfias offered Griffin the unprofitable ranch in exchange for the debt plus another two thousand dollars for the now-useless ranch stock and equipment. Griffin accepted the terms but the title went not to Griffin but to Griffin's business partner Benjamin Wilson, which, on the surface, makes no sense. But the business deals of Griffin and Wilson were often part of larger arrangements that we can't untangle from the records that have survived. In 1860 Wilson sold an undivided half share to Griffin.[6]

Again and again in Southern California native *rancheros* who'd grown up in a cashless cattle economy lost their land grants to *yanquis* who were more sophisticated in finance, who lent them money at high rates of interest and took their family land grants when the hapless *Californios* couldn't repay. This does not seem to be the case here, though. Garfias seemed to be happy with the sale. Arturo Bandini, who owned land nearby and who had failed to profit even from sheep raising, thought Garfias had made a shrewd bargain getting cash for such unusable land. Mayor Spence had viewed the property around 1865 and said later that he wouldn't have given twenty five cents an acre for the land. In fact, he said, he probably wouldn't have taken the acreage as a gift. Initially Griffin was satisfied with the deal, telling Wilson, "I think that the general impression is that the purchase is a good one and that we have received full value for our money." But his enthusiasm waned into buyer's remorse as time went on. There was no obvious value of this vast tract. Sheep could not be raised there profitably and cattle could not be raised there at all. Griffin consulted his brother-in-law Benjamin Eaton on the possibilities of farming, but Wilson and Griffin could not find any productive use of their purchase. Trespassers cut down trees in the arroyo for wood and set fires on the property to smoke out bees. Rancho San Pasqual was a white elephant to the two investors. Benjamin Wilson, who would become so famous for buying the land that would become Pasadena certainly didn't look like a hero then.

Dr. Griffin's sister was married to Albert Sidney Johnston, a Southerner who left his family in Griffin's care[7] and marched with the Confederate loyalists he had recruited in Los Angeles to Dixie to lead the South's Army of Mississippi as its general in the battle of Shiloh where he was killed. In December of 1862 the first sale of rancho land was made. Wilson paid Griffin five hundred dollars for 640 acres in the northeast corner, then a few hours later sold 262 acres of that portion to Griffin's widowed sister, Mrs. Eliza G. Johnson for one thousand dollars. Why Griffin allowed Wilson to profit so with a relative of his instead of making the sale himself is another of those Wilson-Griffin deals that can't be fully understood from the records left to history. Mrs. Johnson named her estate after the Virginia plantation of her birth, Fair Oaks,[8] and that name has left a positive influence on Pasadena history, today serving as the name of the street that divides the city's numbering east and west. But "Fair Oaks" had tragic memories for Mrs. Johnson. She'd just lost her husband in the Civil War when she bought it, and two years later her only son, Albert, was among the twenty-six people who died in the explosion of the fated transfer steamer, Ada Hancock, when it exploded at San Pedro in 1863. She left Fair Oaks and never returned. Other sales were made, reducing the amount still held by Griffin and Wilson to 5,328 acres.

In 1869 Griffin wanted to sell and Wilson was ready to subdivide San Pasqual, since lands in the area were "doubling up every few months."[9] Margaret urged her husband to buy Griffin out. "Dr. Griffin would like to sell his share of the San Pascual Ranch to you, now my dear Husband I do not presume to advise you in business matters, but I think you would do well to buy him out if you can."[10] But Wilson did not buy out Griffin at the time. Griffin was using agents in his efforts to sell the rancho and Shorb complained bitterly that he could represent the partnership more economically, eliminating surveyors, attorneys and others.[11] Wilson then let Shorb handle his interest in the ranch.

Wilson and Griffin decided to use 1,750 of the best acres of *Rancho San Pasqual* for a fruit-growing corporation to grow oranges, lemons, grapes, olives, nuts and raisins. They brought in Phineas Banning, P. Beaudry and some others, divvying up four thousand shares at fifty dollars a share, and the investment opportunity was advertised. Officers of the corporation were to be John Archibald, president; R.M. Widney, vice president; W.J. Taylor, secretary; and the London & San Francisco Bank, treasurer.[12] Before this plan matured, though, a man named Daniel M. Berry entered the picture.

Berry arrived in Southern California in early September, 1873, as an agent for a group of snowbirds in Indianapolis. The Midwesterners he represented had formed themselves into an association called "The California Colony of Indiana" vowing to sell their property and move to Southern California to form a community in a climate of sun and health. The reputation of California as a lawless Gold Rush frontier had been dispelled by a widely-read book, *California for Health, Pleasure, and Residence—A Book for Travellers and Settlers*, by Charles Nordhoff. A group of friends had gathered in the home of community influential Dr. Thomas Elliott in the winter of 1872-73 and, influenced by Nordhoff's book, had decided to move to the Eden of Southern California, with its warm, heath-giving climate. They had named a committee composed of Nathan Kimball, John Baker, Albert Ruxton and Daniel Berry to visit Los Angeles and report back. The other three committee members went their own ways, leaving the job of representing the group's interests to Berry. And Berry, fresh off the train, consumed himself in the job of finding just the right land for their Indiana Colony.

Daniel M. Berry was born in New York, taught school and was making his living in journalism and the grain business with his brother-in-law, Dr. Elliott when he was tapped for the job of scouting out a site for a community in a far-off land. With no prior experience in large real-estate transactions, he had found his niche. Berry trooped "canyons, cactus nettles, jungles, dry river bottoms, etc." through "a hundred pieces of land recommended for our use," trying in vain to find the right spot for the Midwest community. He rejected "at least a half a dozen pieces a day," becoming so sick of the duty that he threatened to quit, but Dr. Elliott convinced him to keep at it. The group's direction was to find property at no more than five dollars an acre. Each of the members would hold between forty to one hundred sixty acres "besides a town lot." They agreed that "no spirituous distilled liquors shall be allowed on the lands of the Colony for traffic."

The town established by the Midwesterners, which they named Pasadena, might have been in the counties of San Diego, San Bernardino, Orange or in the San Fernando Valley. Berry was offered the entire twenty-five-thousand-acre El Cajon Valley for the Colonists' agreed-upon price of five dollars per acre, but water on that land needed windmills, and for some reason the Indiana Colonists loathed windmills. So, windmills turned out to be the reason that community is El Cajon today and not Pasadena. National City, in the southern part of San Diego County, offered land free—ten acres for each Colonist—with the condition that they organize like a chessboard, with the colonists settling on the red squares and leaving the black squares to the owners. Goofy, Berry thought.

Harris Newmark's *Rancho Santa Anita*, the site of present-day Arcadia, was an early contender. Berry wrote Elliott, "If I owned it I think I could easily make it worth $1,000,000. Everything seems favorable about it." Newmark was offering the land for twenty dollars an acre. Even though the Indiana group was awed by the fact that orange trees there were producing two thousand dollars per acre, the price tag was four times their limit. Anaheim was offered. Anaheim had been settled by Germans, giving their community a name which combined the Santa Ana River with the German word *heim* for home. Berry was not impressed with the future Disneyland home. "Fleas, 'musketeers,' sand, dead level, Dutchmen, lager two drinks and warm at that for twenty-five cents," he scoffed. Anaheim would stay Anaheim and not become Pasadena. The price of *Rancho San Fernando*, at the attractive price of two dollars per acre, was considered, but the lack of water ruled it out. He liked the price of San Bernardino, at $2.50

an acre, but not the weather.

On September 12, 1873, Berry visited Wilson and Griffin's *Rancho San Pasqual*. Berry described it as 2,800 acres with "heavenly scenery," a wooded and watered canyon and delicious and cool water on "elevated land up near to God and the Mountains." Berry was an asthmatic, and he enjoyed the first full night of sleep in three years. He "awoke to the music of a thousand linnets and blackbirds in the evergreen oaks." Berry was sold, perhaps for personal reasons related to his own health, and Benjamin Eaton would often state in the future that Pasadena's location was predetermined by a case of asthma. Berry reported that "one-half belongs to Wilson who is getting one thousand five hundred dollars yearly per acre from his orange trees and he has quit selling land. . . . The owner (Griffin) is rich and don't care about selling, but would sell to oblige his brother-in-law, Judge Eaton, who is developing some land near it." Berry was dealing with Eaton, who was obviously working to help his brother-in-law Griffin. Eaton (attorneys were commonly called "Judge" in those times) cast Griffin as a reluctant-but-potential seller, when in fact, Griffin was desperate to sell.

Griffin was eager to take advantage of this offer to be rid of this problematic parcel and convert it to much needed cash. The easy relationship of Wilson and Griffin was rocked by his dealings with J. De Barth Shorb, who was now handling Wilson's business affairs. Wilson and Griffin owned *Rancho San Pasqual* as partners together, "undivided," so neither could act on the property without the other's concurrence. Griffin was pressed to the wall with debt and was frantic to sell his share of the property and take the cash, but Wilson wanted to wait. Shorb was suspicious of Wilson's long-time business friends including Griffin and Banning, feeling that they were taking advantage of Wilson. In this case he wrote letter after letter to Wilson expressing his contempt for Griffin's "offensive manner," writing that "Dr. Griffin is simply acting like a child or a damned fool." Shorb wrote, "Dr. Griffin has tried in a most unfriendly unbusiness-like manner to take advantage of you." The business relationship had been so casual prior to Shorb's involvement that Griffin had sold parts of the common property without Wilson's advance knowledge and Wilson had promised twenty acres each, at twenty dollars an acre, to the Cauthorn and Pitts families, and had paid for certain improvements on their land, on which they were already living on. Now Griffin demanded the north part of the ranch, the better half, and offered one thousand dollars compensation to rid the property of the Cauthorn and Pitts clans, but nothing to Wilson for his investment in the improvements. On his own Griffin hired a surveyor to plot the land so it could be divided,[13] then tried to bill Wilson for half the expense. Wilson continued to deal with Griffin through Shorb, being afraid to meet personally with his old friend when tempers were running so hot.[14] The interchange between Griffin and Shorb became so heated that at one point Griffin demanded that Shorb return all his correspondence.[15]

On September 19, 1873, the Colonists back in Indiana wired Berry to offer fifteen dollars an acre to Harris Newmark for *Rancho Santa Anita* (Arcadia). Newmark was out of town and probably would have rejected the lowball offer anyway, but before he returned the worst depression in the country's history hit. The California Colony of Indiana folded because the Colonists were unable to sell their Midwest property to raise funds for their Southern California land purchase and move west. Berry went ahead with plans to purchase land for a community nevertheless, forming a new organization of buyers composed of some of the Hoosiers and some Southern California residents, as well. Those in Indiana still interested met on November 11 to form a new organization, the San Gabriel Orange Grove Association, capitalized at $25,000 through a hundred shares at $250 each.

On December 18, 1873, Wilson finally signed the deed dividing the land between himself and Griffin. Wilson released 3,962 of the western acres to Griffin. Some 2,576 of these acres were in the southwest corner of the rancho and 1,386 were above them in the northwest corner. Griffin quickly sold the southern portion to Thomas Croft on behalf of the association for $6,250 down and notes for $18,750 more. Croft then transferred the property to the San Gabriel Orange Grove Association a few days later. Since the northern 1,386 acres were without any means of water Griffin considered them worthless and offered them to the association free, as part of the bargain. The association considered them worthless, too, but since the taxes had already been paid for the year, they accepted them. The "worthless" land is today the community of Altadena. Griffin was ecstatic to finally be rid of problematic land, and at a nice profit at that. A legend says that he told a friend that the entire parcel (Pasadena and Altadena) would not support one family. He is on the record as saying, "I've finally got the best of those damn Yankees!"

The investors could not decide on a division of the property so they simply rode out to the property and chose their lots on the site on January 27, 1874. The far eastern boundary of the city was what is today Fair Oaks Avenue. Wilson watched with great interest as this improbable community, planted on land so long considered problematic, took root alongside the portion of *Rancho San Pasqual* that he had kept for himself. He bought back a parcel of land he had previously sold to Alexander Grogan and made plans for a new subdivision of 172 lots of nine or ten acres which he named the Lake Vineyard Land and Water Association. This section opened formally in January of 1876. Wilson priced the lots at seventy-five dollars an acre, and although he discounted some of these to fifty-five dollars it showed Don Benito's business acumen. Dr. John Griffin had wanted to sell at the first opportunity and Wilson had wanted to hold out. Griffin had gloated over the sale of his part of the *rancho* for $6.31 an acre (including the free portion). By waiting two years longer Wilson sold his acreage for up to seventy-five dollars, twelve times Griffin's amount.

L.D. Hollingsworth thought the community had grown large enough to support a store and post office and planned to build on the northeast corner of Fair Oaks and Colorado, the boundary between the "Westsiders" and "Eastsiders" as the two Pasadena communities were known. Seeing a community center quickly developing, Wilson gave five acres of land on the southeast corner for a schoolhouse and community center. By the end of 1876 Fair Oaks and Colorado had become the "crossroads" of the city. In another ten years property at the center of the city was too valuable to be used for a school, so the citizens, with permission from Wilson's family, auctioned off the five acres Don Benito had donated. The parcel was divided into thirty-five lots, and fetched a total of $44,772, double what the colonists had paid for the original city of Pasadena. A new school was built with the proceeds and named Wilson School in Don Benito's honor.

The settlers wanted a name that suggested beauty and fertility, considering an rejecting Hesperia, San Pasqual, Buena Vista, and Kleikos, a variant of Greek "*Kleigkos,*" meaning "key of the valley," a phrase Garfias had used to describe the place. Perhaps an Indian name would serve, they reasoned, so Dr. Elliott wrote to a schoolmate back east who'd been a missionary to the Indians. The friend suggested the Ojibwa word of *pas a de na,* which he said meant "crown of the valley" or "key of the valley." To this day the official crest of the City of Pasadena reflects that confusion, showing both a key and a crown. The Ojibwa word is better expressed simply as "valley." Thus Pasadena was given a name mistranslated from a language spoken by an Indian nation that never lived closer than a thousand miles from the city. Wilson, California, might have been more appropriate.

Notes for Chapter 22

1 For a detailed study of Pasadena's history, see Page, *Pasadena: Its Early Years,* and Reid, *History of Pasadena.*

2 *Los Angeles Star,* January 15, 1859 reported 13,500 acres; Confirmation of title, September 18, 1858, documented 13,693.95 acres surveyed by U.S. Surveyor General Henry Hancock, Heslop Family Collection, Huntington Library.

3 Rose, L.J. *Rose of Sunny Slope,* 44.

4 Lindley, *California of the South, Its Physical Geography, Climate, Resources, Routes of Travel and Health-Resorts,* 110.

5 Ferris, *With Open Hands: A Story about Biddy Mason,* 43.

6 Letter from John S. Griffin Wilson, January 15, 1859, B.D. Wilson papers.

7 Johnson, *Dictionary of American Biography,* 136.

8 Newmark, *Sixty Years in Southern California 1853-1913,* 316, and Rose, L.J. *Rose of Sunny Slope,* 47.

9 Wilson letter to J. Lancaster Brent, January 17, 1869, Brent papers, Huntington Library Collection.

10 Letter from Margaret Wilson to her husband, January 15, 1870, B.D. Wilson papers.

11 Letter from Shorb to Wilson, B.D. Wilson papers.

12 Newmark, *Sixty Years in Southern California 1853-1913,* 411.

13 Map of *Rancho San Pasqual* surveyed by W.P. Reynolds, October, 1873, Huntington Library.

14 Letters from Shorb to Wilson November 4, 21 and 23, 1873; Letter from Wilson to Griffin, November 20, 1873 and letter from Griffin to Wilson October 15 and 21 and November 22, 1873, B.D. Wilson papers.

15 Letter from J. De Barth Shorb to John Griffin, December 3, 1873, B.D. Wilson papers.

CHAPTER 23

Lake Vineyard

I n 1856, Wilson had been living in the heart of the violent Los Angeles pueblo for about seven years. During that time he'd launched American government in Los Angeles County, had served on the Common Council and County Board of Supervisors and had led the city as its mayor. He'd lost his wife, had remarried, had passed from his late thirties into his early forties and was trying to raise two sons and two daughters. Ready for a less frenetic life, he moved to a piece of property he had bought for eight thousand dollars two years earlier, a cultivated property seven miles east of the pueblo, near the San Gabriel Mission. He had bought the 128.5 acre[1] *Huerta de Cuati* (Cuarti's Orchard) property of María Victoria Bartholomea Reid, an Indian of distinguished local lineage and widow of a respected white pioneer, Hugo Reid.[2] *Huerta de Cuati* today would more or less be San Marino. Mrs. Reid, the seller, was an anomaly in Southern California, an Indian in polite society, an Indian married to a distinguished white man, and one of the few Indians to receive a land grant.[3] The land had been granted to her by Governor Juan B. Alvarado in 1830, in consideration for her faithful work at the Mission. Did Wilson buy the property as an act of consideration for a widow who badly needed the money, did he take advantage of a widow in distress, or was it strictly a business deal that met both parties' needs? Speculators in years to come would make all three arguments.

Wilson sold his pueblo house and fruit fields to the Sisters of Charity on June 3, 1856, and sold his merchandising business to Wheeler & Morgan.[4] Because he intended to plant vineyards on his new property overlooking the lake he named his estate Lake Vineyard. This is the estate that would be linked to his name for the rest of his life.

In a region where cattle ranching had been the usual use for land, this parcel of the once powerful mission was heavily cultivated. After life in the busy, crime-ridden pueblo, the new estate was like heaven to the Wilsons. Two months after moving in he wrote to his brother, "I am so comfortable here and enjoy such fine health with all my family in fact, no Country can be more healthy than this . . . I feel certain that I never could find another place so healthy and affording so many comforts, here besides the finest climate in the world we produce every species of grain and fruits in the greatest abundance as a proof I will just give you a list of the different fruits on a place I bought a few days since there is on the farm growing Grapes pears Oranges apprecots Amonds peaches apples English Walnuts cherries figs olives quinces plumbs & other fruits of the smaller kinds two numerous to mention now those fruits all grow So luxuriant that we dont know which grow the best the above purchase I made is one of the most beautiful places that heart could disire fine water and land and about 30 acres in fruits of the kinds just mentioned above this place lies about Seven miles from . . . town. (sic)"[5]

He also wrote to his wife, who was traveling at the time, "I am living comparatively with very little expense since I sold the place in Town . . . I feel much better satisfied here than I ever did in the City here I have nothing to do but work when I feel like it in the garden and when I am tired I come to the house and read and smoke the pipe."[6]

Wilson built his house on a hill above Lake Mission, later known as Wilson's Lake, on a site that would today be on the north side of Euston Road at Patton Place.[7] The lake was kept full by a natural stream that descended between Los Robles and Mill Canyons.[8] Wilson dug a wine cellar into the side of a hill, where wagons could be driven directly to it, and built the house over the wine cellar.[9] The house cost him about five thousand dollars.[10]

At Lake Vineyard, Wilson installed one of the largest vineyards in California. He raised cattle[11] and sheep, alfalfa,[12] corn,[13] wheat, barley and oats.[14] Watering his land through twelve- to fifteen-inch pipes from reservoirs collected by dams,[15] he raised the varieties of fruit mentioned in the letter to his brother quoted above, and he planted one of the earliest major citrus orchards in the Southland, with 1,650 trees, each producing 1,500 oranges.[16] He also grew lemons, limes and olives.[17] Always thinking in new spaces he experimented with sugar cane and even planted mulberry trees as part of California's effort to create a domestic silk industry that could rival that of China. Despite early glowing reports from the *Los Angeles Star*,[18] both the sugar cane and silk ventures failed, however.[19] At one point Wilson grew tobacco at Lake Vineyard, which he made into cigars, which "connoisseurs pronounce equal to the famed Vuelta Abajo brand," according to the *Los Angeles Star*.[20] But the praise of the *Los Angeles Star* was not enough, and this experiment failed, as well. Wilson and his son-in-law tried to grow chiramoya, a fruit native to Ecuador and Peru and planted a banana grove,[21] and these experiments failed, too.

The large Lake Vineyard house took on the character of a hotel, teeming with family, employees and guests, and continued to keep this character after the Wilson home became the Patton home. Wilson's wife, Margaret, and daughter Ruth lived there till their deaths, and daughter Annie lived there most of her life. Margaret's mother and sister Medora lived there. When George and Ruth Patton took over the house, they included in their household Ruth's sister, Annie; George's unmarried sister, Susan; and his widowed sister, Nellie Patton Brown and her six children; as well as the family nurse and nanny Mary Scally.[22]

In the new house was the bed Wilson had bought for his marriage with Margaret. It would be the bed in which Ruth Patton was born, and also her son, (General) George Patton.[23]

The Lake Vineyard estate came to fold in lesser estates of various family members, including acreage of his son-in-law and daughter, Mr. and Mrs. J. De Barth Shorb immediately to the east and the home of

Margaret's son, Edward, to the south.[24] Margaret's widowed sister, Mary Catherine Hereford Cooper lived with her daughter Mamie and grown sons, Isaac and Thomas on a patch of Lake Vineyard.[25]

As years went by and his wealth increased Wilson considered tearing down his large, but simple, Lake Vineyard house to build something more grand, but he "had never found time to pull down his roomy and comfortable original ranch house."[26] He also seriously considered selling Lake Vineyard because the costs of producing his wine, along with the taxes and shipping costs, seemed to leave little profit at the end of the day. He asked John Ross Browne in San Francisco to seek a buyer. Browne wrote "Mr. Butterworth . . . regards your [property] as the most magnificent estate in California . . . I do not intend to ask less than $250,000 for the whole property."[27] His wife, Margaret, was beside herself. She wrote a friend, "The idea of selling our home makes me very sad and I would not consent to it at all, but for the reasons Mr. W gives which seem to be good ones. Our property here is more valuable & productive now than it ever has been, and I think the country generally is more prosperous . . . If I thought Mr. Wilson could live easier, and would be more happy & contented, I should feel better reconciled to the idea of selling our home, but I have many doubts about it. . . . Our home is very dear to me and money could not induce me to sell it. I know that Mr. Browne will do all he can to make a sale of our property as it will be to his interest to do so, but I hope he will not succeed."[28]

The Old Mill

Immediately west of Lake Vineyard was the Old Mill (El Molino Viejo), the first powered grist mill in California. The Old Mill had been built in about 1816 by Father José María de Zalvidea to literally provide the daily bread for the San Gabriel Mission. The mill was powered by water from Mill and Los Robles Canyons, with the run-off flowing along a cement channel into what would become Wilson's Lake. The industrious Father Zalvidea dammed Wilson's Lake, using this additional water power to run a sawmill, tannery and wool works. Flaws in Zalvidea's design had left the mill with a shaft too short and a second story too low, resulting in water splashing up through the shaft housing and wetting the grain. So after only seven years the mission built another grain mill just outside its walls, essentially abandoning the original mill. Just before the American occupation, Governor Pío Pico granted the Old Mill lands, including three-fourths of Wilson's Lake, to William Workman (the Workman of Roland-Workman Party fame) and Hugo Reid, but the confusion of the military occupation and the post-war grant titles meant that Workman and Reid never profited from their grant. An alert squatter, James S. Waite, moved into the Old Mill in February of 1850 and his right to the property was ultimately upheld by the U.S. Supreme Court. Waite was an ardent Democrat who later owned the *Los Angeles Star* and later still was postmaster of Los Angeles. Waite was an ardent Democrat who sought to "maintain the supremacy of the only party that ever has been, or can be, of benefit to the human race."[29]

When Waite moved on he sold the Old Mill property, including three quarters of the lake, to Dr. Thomas J. White for five hundred dollars. Dr. White, in turn, deeded the property to his daughter Fannie J. Kewen, for a dollar, in 1860. Fannie's husband, Edward J.C. Kewen, was later the district attorney of Los Angeles, was arrested and imprisoned for his Southern sympathies, and was later elected to the State Assembly. Fannie Kewen would walk around the patio in the middle of the night holding a candle and covered with a sheet to scare away Indians. The lake shared with Wilson and his Lake Vineyard estate was known for a while as Kewen's Lake.

Mount Wilson

Despite a life of kaleidoscopic accomplishments, he is remembered by most of today's generation for nothing more than leaving his name on the highest peak over Los Angeles: Mount Wilson.

Wilson felt a special kinship with the mountains along the semi-arid San Gabriel plain that surrounded his home. For the Fourth of July in 1860 he gathered his party of invited guests in carriages and on horse-back and guided them to a waterfall, which the reveling guests named "Benito Cascade" for the occasion. When the carriages could go no farther, the women were transferred to horseback and the party continued until even equine travel was impossible. The guests then hiked another two miles into the canyon before returning to Lake Vineyard for dinner, music, dancing and fireworks, forgetting for the moment the great sectional war that had been raging for less than three months at the time.[30]

In the spring of 1864 he took a work party up the mountain that rose eight miles north of Lake Vineyard to clear a trail along a former Indian path.[31] At the mid-point of their climb he built a camp consisting of a three-room cabin, blacksmith shop and stable. Wilson, his twenty-one-year-old stepson, Edward Hereford, and the tutor William McKee advanced through difficult brush and crumbling mountainside up to the 5,710-foot summit one day in April, arriving in the late afternoon. Bear tracks led them to a spring where they made camp. The next morning they found two long-abandoned log cabins, perhaps built as hideouts for out-laws. By late summer the work party had finished the crude, but passable, trail to the summit, where Wilson had his workers build a small log cabin. Work parties then harvested pine and cedar trees, hauling them down the mountain to Lake Vineyard.[32] Hereford brought down the first load. The wood proved unsuitable, or the effort unprofitable, because Wilson soon abandoned the enterprise after only a few weeks and made no important use of the trail or the mountain peak during the rest of his life.

NOTES FOR CHAPTER 23

1 Carpenter, "Benito Wilson: Yankee to California," 34.

2 Deed of *Rancho Huerta de Quate* from Reid, María Victoria Bartholomea to Wilson, February 6, 1854, B.D. Wilson papers.

3 Carpenter, "Benito Wilson: Yankee to California," 34.

4 *Los Angeles Evening Express*, March 11, 1878.

5 Letter from Wilson to his brother, Wiley, April 12, 1854, B.D. Wilson papers.

6 Letter from Wilson to his wife, Margaret, June 15, 1856, B.D. Wilson papers.

7 Peterson, "The Callahan Adobe Ranch House" 1973, and Ross, *Side Streets of History*, 9 and 25 (map).

8 *The Golden Years*, 3.

9 Interview of Mary Agnes Richardson, 1952, Huntington Library.

10 Letter from Wilson to his wife, Margaret, June 15, 1856, B.D. Wilson papers.

11 Letter from Shorb to Wilson, January 28, 1872, B.D. Wilson papers.

12 Letter from Shorb to Wilson, January 3, 1869, B.D. Wilson papers; *Los Angeles Star*, June 2, 1860.

14 Letter from Shorb to Wilson, March 12, 1872, B.D. Wilson papers

15 Truman, *Semi-Tropical California*, 127.

16 Hittell, *History of California*, 875.

17 Truman, *Semi-Tropical California*, 125.

18 *Los Angeles Star*, October 23 and October 30, 1858.

19 Carpenter, "Benito Wilson: Yankee to California," 37.

20 *Los Angeles Star*, December 29, 1860.

21 Truman, *Semi-Tropical California*, 127.

22 D'Este, Patton: *A Genius for War*, 35.

23 Ibid., 150.

24 Graves, *My Seventy Years in California: 1857-1927*, 173-174.

25 Rose, L.J. *Rose of Sunny Slope*, 45-46.

26 Starr, *Inventing the Dream*, 76.

27 Letter from J[ohn] Ross Browne to Wilson, April 5, 1866, B.D. Wilson papers.

28 Letter from Margaret to J[oseph] L[ancaster] Brent, April 10, 1866, B.D. Wilson papers.

29 Cleland, *El Molino Viejo*, 25-26.

30 *Los Angeles Star*, July 7, 1860.

31 For a detailed account of the building of Wilson's Trail and the growing commercial and scientific activity on the mountain see Robinson, *The Mount Wilson Story*.

32 Notes made by Dorothy Bean (Geer) from Richardson, c. 1927. Standlee collection, Huntington Library.

CHAPTER 24

Vintner
and Orchardist

Those in Los Angeles in the 1860s and 1870s would know B.D. Wilson as a winemaker and orchardist. He was an "old pioneer" with colorful stories about the frontier past, but for the last two decades of his life he was known by his contemporaries as a wealthy man at Lake Vineyard who grew grapes and oranges and shipped wine and fruit to other parts of the country. He and his son-in-law J. De Barth Shorb would expand the winery over the years,[1] and after Wilson's death Shorb would further build the winery into what he envisioned as the largest in the world, reinforcing the memory of Don Benito as a winemaker.

The fathers at the San Gabriel Mission had been growing grapes and making wine in the area three-quarters of a century before Wilson planted his vineyard near the pueblo in the late 1840s. The Sisters of Charity had been especially interested in buying Wilson's Los Angeles property because of those vineyards and the opportunity it gave them for income from the site. When Wilson moved to Lake Vineyard his land was already teaming with fruits of different kinds, but it was he who brought grapes to this acreage.[2]

Mission fathers had used a single grape for all the wine and brandy they produced, whether red or white, sweet or dry. Their one-fruit-fits-all was the *Vitis vinifera* grape, believed to be an import from Europe, although it matches no present-day Spanish grape.[3]

Although many growers found it more profitable to ship their grapes to San Francisco to be made into wine,[4] Wilson made his grapes into wine and brandy before shipping them north and east. His grapes were crushed the old fashioned way, with naked human feet, "treading the wine press."[5]

Wilson was the commercial wine pioneer in the San Gabriel Valley,[6] but he was by no means the first grape grower and wine producer in Los Angeles. At the time Wilson began growing grapes at Lake Vineyard there were about 125 other grape growers in Los Angeles County, each producing about seventy-thousand pounds a year, for a total of about nine million pounds, accounting for ten percent of the spirits produced in the U.S.[7] About 1,500 acres in Los Angeles County were committed to grapes at the time, each acre producing about four hundred gallons per year and yielding an income of about two dollars per gallon.[8] About the same amount of wine was being exported from Los Angeles County as was being imported to the U.S. from other countries.[9] About half of the Los Angeles County crop was turned into wine and brandy and exported, about a fourth was sold as grapes, and the rest was used locally or suffered from spoilage or mismanagement.[10] In the 1850s Wilson and other wine pioneers were planting the vineyards and perfecting their art for the local wine boom of the 1860s. By 1859 Wilson ranked number four in the county in total gallons of wine.[11] Wine production in the Los Angeles area grew eight hundred percent between 1860 and 1866, to 2.25 million gallons.[12] After Wilson's death the *Los Angeles Times* labeled Wilson, one of the two "fathers of the wine interest."[13]

Wilson's production of citrus fruits, wine and brandy from Lake Vineyard was great enough that he had his own office in San Francisco and agents in the East selling the estate's products. His son, John, staffed the San Francisco office in 1865,[14] and Wilson even called his business B.D. Wilson & Son for a short time,[15] but by 1868 his son-in-law J. De Barth Shorb had replaced his son.[16] In 1869 Shorb wrote, ". . . we have every prospect of increasing trade, and really do stand to-day at the head of the wine trade of the State . . ."[17] Shorb and a partner, Carlton Curtis, had formed a business to buy and sell Wilson's fruit and wine, among other things. They operated under the name of B.D. Wilson & Co. to take advantage of "the reputation and established character" of his wines. But with extensive experience in the courts of law, Wilson sought a legal opinion on his liability. When the San Francisco law firm of Wilson & Crittenden (no relation) opined that "you are, so far as third persons are concerned, as much a member of the firm as if you were interested in its business and profits. It makes no difference what may be the real relations existing amongst yourselves. You are held out to the world as a partner, by the use of your name, with your knowledge and acquiescence, and all persons dealing with the firm, and giving it credit, have a right to look to you for payment, and to treat you in all respects, as a partner in the firm."[18] Shorb argued that "It would very seriously interfere with our arrangements now to change the name of the firm as all our business connections have been already formed under that name."[19] Wilson, however, was not about to risk liability for Shorb and Curtis's debts, and Shorb changed the company name to Lake Vineyard Co.[20] For the same reason the name of the New York distributor was changed to Norman Chamberlin and Co., to remove Wilson's name from the East Coast business.[21]

In 1869 Shorb grew impatient with the office in the big city of San Francisco and longed to settle on the farm near Wilson. He wrote to his father-in-law, "I considered it better for myself and Sue to settle near you; and build up a home for ourselves . . . I have never cared for city life and now that I have a family I am anxious to get out of it as soon as possible. I think I could make as much money in Los Angeles Co as here; with more peace and happiness with it; hence my determination. I hope you will not change your mind in regard to the sale of the land back of Sue's place."[22]

Don Antonio María Lugo had first produced wine commercially in Los Angeles shortly after he moved to the pueblo in 1809, and by 1818 he and his fellow vintners were tending 53,000 vines around the town.[23] By 1847 vineyards were literally taking root in what today are Riverside, San Bernardino, Santa Anita, Rancho Cucamonga, Azusa and around the pueblo itself.[24]

After Wilson bought the land that he would name Lake Vineyard, but before he had moved his home there, he made the first champagne in California.[25] News bubbled through the state and his sparkling wine earned high marks from critics of the day, but he soon dropped the line,[26] perhaps because his champagne did not endure well in the bottle.[27]

Wilson's white wines and port won prizes in the 1860s, maybe because he aged his wines more than most vintners in the state.[28]

Among Wilson's competitors was the Sunnyslope Ranch of his next door neighbor, Leonard J. Rose, a German who was also famous for breeding race horses. Rosemead is named after him. Wilson served as a mentor to another neighbor, E.J. "Lucky" Baldwin.[29]

Shorb had come to his lofty position in the Los Angeles constellation by watching his father-in-law think big. Shorb rounded up investors from England to bankroll an expansion of the family business into the San Gabriel Winery, with 1,500 acres of vines and storage for 250,000 gallons. It was to be the largest winery in the world, but it never made it.[30] Shorb did not have Wilson's uncanny sense of when to get in and when to get out of a business. Wilson had entered the wine business in its infancy in Los Angeles. Six years after Wilson planted his Lake Vineyard fields Los Angeles produced two-thirds of the state's wine. A decade later it was down to a half and by 1890 Los Angeles wine accounted for less than a tenth of the state's total.[31] The climate around Los Angeles was fine for sweet wines and brandy, but Northern California, which was able to produce fine dry wines as well displaced Los Angeles as the principal wine region of the state.[32] Wilson was best known for his angelica (a sweet white wine), white wine, port and brandy.

Wine was not produced in commercial quantities in the Napa Valley until about the time Wilson launched his Lake Vineyard operation.[33] A San Francisco dealer wrote to Wilson in 1863 that "the Anaheim & Sonoma Wines are not as good as the Wine from Los Angeles."[34]

Wilson forged a strong friendship with J. Ross Browne who lobbied Congress on behalf of the California wine industry, fighting against increased taxes on wine and brandy. Although all California vintners would benefit from Browne's successes, the expense seems to have been borne mostly by Wilson in Southern California and Colonel Agoston Haraszthy in Northern California. Browne was able to eliminate the federal tax on domestic wine altogether, although Congress did raise the tax on brandy. Wilson's relation with Browne was so close that Don Benito's daughter, Sue, lived in Oakland with the Brownes for a short time and Wilson engaged Browne as an agent to find a buyer for his Lake Vineyard home, since Browne was active in the East where the highest offers were likely to come from.[35] To Margaret's relief Browne found no buyer for Lake Vineyard at a price satisfactory to Wilson.

Since Wilson moved to his Lake Vineyard property after two years of cultivating it remotely, his production was already large enough to warrant a San Francisco sales office.[36] He later opened a New York office and sold his wine throughout the country. By 1860 he was the largest vintner in Los Angeles County, with one hundred thousand vines; in 1864 he out-produced all vintners countywide with 140,000 gallons.[37] In 1880 he and Shorb expanded their operation under the name of San Gabriel Wine Company, with a huge vineyard in present-day western Alhambra.[38]

In addition to his wines, Wilson was known for this large business in oranges, lemons and other fruit. Prior to the American era the northern part of California was fed from the gardens of Southern California.[39] Oranges had been grown at the San Gabriel Mission and in the pueblo from about 1815. In 1840, the year Wilson arrived in Southern California, William Wolfskill planted orange orchards large enough to yield commercial quantities, thus launching an industry that would become an icon for the region,[40] but as late as 1855 oranges not been "very extensively cultivated," according to the Los Angeles Star.[41] Wilson took orange production to a new level. Wilson's neighbor, L.J. Rose, wrote that "Mr. Benjamin Davis Wilson (was) the first real apostle of both the orange and the vine.[42] Major Ben C. Truman, who published a book of his observations from traveling in Southern California in the early 1870s, called Wilson "the most successful orange grower in the county." Wilson began with the orange trees already on the property, trees from the Mission days, or planted by Hugo Reid, the previous owner. He added to this orchard, growing trees in his own nursery. [43] Years later an ad in the Los Angeles Times promoting lots in a co-operative nursery tract growing oranges crowed that "Colonel B.D. Wilson once sold $1,800 worth from a single acre." The ad asked, "Can you now hesitate in buying lots . . . containing fourteen-year-old-trees."[44]

By the mid-1870s, as Wilson was slowing down and Shorb was succeeding more and more in his own right, Shorb's Mount Vineyard and Wilson's Lake Vineyard estates existed side by side, with Shorb managing both properties.[45]

	Lake Vineyard 1,300 acres	Mount Vineyard 500 acres	Combined 1,800 acres
Vines	102,000	129,000	
Bearing orange trees	1,600	450	
Young trees	750	1,200	
Lemon trees	250	250	
Lime trees			300
Olive trees			500
Walnut trees			450

The combined estates produced a million oranges and 75,000 lemons a year. Some 75,000 gallons of wine were produced in 1873 along with five thousand gallons of brandy. Another 85,000 to 90,000 gallons of brandy was stored in the cellars.

Notes for Chapter 24

1 Graves, *California Memories: 1857-1930*.
2 Callahan, Oral history project of the Friends of the San Marino Library, 1975.
3 Pinney, "The Early Days in Southern California," 4.
4 Guinn, *A History of California*.
5 Kip, *Early Days of My Episcopate*, 210.
6 Pinney, "The Early Days in Southern California," 6.
7 *Los Angeles Star*, March 1, 1855.
8 *Los Angeles Star*, April 7, 1855.
9 *Los Angeles Star*, March 1, 1855.

10 *Los Angeles Star*, February 15, 1855.

11 *Los Angeles Star*, December 3, 1859.

12 Pauly, "J. Ross Browne: Wine Lobbyist and Frontier Opportunist," 102-103.

13 J.L. Sansevaine. *Los Angeles Times*, April 29, 1882.

14 Letter from John B. Wilson to his father, April 10, 1865, B.D. Wilson papers.

15 Letter from John B. Wilson to his father, c. Nov. 1865, B.D. Wilson papers.

16 The first correspondence from Shorb in this capacity is dated January 21, 1868, B.D. Wilson papers.

17 Shorb to Wilson, January 19, 1869, B.D. Wilson papers.

18 Letter from Wilson & Crittenden to B.D. Wilson, February 10, 1869, B.D. Wilson papers.

19 Letter from Shorb to Wilson, February 26, 1869, B.D. Wilson papers.

20 Letter from Shorb to Wilson, May 7, 1869, B.D. Wilson papers.

21 Letter from Shorb to Wilson, August 17, 1869, B.D. Wilson papers.

22 Letter from Shorb to Wilson, May 7, 1869, B.D. Wilson papers.

23 Teiser, *Winemaking in California*, 16.

24 Pinney, "The Early Days in Southern California," 5.

25 *Los Angeles Star*, March 21, 1855, April 21, 1855.

26 Davies, "Sparkling Wines," 265.

27 Teiser, *Winemaking in California*, 66.

28 Ibid.

29 Ibid.

30 Pinney, "The Early Days in Southern California," 8.

31 Ibid.

32 Graves, *California Memories: 1857-1930*.

33 Pinney, "The Early Days in Southern California," 17.

34 Letter from HG & Co. to Wilson, September 24, 1863, B.D. Wilson papers.

35 Pauly, "J. Ross Browne: Wine Lobbyist and Frontier Opportunist," 107.

36 Ibid.

37 Teiser, *Winemaking in California*, 66.

38 Graves, *California Memories: 1857-1930*.

39 Barrows, "Los Angeles Fifty Years Ago," 206.

40 Guinn, *A History of California*.

41 *Los Angeles Star*, March 24, 1855.

42 Rose, *L.J. Rose of Sunny Slope*, 44-45.

43 Truman, *Semi-Tropical California*, 85-89.

44 *Los Angeles Times*, June 22, 1886.

45 Truman, *Semi-Tropical California*, 125.

CHAPTER 25

Railroads

Wilson had come to California by mule train and settled into a business environment served by wooden ox carts, sailing ships and the new steamships. It wasn't till after Don Benito was mayor that the first carriage rolled down the streets of Los Angeles in 1853.[1] As one of the leaders of the business community, he'd helped build roads so that wagons could transport goods overland and thanks to the newly cleared roads the stagecoach had finally reached Los Angeles shortly before the Civil War. Railroads had spread like a growing spider web throughout the eastern United States before the war, but had not reached the West Coast before the hostilities. Perhaps no Southern California leader saw the need for railroads more clearly than Don Benito.[2] The leading industry of Southern California was agriculture, but the produce was highly perishable and needed to be shipped quickly to population centers elsewhere. For this particular region, that meant an adequate seaport for shipment by sea and railroads to haul goods overland. Also, because of the agricultural focus of the local economy, almost everything else needed for commercial and private life had to come from outside the area. And so Wilson became an ambassador for both improving the harbor and connecting it to Los Angeles with a railroad.

The city-to-port railroad proposal was not new with Wilson. Abel Stearns, as a state assemblyman, had won passage of a bill for such a railroad in 1861, authorizing Los Angeles County and City to invest one hundred thousand dollars and fifty thousand dollars, respectively, in the connection, but fighting was breaking out between the North and the South as the bill was being passed, and it was not acted on. In the next legislature, Assemblyman E.J.C. Kewen won passage of the same measure but, with the Civil War at full throttle, the opportunity was once again not acted on.[3]

Wilson took up the cause, and with the Civil War still raging, he and Banning and a few others gathered in November of 1864 to renew that process by planning a public rally,[4] which was staged at the County Courthouse the following month. At that event Wilson, Banning, John G. Downey and Dr. John S. Griffin urged public support for the line, but they were unable to spark results. Opposition came from farmers who feared a railroad's impact on the hay and barley they were growing for horses. Large ranch owners foresaw increased taxes but little benefit, and citizens of San Pedro saw only ruinous competition for their own port's business. Phineas Banning himself was in the state senate in 1866 and offered another bill to allow public financing of the railroad that would help his own Wilmington business interests.[5] His measure failed, so he ran for re-election on a campaign focused on the proposed railroad, and after a bruising campaign returned to Sacramento. In 1868 he won passage of bills for investment of $150,000 by Los Angeles County and $75,000 by the City of Los Angeles in the railroad company. Wilson and Banning worked tirelessly to win passage of the measures locally, and at the March 24, 1868, election the measure succeeded, by 102 votes in the city and only twenty-eight votes in the county. The fact that the most vocal opponent, John Tomlinson, the freight-hauling competitor in San Pedro, died two weeks before the election may have been a factor in the outcome.[6]

The board of directors of the twenty-one-mile Los Angeles and San Pedro Railroad included Wilson, Banning, Dr. John S. Griffin and seven others. Former Governor John G. Downey was elected president of the company. Competition for the lucrative $19,000-a-mile construction contract was spirited, and ultimately went to Banning's own firm, Banning and Tichenor, over other bidders, including the son-in-law of the railroad's president, John Downey. Self interest was the code of the day, and when company president John Downey insisted on the line passing through his own property and was not supported by the board, he ultimately quit over the issue.[7] Benjamin Wilson was elected president to replace him.[8] Wilson headed the company during stormy times, with accusations that Banning and Tichenor had over-billed the investors for their construction. When the company assessed the city to help pay the railroad's obligations the city sued the railroad[9] and Banning threatened to run the line to Anaheim to leave Los Angeles as a mere way station. The city dropped its complaint prompting new litigation against the railroad and the city.[10] As the operating line proved more and more profitable the litigation melted away.[11]

Ground was broken in Wilmington on September 19, 1868. The line was opened in a huge celebration on October 26, 1869, two weeks before the Central Pacific connected the Bay Area with the Transcontinental Railroad. In their rush to deliver the first full-sized locomotive to the line, its name was misspelled "Los Angelos" and had to be corrected once the engine reached the city.[12] The crossing signs at intersections with roads read "Look out for the Locomotive" in English. In Spanish they read "*Cuidado de La Maquina de Vaho del Camino de Fierro*" (Look out for the Steel Machine on the Iron Road). This first Los Angeles railroad ran between the upper Wilmington Harbor and a crude terminal at Commercial and Alameda Streets, a few blocks south of the property where Wilson's home once sat and where Union Station sits today. It should have been named the Los Angeles and *Wilmington* Railroad, because those were the two terminals. The railroad never reached San Pedro.

Wilson had been instrumental in bringing steel wheels and steel rails to Southern California. In that moment, horse-drawn freight wagons and stagecoaches were rendered virtually obsolete for travel to and from the port. Travel time between city and port shrank to one hour and the cost of shipping goods and people dropped, benefiting large parts of the local economy.[13] Within two years the new railroad showed a net profit of $46,382 and was paying the local governments returns on their investments. Revenue from the line showed that goods imported into Los Angeles were more than double the amount of goods shipped out of the city.[14]

But still, this was a dead-end line that ran from the city to the port, and there was still no railroad link to the rest of the country. When railroads came to the region, and that was inevitable, Los Angeles must be a major rail hub, not just the end of a stub. "The man who saw that most clearly was Benjamin D. Wilson," according to historian Joseph S. O'Flaherty.[15]

The Transcontinental Railroad was completed only five months before the Los Angeles and San Pedro Railroad was finished. The Union Pacific had built from the east and the Central Pacific had built from the West, meeting up at Promontory, Utah, where former Governor Leland Stanford, president of the Central Pacific, had swung and missed on his first attempt to drive in the famous golden spike. Stanford was one of the Big Four controlling the Central Pacific. The others were Charles Crocker, Mark Hopkins and Collis P. Huntington. The Big Four bought the Southern Pacific Railroad in 1868 and merged the operations of two railroads two years later, under the name Southern Pacific, and began to add a southern route, from San Francisco to New Orleans, to their line. They bought out the Texas & Pacific Railway Co. and its entitlements for a route that cut across the Mojave Desert to Yuma, bypassing Los Angeles entirely, thus shortening their line and saving a great expense. The flat fertile Los Angeles basin is rimmed by mountains along its northern rim. For the railroad to build directly to Los Angeles an expensive tunnel would need to be drilled through the Tehachapi Mountains. The Big Four intended to build south through the San Joaquin Valley to the Tehachapis, then bend eastward toward Yuma along the thirty-fifth parallel to stay on flat land.

Wilson succeeded Banning in the state senate in 1870, and took up the railroad cause and continued Banning's championship of improving the Wilmington Harbor. Wilson fought the notion that county subsidies were no longer needed and succeeded in legislation to keep five percent subsidies in Los Angeles and seven other counties.[16] Wilson capped his efforts in Sacramento by traveling to Washington at his own expense to lobby for a clause in federal railway legislation that required the Southern Pacific to come directly to Los Angeles instead of cutting across the desert.

He was also in Washington to lobby for federal funding to deepen the harbor so that ships could sail directly to a pier in Wilmington instead of loading and offloading their wares onto lighters. He was successful on both goals. Congress appropriated two hundred thousand dollars for a harbor breakwater and inserted words "by the way of Los Angeles" into their legislation to bring the railroad to Los Angeles. Wilson warned constituents back home, though, that they'd better make a deal with the railroad because the Big Four's influence in Congress might well get the six words deleted. Collis P. Huntington did, indeed, work to have Wilson's words eliminated from the railroad act of 1871, but pressure from Los Angeles kept them in.[17]

Wilson and other Los Angeles leaders kept pressure on the Big Four to build "by the way of Los Angeles."[18] In April, 1872, Wilson and Tom Mott advised Leland Stanford that a taxpayers' meeting would soon appoint a committee to confer with the railroad and Stanford replied that he would send E.W. Hyde as the railroad's representative. At the May 18 meeting Wilson and others spoke to the crowd at the Los Angeles County courthouse urging public financial support to the Southern Pacific to entice it to come directly to Los Angeles. A few days later Wilson traveled to San Francisco with L.J. Rose and W.R. Oden to negotiate.[19] J. De Barth Shorb had been very involved in the negotiations with Hyde since the completion of the San Pedro line. Margaret wrote to Wilson two months after the San Pedro line had opened, "Mr. Shorb has been away nearly all of the week with Mr. Heide the Rail-road man, I have not been able to hear whether they thought favorable of the rout or not."[20]

The lure in the negotiations turned out to be the rail line that Wilson and others had built from Los Angeles to the port. If the Southern Pacific controlled this link, it would have a monopoly on land transport and would control the seaborne competition as well. The Southern Pacific would lose $602,000 in Los Angeles subsidies if it didn't link the Bay Area with Los Angeles by November 5, 1876, but to get to Los Angeles directly the company would need to build one of the longest tunnels in the world, seven thousand feet through the San Fernando Mountains, and that could cost more than the subsidy awaiting the railroad. Ultimately the Big Four made the decision, in March of 1875, to build directly to Los Angeles.[21]

The deal worked out between Southern California representatives and the Southern Pacific called for fifty miles of track through the county, twenty-five miles north from Los Angeles and fifteen miles east toward San Bernardino. The Los Angeles and San Pedro Railroad would be given to the Southern Pacific. The County would pay Southern Pacific five percent of its assessed real and personal property value (fifteen million dollars) less the bonds and stock in the Los Angeles and San Pedro Railroad Co. Los Angeles County voters approved the deal on November 5, 1872, 1,896 voting for the Southern Pacific deal and 724 against it. (An alternative from Tom Scott of the Pennsylvania Railroad was also on the ballot, offering a link to the east via San Diego, but the voters soundly rejected this.) The Los Angeles and San Pedro Railroad Co. became a part of the Southern Pacific on April 23, 1873.[22]

A trained tunnel force of 1,500 diggers, mostly Chinese, labored sixteen months, at a cost of two million dollars, to overcome obstacles of water seepage, cave-ins, bad air and encounters with clay-infested fissures. Three shafts were sunk so that work could progress along eight faces simultaneously and a support team of hundreds of cooks, teamsters and other specialists helped from the surface. The railroad was completed north from Los Angeles and south from the Tehachapis awaiting the completion of the dramatic tunnel. On August 12, 1876, telegraph wires hummed with the long-awaited message: "The iron horse poked his nose through the San Fernando Tunnel this evening at six o'clock and neighed long and loud his greeting to the citizens of Santa Clara Valley. Three weeks later, on September 5, 1876, an elaborate ceremony was staged to celebrate the rail linkage of Los Angeles and San Francisco, and thus to the rest of the country. Hundreds of Chinese workers stood at parade rest with their shovels, spaced along the right of way, as an honor guard for the official train. Charles Crocker swung the hammer in Mint Canyon to drive in the Golden Spike.[23]

After the Los Angeles and San Pedro Railroad became a part of the Southern Pacific, the Big Four had common interests with Banning and Wilson in improving the Wilmington port. The water at low tide there was only eighteen inches,[24] so shallow-draft lighters were needed to transfer cargo between ships to piers. Deepening the channel so that ships could tie up directly to the piers would make the port much more efficient and profitable, but to do so would be extremely expensive. Wilson and Banning used son-in-law J. De Barth Shorb as their intermediary with the Big Four. On August 16, 1875, Shorb met with Charles Crocker to argue that the dredging project would not be as expensive as the Big Four's engineers had predicted, and that this was to the Southern Pacific's advantage anyway. Shorb met with Collis P. Huntington the following two days. Huntington said that he and Leland Stanford had almost quarreled over this issue. Stanford thought that the railroad could freeze out seaborne traffic and force freight onto its rail cars. Huntington told Stanford that would be true only when he could do away with gravity. Shorb told Huntington that Wilson and Banning were so confident in their estimates of the costs that they would personally consider bearing any overage. That settled it, said Huntington.[25]

After the Southern Pacific was operating in Los Angeles, businessmen grew angry over the high-handed way the railroad was bleeding them through freight rates and Crocker returned to Southern California in 1877 to face an angry room in the city council chambers. Rates had increased by as much as fourfold. Crocker was treated so rudely by City Councilman J. S. Thompson and the taunting crowd that the railroad owner exploded with a threat to Los Angeles: "If this be the spirit in which Los Angeles proposes to deal with the railroad upon which this town's very vitality must depend, I will make grass grow in the streets of your city." The city businesses, one by one, gradually accepted the high rates as part of doing business in the new transportation era.[26]

Notes for Chapter 25

1 Abel Stearns imported the first carriage in 1853, to please his wife, Doña Arcadia, it was said. Newmark, *Sixty Years in Southern California 1853-1913*, 84.

2 O'Flaherty, *An End and a Beginning: The South Coast and Los Angeles 1850-1887*, 147.

3 Robinson, *Southern California's First Railroad*, 27.

4 Letter from William P. Reynolds to Wilson, November 30, 1864, B.D. Wilson papers.

5 Letter from Phineas Banning to Wilson, January 22, 1866, B.D. Wilson papers.

6 Robinson, *Southern California's First Railroad*, 32.

7 Ibid., 39.

8 Ibid., 60.

9 Los Angeles Superior Court, District 17, Case 1648. The Mayor and Common Council of the City of Los Angeles plaintiffs against The Los Angeles and San Pedro Rail Road Company—H.B. Tichenor—Phineas Banning—B.D. Wilson and D. McAlexander Trustees. Defendants.

10 Los Angeles Superior Court, District 17, Civil Case 1856. Volney E. Howard vs. The Los Angeles and San Pedro Rail Road Company (thirteen defendants plus Common Council of Los Angeles). Class-action suit on behalf of Los Angeles taxpayers alleging mismanagement.

11 Robinson, *Southern California's First Railroad*, 63.

12 Newmark, *Sixty Years in Southern California 1853-1913*, 402.

13 Port of Los Angeles Web site, "Story Rope"of San Pedro Waterfront (spwaterfront.com/PolaGateway/storyRope.aspx).

14 Barsness, "Iron Horses and an Inner Harbor at San Pedro Bay, 1867-1890," 291.

15 O'Flaherty, *An End and a Beginning: The South Coast and Los Angeles, 1850-1887*, 16.

16 Ibid., 147.

17 Ibid., 153.

18 Graves, *My Seventy Years in California: 1857-1927*.

19 Newmark, *Sixty Years in Southern California 1853-1913*, 440.

20 Letter from Margaret Wilson to her husband, December 18, 1869, B.D. Wilson papers.

21 O'Flaherty, *An End and a Beginning: The South Coast and Los Angeles 1850-1887*, 153-154.

22 Newmark, *Sixty Years in Southern California 1853-1913*, 441.

23 O'Flaherty, *An End and a Beginning: The South Coast and Los Angeles 1850-1887*, 154.

24 Ibid., 169.

25 Letter from J. De Barth Shorb to Wilson, Phineas Banning and George Hines, August 19, 1875, B.D. Wilson papers.

26 Newmark, *Sixty Years in Southern California 1853-1913*, 505-507.

CHAPTER 26

Business

B D. Wilson made his mark in the history of early Los Angeles in many ways. He used his money to bankroll one business after another, and his business investments fairly well catalogue the economy of early Los Angeles. Wilson was financially nimble, reinventing himself again and again as the local economy shifted and as technology evolved. He lived on the economic cutting edge as a one-man Standard & Poor's, investing in virtually every aspect of the local economy, from agriculture to manufacturing to utilities to real estate to minerals to transportation.

The economy of the Los Angeles area took enormous turns during Wilson's time there, and he leapt from industry to industry with uncanny timing to build his net worth. When the market for cow hides justified the enormous cattle herds of the *ranchero* days, Wilson raised cattle.[1] When that market fell off, and the population of the pueblo began to grow rapidly, Wilson moved there to use his former skills as a merchant, while growing fruit and grapes and bottling wine on his twelve-acre home site off the downtown streets. In the 1860s when land use favored wheat and barley and California became the world's granary, Wilson bought and cultivated lands accordingly. As the world market for wool exploded, Wilson was raising sheep. As the demand for wheat and barley waned, California became the new center for vines and deciduous fruits, especially citrus fruits, and Wilson was again leading the way.[2]

Money Lender

When Wilson came west, Alta California was a mostly-cashless society. The regional economy of the time was based largely on the byproducts of cattle: hides and tallow. Cowhides in this cash-starved land were known as "California bank notes" or "leather dollars"[3] and were worth about two bucks each. But Wilson had money . . . enough money to act as a bank in a land and time where there were no banks. He lent a lot of money to a lot of people, at interest rates that would be downright felonious in today's highly regulated cash society. Wilson lent money and borrowed money himself at rates up to five percent *per month*,[4] which translates to sixty percent per annum. In Northern California the going rates were even higher. A friend wrote him from San Jose in January of 1850 claiming that money was going for ten to eighteen percent per month (120 to 216 percent interest per year).[5] The interest rates were ruinous to many. Although not related to Wilson, one story of the period was of the man who pledged his *Rancho Santa Gertrudes* behind a poker bet of five hundred dollars. The man had to borrow more and more to cover the five percent per month interest payments, until the interest and principal soared to one hundred thousand dollars and his ranch was lost.[6] Wilson came into ownership of land a number of times as debtors could not repay what they had borrowed from him. In other cases the sheriff sold the property and gave Wilson the proceeds.[7] In one case Wilson was given "six entire pieces of silver ware, comprising a Tea Service" to satisfy a mortgage foreclosure.[8]

Freight Forwarding Agent

This was the business of Wilson's good friend and business partner Phineas Banning, but briefly in 1856, Wilson himself accepted commissions in the freight forwarding business, as evidenced by a receipt of Alexander & Banning on which Alexander's name is crossed out and Wilson's name is added by pen, to read "Wilson & Banning, Forwarding And Commission Merchants."[9]

Manufacturer

Wilson was the first furniture manufacturer in Southern California, and thus one of the first to be involved in manufacturing of any kind in the area.[10] Wilson and his son-in-law, J. De Barth Shorb, invested in a furniture factory and planing mill in Wilmington, called the Wilmington Manufacturing Company. Wilson and Shorb put up two-thirds of the money in 1874, and the manager of the enterprise, J.H. Taffe, was to put up the remaining capital from his share of the profits. When Taffe proved to be a disappointment, Wilson and Shorb installed W.L. Watkins over Taffe. A year after the start-up the venture was such a disappointment that Wilson and Shorb pulled the plug on the business.[11]

Mining Executive

In the late 1840s and early 1850s, California was consumed with the mining of precious metals. Gold in small quantities had been discovered in the San Fernando Valley area of Southern California in 1833,[12] preceding the great Northern California Gold Rush by fifteen years, but it was the latter frenzy which caused prospectors to scour the state for undiscovered lodes. Wilson was still a prisoner of war when gold was discovered at Sutter's Mill, but after he was released, he caught the gold and silver fever that affected most of the state and invested in more than one mining company. When a party containing Mormon missionaries bound to Tahiti reported discovering gold as they passed through Death Valley in December of 1849, Wilson was quick to organize a mining company, the Salt Springs or Margose Mining Company, and outfit an expedition in February of

1850. But gold is profitable only if the costs of mining and transporting it are less than the price of the gold ultimately brought to market. In the case of the Death Valley find, the costs of transporting to the site the necessary timber and a crushing machine were staggering. Wilson soon found that the venture was unprofitable and pulled out in 1850 as two other companies, the Los Angeles Mining Company and the Desert Mining Company, moved expensive equipment to the site. The exaggerated costs of mining in such a difficult and remote area sank the two companies, and they abandoned their equipment, including an expensive crushing mill, that had made it part way across the Mojave Desert before its wagon broke down.[13]

When the other companies folded, however, Wilson realized he now had a monopoly and went back into the area with his merchandising partner, Albert Packard, and their Salt Spring Mining Company. Wilson hired Andrew Sublette, a relative of his future wife, Margaret Hereford, as his superintendent. Sublette had operated one of the failed companies, the Desert Mining Company. But the machinery could not be made to work properly, and the Piute Indians swooped in to mangle the evil machine, so Wilson closed down the company in July of 1852.[14]

Closer to home, gold was discovered by Captain Hannager in 1854 right in Wilson's San Gabriel Valley, and within a few months seven hundred miners were sifting the sand and gravel for nuggets. During the next ten years the number of miners rose and fell as the easy minerals near the water were depleted and miners had to search for the more sparse finds farther away. All in all perhaps four million dollars in gold was extracted from San Gabriel Valley canyons.[15] Three miles up the San Gabriel canyon silver was found by Francisco Zapata, and one of the mines established there was known as the Zapata Silver Mine.[16] Wilson, along with Dr. James B. Winston and others, invested in the Zapata mine and Wilson delighted in showing visitors to his home a goblet made of silver from the mine.[17] At least a quarter of a million dollars in silver was extracted from the Zapata mine and others in the San Gabriel Canyon.[18]

Oil

On August 27, 1859, a salt well driller named William A. Smith stuck oil for his client, Colonel Edwin L. Drake, at Titusville, Pennsylvania, with a technological sneeze that caused an entrepreneurial cold around the country. One might wonder today what use oil might have had before the time of automobiles, but it was a valuable commodity even then. "Asphaltum" was used for roofing, sidewalks,[19] axle grease, fuel for lamps and lubricants for tools.[20] Society wanted something to replace whale oil which reeked with distasteful odors and medicine, among other uses. Benjamin Wilson and other investors were determined to bring the oil industry to Southern California. Behind the leadership of Phineas Banning they formed the first oil company in Southern California,[21] the Pioneer Oil Company, and held their first board meeting on January 1, 1866.[22]

The Pioneer Oil Company raced around gathering permits for drilling. It convinced the City of Los Angeles to give it rights for five hundred acres that had been worth fifty cents an acre, with the promise to pay them ten dollars an acre if oil, or a large reserve of water, were struck.[23] The company also acquired rights to "all brea, petroleum or rock oil" in the *Rancho San Pasqual* of board member Dr. John Griffin,[24] *Rancho Camulos* near Newhall,[25] Palos Verdes and other lands. The venture was more expensive than the investors had first imagined, and former Governor John G. Downey dragged his feet in anteing up the thirty thousand dollars for his three hundred shares. Company president Phineas Banning was reluctant to press too hard. After all, Governor Downey had made him a brigadier general in the California National Guard and Banning wore that title conspicuously. But the board members insisted, Banning sued, Downey paid up, and the two remained friends after all.[26] As the number of dry holes increased, board members were tapped for more money.[27]

These visionaries were right, of course. There *was* oil in Southern California, and lots of it. And the oil lay beneath their own lands, as it turned out, but their company employed no geologist and its equipment was too primitive for the task. The Pioneer Oil Company used heavy hawser rope, and drill bits in twenty-foot, twelve-inch-wide sections. The company claimed a strike on Wilson's old *Rancho Rodeo de las Aguas*, but it turned out to be a false alarm. One particularly deep well, in the San Fernando Valley, did strike oil at 325 feet, but the well ran dry almost immediately. In Pasadena the wells were dry, on the Palos Verdes Peninsula they found only salt water. In 1868 the Pioneer Oil Company folded.[28]

"Chamber of Commerce"

A nother business connection must be mentioned. In those early days Wilson served the area as a sort of one-man chamber of commerce, conscientiously answering questions of strangers who knew that he was the man to ask in Los Angeles. He was an unqualified booster of the area and he took time to answer the questions he received in detail. One man asked if one thousand dollars was enough for orchard land to guarantee him a livelihood while he learned the craft as an employee of another grower. Another man asked, "Is the population Spanish, Yankee or French?" Of course, those who took his advice and came West would be prospects for his subdivisions.

NOTES FOR CHAPTER 26

1 Graves, *My Seventy Years in California: 1857-1927*, 167.

2 Ibid.

3 O'Flaherty, *An End and a Beginning: The South Coast and Los Angeles 1850-1887*, 28.

4 Wilson borrowed at five percent per month in 1853 on his $600 purchase of pueblo property on Main Street. Mortgage deed, B.D. Wilson papers. Wilson lent Tomas Talamantes $1,500 in 1854 at five percent per month interest. Los Angeles Superior Court, First District, Civil Case #604.

5 Letter from Montgomery Martin to Wilson Jan. 23, 1850, B.D. Wilson papers.

6 Guinn, *A History of California*, 201.

7 Los Angeles Superior Court, First District, Civil Case #55 (another record shows Case #39) Wilson & Packard vs. Samuel R. Drummer "for principal and interest on the note & mortgage . . . with three percent interest per month . . . and the sum of ($164.46) and frame house, El Dorado House . . . on Main Street." The sheriff sold the house for $750 and gave Wilson $611.

8   Los Angeles Superior Court, First District, Civil Case #362, Wilson vs. John O. Wheeler. Wilson won a judgment of $1024.56 for foreclosure of a chattel mortgage and was paid with the silver.

9   Printed receipt, August 11, 1856, B.D. Wilson papers.

10 *Los Angeles Times*, February 21, 1887, 4.

11 Los Angeles Superior Court, District 17, Civil Case #3068.

12 Truman, *Semi-Tropical California*, 96.

13 Vredenburgh, "Fort Irwin and Vicinity History Of Mining Development."

14 Wynne, "Salt Springs, Death Valley!"

15 Truman, *Semi-Tropical California*, 97-99.

16 Robinson, *Mines of the San Gabriels*, 15.

17 *Los Angeles Star*, February 2, 1861.

18 Robinson, *Mines of the San Gabriels*, 15.

19 Truman, *Semi-Tropical California*, 104.

20 Vickery, *Harbor Heritage: Tales of the Harbor Area of Los Angeles, California*, 62.

21 The Pioneer Oil Company is generally cited as the first company to explore for oil in Southern California, but Gerald Taylor White in *Formative Years in the Far West: A History of Standard Oil Company of California*, page 593, cites the Los Angeles Brea Co., organized June 8, 1861, by Wilson's close friend, Dr. John S. Griffin, as the first oil company to incorporate for this intention. Griffin's company apparently never got to the drilling stage, however.

22 Notice of first regular meeting, B.D. Wilson papers.

23 Letter from Dr. John Griffin to Cave Couts, Couts papers, Huntington Library.

24 Newmark, *Sixty Years in Southern California 1853-1913*, 346.

25 O'Flaherty, *An End and a Beginning: The South Coast and Los Angeles 1850-1887*, 145.

26 Court Case 897, cited by Vickery, *Harbor Heritage: Tales of the Harbor Area of Los Angeles, California*, 55.

27 Letter from Patrick Downey to Wilson, January 31, 1866, B.D. Wilson papers.

28 Vickery, *Harbor Heritage: Tales of the Harbor Area of Los Angeles, California*, 62.

CHAPTER 27

Religion

Don Benito Wilson was deeply religious. The mountain men were famous for their lack of religion as a group. Theirs was a world beyond the white man's churches, and to many of them, beyond the white man's God. Many of them depended more on the religious men of the native campfire than the portable scripture that was just one more thing to weigh them down. Not Wilson. Like Jedediah Smith, the clean-living young mountain man who first ventured into California from the landward side, Wilson trusted in God, prayed to God and talked of God. His Protestant religion, like his American citizenship, was too important to him to treat as a commodity to be traded for advantage. Most of his American peers in Mexican Santa Fe and early Los Angeles took Mexican citizenship and converted to Catholicism for the advantages they brought in Mexican society. Wilson sought out Protestant ministers and helped found Protestant churches in Los Angeles and laced his letters to Margaret with talk about God's love, God's mercy and God's help.

When Wilson was mayor there were no Protestant churches in Los Angeles. In 1822 a parish Catholic church, *Los Fieles de Nuestra Señora la Reina de los Angeles*, was built to face the plaza. It still faces the plaza today. This church with its adobe walls and dirt floors was only served by a visiting priest since the religious center was in the San Gabriel Mission. It would be almost the very end of Don Benito's life before a cathedral, St. Vibiana, was built in the city, in 1876.[1] By the early 1850s few men went to church and pews of the Catholic church were filled mostly by women.[2] Protestants were no different. A pastor held services in city hall with only a few women attending, then, in ill health, became discouraged and quit.[3]

There were no Protestant churches and no Protestant clergyman in town.[4] An upscale drinking emporium called El Dorado, (no Indians or vagrants allowed), in a poetic twist of karma, would become a Methodist Church[5] around 1852.[6] And the minister of this boisterous den-turned-sedate-refuge would be (no kidding) Rev. Bland.[7] The first Black church in town, the African Methodist Episcopal Church, was formed in 1854.[8] Gatherings of the numerous Jewish worshippers were held in private homes in those days, as the first synagogue was not built till after the Civil War.[9]

In 1855, Wilson wrote to his brother, Wiley, saying, "I fear I shall fall far short at the great day of judgment in fact my only hopes are in His continued mercy in which I have entire confidence and my obedience to. This will has been my first duty although I never have been a member of any Church and I think it probably I never will."[10] But beginning almost immediately after he wrote this letter, he became not only a member of, but a leader in, several new churches. Don Benito used his wealth and position in Southern California to establish a number of Protestant churches and forge friendships with a number of Protestant clergymen who came to the godless frontier town of Los Angeles. Margaret wrote to Rev. Samuel Hopkins Willey, "Our town is improving rapidly—and I hope for a better state of morals soon, in our community. We have another Minister (a Presbyterian) Mr. Woods from San Francisco. The people seem much pleased with him."[11] The Wilsons carried on correspondence with a number of ministers. and both the Wilsons and the men of the cloth expressed frustration with the difficulties of starting a church in the frontier city. Rev. Joshua Phelps expressed such discouragement in trying to preach in Los Angeles that he was ready to give up the ministry altogether.[12]

The first Protestant society of Los Angeles evolved into the First Presbyterian Church. On July 25, 1855, Wilson and other trustees of the start-up church bought a 60-×105-foot lot at the corner of Temple and New High Streets from Mr. and Mrs. Francis Meline. In 1860 the mayor and Common Council wanted to extend a road through the church's property and gave the church 120 feet of land along Temple Street. The First Presbyterian Church was built on this 120-×165-foot lot. Wilson, along with Isaac S.K. Ogier and H.R. Myles, signed an indenture with the mayor and Common Council for one dollar.[13] But the Presbyterians could not pay for the supplies they had bought from Perry & Woodworth, so the firm sued, and the church went under. The Los Angeles Star lamented, "What heathens we must be, sure enough, when we find the church offered for sale by the Sheriff, on Monday next."[14] The forfeited Presbyterian Church was born again as the Episcopal church.[15]

The town was divided on the subject of religion. A law forbidding business on Sunday was passed in 1858,[16] but two years later the Los Angeles Star reported a protest against the Bible being used in public schools, the opponents saying that this was "contrary to law and decent respect for dissenters."[17]

On October 7, 1855, the first Episcopal bishop of California, William Ingraham Kip, came to Los Angeles to conduct the first Episcopal service[18] in Los Angeles, in the Plaza's tavern-turned-Methodist church, and his visit sparked a lifetime friendship with the Wilsons. The bishop would from then on stay with the Wilsons when he traveled to Southern California,[19] but his denomination would not gain a foothold in the town for another nine years. In 1864 a Missionary Committee appealed to Bishop Kip complaining that "Americans and other Protestants settled here are left to a life of simple heathenism . . . It is pitiable to think that if a Protestant dies here he must be buried like a dog; that an infant can never be baptized, and that a justice of the peace is the only authority to whom a couple can go to get married."[20] In response an Indiana missionary named Elisas Birdsall, who had come to California for his health, was dispatched. The following year a parish was formed under the name of St. Athanasius,[21] and the Wilsons may well have been among the ten souls who attended the parish's first service.[22] Rev. Birdsall wrote that "We have united the whole Protestant element in our own new parish . . . in a wide field here that is almost entirely neglected."[23]

One pioneer remembered that Wilson gave the land for this church.[24]

A decade later Wilson and other major San Gabriel Valley landholders heard about a philanthropist named Mrs. Amos Maine Vinton who wanted to pay for a new Episcopal church somewhere in Southern California. Mrs. Vinton's dream was to underwrite three churches, each named Church of The Savior, stretching from the Atlantic to the Pacific. The first was in her home town of Providence, Rhode Island, and the second was in Clermont, Iowa.[25] She contacted Rev. Henry Messinger, who had replaced Rev. Birdsall as the rector of the St. Athanasius church in 1866. Wilson, his immediate neighbors to the west and east, E.J.C. Kewen and Leonard J. Rose, and a fourth area landholder, Luther Harvey Titus, persuaded Mrs. Vinton on a San Gabriel Valley location, and she donated four thousand dollars to the task.[26] Rev. Messenger agreed to be the new church's rector.

Benjamin Wilson gave the land for Mrs. Vinton's third Church of The Savior, and offered lodging to Rev. Messinger while his parsonage was being built.[27] A Mexican brick maker used soil for the knoll behind Wilson's house where the Patton house would be built in years to come.[28]

The first services were held in a temporary structure in 1869. In 1872 the Wilsons took great offense "after the way he acted with regard to that Dr. Stevens," and they withdrew from the church until after he had left. Rev. Messinger had written to Wilson on January 20, 1872, announcing that he had written a draft for Wilson's entire pledge of one hundred dollars to Griffith Lynch & Co. He immediately asked for more money for seats ($6.50 each) and "a pulpit & reading desk . . . & a nice partition work behind the chancel." He also wrote, perhaps hinting for even more money, that a tower and bell "must perhaps wait . . . for a while." He wrote, "I hope you will find it convenient to cancel your subscription thus & soon be able to renew it, & that blessings may ever rest upon you . . ."[29] In the end, Mrs. Vinton, not Wilson, paid for the bell, forged in Cincinnati.[30]

Wilson dutifully paid the draft,[31] but shortly after that Margaret wrote to Wilson, saying that she had no idea whether the church was finished since she had not been back there since Wilson had left for Sacramento.

She wrote, "I did not think it was right to go to hear him, after the way he acted with regard to that Dr. Stevens. I feel very badly about it, as

I would like to be able to take my children to Church."[32] Rev. Messinger responded to the umbrage and withdrawal from his church of perhaps his most influential family with a four-page letter of obsequious, submissive toadying. On and on he wrote trying different words to express his regret at the affront he was guilty of. "Dear Mrs. Wilson,

> Whatever blindness I may have been guilty of in past time please allow as past & do not attribute evil to me. I do not feel wicked. I wish to be your pastor still. I can live, I believe, without the help of any body. I am independent now. . . . Do not hold anything against me longer. It is not Christ-like. I believe he has forgiven me. . . . If he owns me, why should you disown me?"[33]

For four pages he purveyed, but Margaret wasn't buying. The church itself was finally finished in 1875, without further help from the Wilsons, having been delayed by the financial panic of 1873.[34] Although Mrs. Vinton had very specifically funded three churches across the country with the same name of The Church of The Savior, and always referred to all three by that name, the San Gabriel church for some reason was called by its parishioners The Church of Our Savior.[35]

After Rev. Messinger left the church in 1873[36] the Wilsons returned and made The Church of Our Savior the cornerstone of their family's religious life. Their daughters Ruth and Annie were confirmed there,[37] and Ruth was married to George S. Patton in the church.[38] The funerals of Ruth Wilson Patton, Anne Patton and Margaret Wilson were held in the church. Today a number of the stained glass windows of the church celebrate the lives of Benjamin D. Wilson and various members of the Wilson/Patton family.

Wilson gave land for other churches as well. In 1876 he gave two and a half acres for a Methodist church in the town he was founding, Alhambra.[39] In 1877 he gave land for the San Gabriel Methodist Episcopal Church.[40]

After they moved to San Francisco for the wine business, they grew tired of city life and moved back to Lake Vineyard in 1869.

228

Notes for Chapter 27

1 Newmark, *Sixty Years in Southern California 1853-1913*, 490.
2 According to Judge Benjamin Hayes, who arrived in Los Angeles in 1851, quoted by Krythe, "Daily Life in Early Los Angeles," 28.
3 de Packman, "Landmarks and Pioneers of Los Angeles."
4 Ibid., 62.
5 Layne, "Annals of Los Angeles: Part II," 321.
6 Newmark, *Sixty Years in Southern California 1853-1913*, 103.
7 de Packman, "Landmarks and Pioneers of Los Angeles," 75.
8 Layne, "Annals of Los Angeles: Part II," 332-333.
9 Ibid., 333.
10 Letter from Wilson to his brother, Wiley, May 5, 1855, B.D. Wilson papers.
11 Letter from Margaret Wilson to Rev. Samuel Hopkins Willey, November 1854, B.D. Wilson papers.
12 Letter from Rev. Joshua Phelps to Wilson, September 7, 1863, B.D. Wilson papers.
13 A full account of the legal matter was described in a letter to the editor of the *Los Angeles Times*, July 9, 1882, by John W. Ellis. Ellis did not mention an indenture now in the B.D. Wilson papers of the Huntington Library collection from the Mayor and City Council to Church trustees Wilson, Isaac S.K. Ogier and H.R. Myles, dated November 17, 1860, for one dollar, which was apparently succeeded by the deed of December 5, 1860.
14 *Los Angeles Star*, January 31, 1863.
15 *Los Angeles Times*, July 9, 1882.
16 *Los Angeles Star*, June 5, 1858.
17 *Los Angeles Star*, July 28, 1860.
18 Kelley, *History of the Diocese of California From 1849 to 1914*, 35.
19 Shoop, *Pasadena Star-News*, June 28, 1955.
20 Kelley, *History of the Diocese of California From 1849 to 1914*, 53.
21 Ibid., 35, 381.
22 Beverly Wayte, in her "A History of the San Gabriel Cemetery," wrote that the Wilsons were "almost certainly" among the ten.
23 Kelley, *History of the Diocese of California From 1849 to 1914*, 35, 54.
24 Interview transcript of Mary Agnes Richardson. Standlee papers, Huntington Library.
25 Truman, *Semi-Tropical California*, 143.
26 Ibid., 143
27 Wayte, "A History of the San Gabriel Cemetery."
28 Dryden, "Church of Our Savior: The Early Years (1853-1875)."
29 Letter from H.H. Messinger to Wilson, January 20, 1872, B.D. Wilson papers.
30 Truman, *Semi-Tropical California*, 143.
31 Letter from Wilson to his wife, January 31, 1872, B.D. Wilson papers.
32 Letter from Margaret Wilson to her husband, February 4, 1872, B.D. Wilson papers.
33 Letter from H.H. Messinger to Margaret Wilson, February 25, 1872, B.D. Wilson papers.

34 Wayte, "A History of the San Gabriel Cemetery."

35 Ibid.

36 Ibid.

37 *Pasadena Star-News*, June 28, 1955.

38 December 10, 1884, Hirshson, *General Patton: A Soldier's Life*, 19.

39 Northrup, *History of Alhambra*, 83.

40 Carpenter, "Benito Wilson: Yankee to California," 31-43.

CHAPTER 28

The Shorbs
and the Pattons

Benjamin Wilson was one of the richest men in Southern California, so it is no surprise that his daughters married well. Wilson's beloved daughter, Margaret, known to the family as Maggie, died in her third year of life; his other three daughters lived full lives. Two of them married, and married well. Both of Wilson's stepsons were ambitious, wealthy, prominent in Southern California social circles and both were elected to County-wide office as he had been, but they were as different from each other as were their two mothers-in-law, Wilson's two wives. One of the Wilson girls' husbands was Catholic, the other Protestant. One lived a life of regal splendor, the other wore his wealth quietly. One was tolerant; one was famous for his misogyny and bias against the region's original Hispanic settlers, the Hispanics and Catholics.

Sue Wilson and James De Barth Shorb

María de Jesús Yorba Wilson, known as Sue, was Wilson's first child, born of a mother who'd been part of the *Californio* aristocracy in the days before the region lived under an American flag. Sue, daughter of a Catholic mother, married James De Barth Shorb, also a Catholic. Shorb was born into a prominent family on April 4, 1842, in Frederick County, Maryland, and graduated from Mount St. Mary's College. He studied law, and came to California in 1863 as assistant superintendent of the Philadelphia & California Oil Company. In 1867 he purchased a mining interest. While calling on Benjamin Wilson on a business matter he met Sue and the two were married at Lake Vineyard on June 4, 1867.[1] After their marriage they moved to San Francisco, where Shorb handled Wilson's wine and produce business. Growing tired of city life in 1869,[2] Shorb moved his family back to the family domain where they lived in the Lake Vineyard house and tended their own part of the estate, immediately east of the Wilson house.[3] Mr. and Mrs. Shorb lived in the Lake Vineyard house until they built their own elegant house in the mid-1870s on a commanding hill east of the Lake Vineyard abode. Shorb named this new family home "San Marino" after his grandfather's plantation in Maryland.[4] It would be this house that hosted Henry E. Huntington on his very first visit to Southern California, and when the estate was sold in insolvency, Huntington would buy the place, raze the Shorb home and build his own grand mansion on the same plot. Huntington didn't like the name *San Marino* however, preferring the name *Los Robles*.[5]

Shorb was the ambitious, super-achieving son Wilson had wanted, but hadn't found in his own son, John, or his stepson, Edward, and under Wilson's tutelage and encouragement Shorb ran and expanded Wilson's wine and agricultural operations, and participated in his land and railroad ventures. Shorb was president of the family San Gabriel Wine Company, the San Gabriel Valley Railroad, the Pasadena & Alhambra Railroad, and was also president of the Los Angeles Chamber of Commerce.[6] Shorb was elected the treasurer of Los Angeles County in 1892 as a Democrat, riding the shirttails of Grover Cleveland in the presidential election. But, while Wilson had lived relatively modestly for a man of his financial comfort, Shorb wore his wealth like a flashing neon sign. He traveled in a private railway car and hosted parties in the Great Gatsby style.[7]

Sue and James De Barth Shorb had eleven children: Ynez; James De Barth, Jr.; Margaret Nina; Edith Octavia; Ramona; Benito Wilson;

Joseph Campbell; Ethel Rebecca; Donald McMeal; Norbert Newlands; and Bernardo Yorba.

Ruth Wilson, Annie Wilson and George S. Patton

The tale of the two surviving daughters of Benjamin and Margaret Wilson must be told as one. Anne was older, by three years, and was thought to be prettier and smarter than Ruth. Anne was known to the outside world as Annie, and to her family as Nannie. Annie had a childhood crush on a young man named George Smith Patton II, who went away to Virginia Military Institute. Shortly after he returned from school he stood in for his stepfather, State Senator George Hugh Smith, at Don Benito's funeral at the Lake Vineyard estate, renewing his acquaintance with the sisters at that time. He fell in love with the younger sister, Ruth, and married her on December 10, 1884, five years after Wilson's death, at the family's church, Church of Our Savior in San Gabriel.[8]

But this is not the end of Annie's love for George, but the beginning. When Ruth and George were at the train station ready to begin their honeymoon, Annie showed up with all her luggage, expecting to be a part of the trip. Only after earnest reasoning did Annie give up her resolve to accompany the man she, too, loved. When the couple returned home to take up residence in the fabled Lake Vineyard estate, Annie moved into their house, her old house, the house where the two sisters had grown up. George had, in effect, two wives. As long as George lived Annie was a part of the household, sharing everything, except, apparently, George's bed. When Ruth gave birth to a son, named George, Jr., (Georgie to the family) Annie viewed him as her own, the son she should have borne with George. So Georgie, the future World War II General George S. Patton, Jr., was, for all practical purposes, raised by two mothers. Annie never married and never had a romantic notion for any other man. She was an intrinsic fixture in the family landscape, traveling with George and Ruth, attending social events with them and constantly with them at home.

George was patrician and very class conscious. Blacks, Asians and Catholics were in a class beneath him, he once told an audience at a private club. He denounced "any plan . . . which shall in the slightest degree imperil the continued supremacy of our own race, or threaten the pollution of its Aryan blood."[9] A leader of the Men's League Opposed to Suffrage Extension, he fought vigorously against women's right to vote.[10]

George Patton, an attorney, gained wealth, as most of the Southern California rich did, through real estate. Like his father-in-law he had partnerships with the Banning family, now with the next generation. Patton's half-sister, Anne Ophelia Smith, married Hancock Banning, Phineas's oldest son. Patton owned a seventh of the Catalina Island Company with the Bannings. He also invested in wine making and in oil.[11] He had a close business relationship with Henry Huntington, best known for his Pacific Electric railway system, but it was an adjunct to the remote land he bought. By building a transportation link, he increased the value of the land, which he then subdivided and sold. Patton oversaw that business. Patton was district attorney of Los Angeles County for two terms[12] and ran for Congress in 1894 and again in 1896, coming so close the second time that the result had to be decided in the Democratic State Convention, the delegates finally leaning to the other candidate.[13] In 1916 he ran unsuccessfully as the Democratic candidate for the U.S. Senate against Hiram Johnson.

When George built a new, five-bedroom house and moved the family out of the Lake Vineyard home close by, Annie moved with them. When George died of the life effects of alcohol abuse the family held a vigil of mourning. Annie, who shared George's reckless dependence on strong drink, retired to her room upstairs where she shouted and cried that George had always loved her, not her sister. She screamed that she, not Ruth, was meant to be George's wife and that Georgie should have been her son. She screamed for George to come and take her with him. "Wait for me, George! Wait for me!" she wailed in high decibels. From that night on Annie made no more entries in the diary she had kept virtually her entire life.[14] She moved out of her sister's house, and into a house at 1540 Oak Grove Ave., on the Lake Vineyard grounds. Ruth died in Albuquerque on April 28, 1928, at sixty-seven years of age. Annie died at Lake Vineyard on

November 26, 1931, at the age of seventy-three, the last surviving child of Don Benito Wilson.

George Smith Patton II

George Smith Patton, II, the object of the two Wilson daughters' affection, was a descendent of the blueblood Patton family of Virginia. His father had been a Confederate Army brigadier general, who had died of wounds suffered in the third battle of Winchester, when General Jubal Early's army was defeated by the Union army of General Philip Sheridan outside Washington, D.C. The father of this Confederate officer, in turn, had been a Virginia Congressman. Ruth Wilson and George Smith Patton had two children, George Smith Patton, Jr., the famous World War II general (1885-1945), and Anne (1887-1971).[15] Anne, known to the family as Nita, was born August 24, 1887, just after the family moved to the family home.[16]

General George Smith Patton, Jr.

George Patton, Jr., (the World War II general, known to his family as Georgie) was born in the Lake Vineyard house of his grandfather, Benjamin Wilson, but after Don Benito had died. Georgie lived there till he went away to VMI and then West Point. Georgie was born in the same bed his mother and aunt had been born in. General George S. Patton, Jr., graduated from West Point, was badly injured in World War I and is credited with creating America's tank corps between the two world wars. He became famous for his leadership in the Second World War. The legendary General Patton was the grandson of the legendary Don Benito Wilson. Many of the famous traits of the *Rambo* mountain man were repeated in his grandson. Both were filled with bravado, courage and a sense of adventure. Both were men of the old South and full of sympathy for the Confederate cause. And both had enormous tempers. General George Patton was certainly a chip off the old mountain-man block, and yet, Patton disdained his famous grandfather and bristled at the notion that he bore his progenitor's traits. Patton viewed Don Benito as a coarse backwoodsman, an unpolished self-made man. Patton pointed instead to his blueblood Patton roots. Patton was ashamed that his grandfather had married a Mexican and thus "sullied" the family's blood lines. Don Benito Wilson's most famous descendent, the descendent who best reflected his qualities, railed against any comparison with his grandfather.

General Patton did not share the family appetite for politics. One of his biographers, Robert H. Patton, quotes him as saying, "I have no more gift for politics than a cow has for fox hunting." "To hell with the people!" he said. "The few must run the many for the latter's good," he opined, and said, "I have never voted and do not intend to."[17]

NOTES FOR CHAPTER 28

1 Wilson-Patton Bible, B.D. Wilson papers.

2 Letter from Shorb to Wilson, May 7, 1869, B.D. Wilson papers.

3 Rose, L.J. Rose of Sunny Slope, 48.

4 City of San Marino Web site.

5 Letter from Henry E. Huntington to George S. Patton, April 26, 1904. Henry E. Huntington papers, Huntington Library

6 History of Los Angeles County, 813.

7 Patton, The Pattons: A Personal History of an American Family, 78.

8 Hirshson, General Patton: A Soldier's Life, 19.

9 Patton, The Pattons: A Personal History of an American Family, 124.

10 Hirshson, General Patton: A Soldier's Life, 23.

11 Blumenson, The Patton Papers, 146.

12 Hirshson, General Patton: A Soldier's Life, 21.

13 Patton, The Pattons: A Personal History of an American Family, 99.

14 D'Este, Patton: A Genius for War, 35-36. Blumenson, Patton: The Man Behind the Legend, 1885-1945, 339; Patton, The Pattons: A Personal History of an American Family, 98-99.

15 D'Este, Patton: Genius For War, 9-17.

16 Hirshson, General Patton: A Soldier's Life, 19.

17 Patton, The Pattons: A Personal History of an American Family, 159.

CHAPTER 29

Death
and Funeral

Benjamin Wilson was beside himself about a pending action in the state legislature that would have a negative impact on his Wilmington interests. On Saturday he was in Los Angeles, greeting old friends on the street, and venting his anger about Sacramento. He appeared as hale and vigorous as ever.[1] On Sunday evening at Lake Vineyard he stayed up till about 10:30 talking with a close friend named McKee. He became ill during the night and died around seven the next morning, March 11, 1878. Doctors of the day diagnosed it as a heart attack, but many mysterious deaths were labeled heart attacks in those days. Wilson had had a similar attack in Wilmington a month or six weeks earlier.

His funeral was held in his great house at Lake Vineyard on March 13. It was one of the largest funerals, if not the largest, in the history of the city, and certainly the largest ever in the San Gabriel Valley. The new rector of The Church of Our Savior conducted the service, a man coincidentally by the name of Wilson. Rev. Wilson spoke of Don Benito's "sterling integrity of character" and his "goodness of heart." The mourners then sang the hymn, "Rock of ages cleft for me; Let me hide myself in thee." The pallbearers were a mix of the pre-American pueblo and the Yankee Los Angeles that followed. They included Don Pío Pico, the last governor of Mexican California, Judge V. Sepúlveda and Antonio F. Colonel, the first Mexican-American mayor of Los Angeles. Also serving were the current mayor, Prudent Beaudry; General V.E. Howard; ex-Sheriff D.W. Alexander, L.J. Rose, L.H. Titus, H. Hamilton, and Major E.M. Ross. Veterans of the Mexican War and fellow Masons swelled the crowd. A hundred carriages formed a procession from Lake Vineyard to the cemetery next to The Church of Our Savior.[2]

Among the assets he left (partial list):

Real estate: 250 acres in *Rancho Santa Anita*
588 acres in the Oak Knoll Tract
161 acres in or near Lake Vineyard
41 acres in Wilmington
160 acre warrant of land for service in Mexican War
72 acres in Alhambra
Interests in the Soledad Township Road Company, Wilmington Manufacturing Co., iron pipe laid from Lake Vinyard to the Alhambra tract and two reservoirs in Alhambra tract.
Total real-estate value: $165,590

Stock: All 500 shares of Lake Vineyard Land & Water Assn. ($50,000)
10 shares of Los Angeles Bank Stock ($10,000)

Other assets: Carriage, Buggy, Spring Wagon
2 half-breed horses
6 American Cows
4 calves
5 hogs
2 watches
Library
16 tanks ranging from 1,500 to 6,000 gallons
Large copper still
Small boiler

Wine:	Vintage	Gallons	Value
	Port wine		
	1873	4030	$1600
	1875	1770	650
	1876	11345	4500
	Damaged	2730	0
	Muscatel		
	1876	1180	480
	M. V. Wine		
	1873	1768	500
	1876	4500	1800
	Angelica		
	1873	150	60
	1874	600	360
	1875	1500	600
	1876	600	240
	10 cases Musacatel		50
	Sedement BT Muscatel		50
	162 Barrels Brandy:		
	7008 gallons (Bonded)		$2,800

His will, signed in 1870, left "All property, real, personal and mixed, to my three daughters . . . "To my son, John B. Wilson, in view of his disobedience and undutifulness, I give nothing, further than the affirmance of such gifts and conveyances as I have made or may hereafter make to him during my life." It didn't matter. John had been dead for nine years.

He left a fifty-five-year-old wife. Sue was thirty-three, Annie was nineteen and Ruth was sixteen.

The monument over his grave, fashioned by Deelez & Gilbert, was not erected until five years after his death. According to the *Los Angeles Times*, it was "one of the largest monuments in Southern California."[3]

It reads: COMING TO CALIFORNIA AMONG THE
             EARLIEST OF PIONEERS IN 1841 HE
             DEVOTED THE BEST ENERGIES OF HIS
             PRIVATE AND PUBLIC USEFUL LIFE IN
             HIS STATE AND PROMOTING THE WELFARE
             AND HAPPINESS OF ALL
             THE BEAUTY, PROGRESS AND WEALTH OF
             SAN GABRIEL VALLEY IS THE BEST
             MONUMENT OF HIM WHO RESTS BELOW
             HONEST, PURE, BRAVE AND INCORRUPTIBLE
             HE LIVED REVERENCED AND RESPECTED
             AND DIED MOURNED BY ALL

             MAY HIS SOUL REST IN PEACE

NOTES FOR CHAPTER 29
  1 *Los Angeles Evening Express*, March 11, 1878.
  2 *Los Angeles Evening Express*, March 14, 1878.
  3 *Los Angeles Times*, June 24, 1883.

CHAPTER 30

Sizing Up Don Benito

So let's take stock of this larger-than-life icon of the century-before-last. Physically, Benjamin Wilson was a bit above average in size, six feet tall and two hundred pounds.[1] He carried in his body a deep scar from being mauled by a grizzly and part of an Indian arrowhead, decorations from his triumph over animal and human adversaries. A pronounced brow overarched piercing eyes, bespeaking fierce ambition and uncommon courage. He smoked a pipe.[2] We know from the fact that he was a mountain man that he had to be an exceptional rider and an excellent shot, because he could not have survived in that genre otherwise. He may well have been plagued with rheumatism from his years of wading in ice-cold rivers, because that was the occupational disease of the profession. Wilson was shaped by a frontier childhood, an early springboard into adult survival, and by life in a kill-or-be-killed environment. The vicarious thrill of today's paintball or computer games was his everyday reality show.

He was a natural leader, comfortable in command outdoors and at the head of a meeting table inside. He did not have the kind of ego that demanded recognition. Although he agreed to have Wilson College bear his name, this was an exception. When he subdivided part of his land to form a town he let his daughters name the new city, rather than calling it Wilson, California. (They called it Alhambra.) Although one of the wealthiest men in the region, he did not surround himself with the trappings of obvious wealth. His house, although large, was no palace. He did not dress expensively or ride in elaborate carriages.

Don Benito Wilson was rough-hewn and unrefined, a man of imperfect English. His writing style was sometimes ungrammatical, often plagued with misspellings and almost completely devoid of punctuation. He was not the backwoods buffoon of a congressman like David Crockett, but he was viewed as a simple frontiersman even in the relatively unsophisticated legislative halls of Wild West Los Angeles and California. The president of Wilson College described him as "very much above an average man, especially in those characteristics necessary for frontier life and civilization."[3] The *Los Angeles Star* said that he was "a man peculiarly adapted to the bold, independent life of a frontiersman."[4] His contemporaries' descriptions praised his intelligence, honesty and generosity, but generally began with a phrase such as "Mr. Wilson had not the advantages of a liberal education, but. . . ."[5] "He was not among those fortunates who enjoyed a formal education, yet. . . ."[6] or "Uneducated, but. . . ."[7] One newspaper said "there was nothing . . . about him of the superfine veneer of conventional life."[8] So his lack of sophistication must have been so jarring that commentators felt the need to mention it first. Clearly, it was his wealth and position, not his social graces, that gave him entry into the right rooms with the right people. (Margaret Wilson, on the other hand, was described as "finely educated and refined.")[9] The *Daily Los Angeles Herald* said of Wilson, "His most marked characteristic was . . . frankness."[10]

He was viewed as a man of great intelligence, albeit not of the kind earned in halls of ivy. He was described as an "indefatigable reader"[11] and of course legendary for the field smarts and common sense that led to a net worth far beyond that of his better educated peers. His business books show a careful accounting and a sophisticated understanding of double entry bookkeeping.

The *Daily Los Angeles Herald* said, "He was above all things, a native born gentleman. The instincts of courtesy and delicacy were ingrained in the man himself . . ."[12]

Commentators of his time inevitably spoke of his character. He was a man of principle who was trusted and respected by those who knew him. The Los Angeles Star eulogized, "He has left behind . . . a name which is a synonym for unbending integrity."[13] In a landscape where the far edge of Second World civilization had outstretched the supply line of formal justice and polite remedy, he was a public example of ethics and decency. The Los Angeles Star found it noteworthy that despite his survival in the roughest of times and places, his code was that of a model citizen. "His life has been of vicissitude, trial, toil and danger, and yet he passed through the furnace and came out without the smell of fire upon his garments," the newspaper wrote.[14] This ethical reputation has to be measured by the yardstick of his day, not ours. He made his initial bankroll by smuggling and other illegal activities, this in a cat-and-mouse environment which pitted American practices against a rigid Santa Fe structure where legal compliance was felt by the yanquis to be impossible. There is no hint that he engaged in similar practices in Mexican Alta California or in the American system that followed. His business dealings show a man who insisted on living by whatever bargain was struck, and not one to engage in slippery practices. He would take a fellow's land if that land had been the security for a loan not repaid, but that had been the agreement all along, and part of the rules he'd have played by if the roles had been reversed. Writers in later generations have accused him of ignoble motives and underhanded dealings, but his contracts and court records reveal nothing more sinister than a man who stuck by his word and expected others to do the same. His use of public office to advance issues where he stood to gain financially would be cause for ethics investigations today, yet in his own time he was called "an opponent of jobbery (corruption) in every form."[15]

He was, for his times, tolerant of class, race and religious differences. Although a partisan Protestant and proud American, he married a Mexican Catholic woman and raised a Catholic daughter whose blood lines were Mexican and American. Although his views on justice for Indians would be deemed paternalistic today, in his time he was known for his fierce defense of Indian rights and his work for justice for the Indians still living independently at the time. Those Indians themselves viewed him as one of the White leaders they could trust and they came to Los Angeles to seek his advice and intervention. Horace Bell, a contemporary, wrote, "Don Benito seemed to love all mankind . . . and . . . seemed to have a special love and regard for the red branch thereof—the poor Indians."[16] He denounced slavery (at least in retrospect) and lived a life of tolerance in his multi-cultural pueblo.

He welcomed his own, and his wife's, family to live in the shade of the advantage he had created in Southern California. He was famous in his time for his generosity to charity, especially the causes of religion and private education. The *Los Angeles Star* said, "in times when charity was wanted he was ever open-handed; when public enterprises asked the aid of his purse, or personal influence, he gave them cheerfully. . . . He was a friend to all, rich and poor alike. . . . He was not forgetful to entertain strangers, nor did he turn the beggar away empty from his door."[17]

His letters to Margaret were long and loving. They reveal a man genuinely concerned about her, his children and members of their extended family. The husband and wife letters in both directions are formal and correct, devoid of romantic suggestion and betraying no humor. Life was serious. But the letters were laced with sentiments of love and commitment.

He had a violent temper. His wife, Margaret, could get angry, too. One student of the period reported, "The Herefords were said to have tempers 'equal to brimstone.'"[18] If so, Margaret Hereford had met her match. Wilson expressed fear that his material comfort would disappear. He remembered all too well desperate times as a mountain man when he'd had to kill his own faithful mule to keep from starving.

Don Benito purred in his final year of life that in the California he first knew "There were no courts, no juries, no lawyers, nor any need for them." For one who waxed romantically about a lawyer-free world, he certainly helped make that profession wealthy in Los Angeles. He used the courts in legal combat, and his opponents attacked him as well, beginning with Case Number Seven in the new American government in Los Angeles. He sued, or was sued in scores of cases, but in the majority of these he was the plaintiff. He sued Francisco Ocampo and José Sepúlveda for repayment of a $440 debt (payable with "fifty head of good cattle over two years of age").[19] Wilson owned so much land, with so many partners that he was listed in one case among both the plaintiffs and the defendants.[20]

Perhaps Don Benito Wilson would not deserve a major place in Los Angeles history for any one of his accomplishments alone. An editor who had known him for only three years praised him, although commenting, "While he has never filled any post of overshadowing importance he has been a legislator . . ." Say what? Mayor of Los Angeles and state senator were unimportant posts? This editor concluded, "He was not a great man, but he was emphatically a good man."[21]

We might differ. Other actors in the great drama of that unfolding City of Los Angeles were briefly mayor, others amassed large amounts of land, others came and went in the state legislature. Others led American troops, owned mines, drilled for oil, started railroads, fought Indians, helped Indians, bottled wine and exported oranges. But Don Benito Wilson is worthy of our memory and reverence because of his incredible span of distinctions. He is a one-man *Who's Who* across the board in the early history of the American West and Los Angeles in particular. He, in one incredible life, represents a bridge between post-Revolutionary America to the dawn of the modern city.

NOTES FOR CHAPTER 30

1 "Recollections of Samuel Butler," oral history interview by Elizabeth I. Dixon, Oral History Program, UCLA, 1962. This is the only known physical description of Wilson. Referenced by Kurutz, "Don Benito Wilson: A Pioneer In Transitional Southern California, 1841-1854."

2 Letter from Wilson to Margaret, June 15, 1856, B.D. Wilson papers.

3 *Los Angeles Star*, March 15, 1878.

4 *Los Angeles Star*, March 12, 1878.

5 *San Gabriel Valley News*, March 14, 1878.

6 *Los Angeles Star*, Tuesday, March 12, 1878.

7 Brewer, *Journal*, Book 1, Chapter 2, "Los Angeles and Environs."

8 *Daily Los Angeles Herald*, March 12, 1878.

9 Brewer, *Journal*, Book 1, Chapter 2, "Los Angeles and Environs."

10 *Daily Los Angeles Herald*, March 12, 1878.

11 *Los Angeles Star*, March 12, 1878.

12 *Daily Los Angeles Herald*, March 12, 1878.

13 *Los Angeles Star*, March 12, 1878.

14 *Los Angeles Star*, March 12, 1878.

15 *Los Angeles Evening Express*, March 11, 1878.

16 Bell, *Remeniscences of a Ranger: Early Times in Southern California*, 113.

17 *Los Angeles Star*, March 12, 1878.

18 Sunder, *Bill Sublette: Mountain Man*, 194.

19 Civil Case #50 (another record shows Case #43), Los Angeles Superior Court,
    First District, August 30, 1851.

20 Los Angeles Superior Court, District 17, Civil Case #3816, Joseph J. Bullis et al.
    (including Wilson) vs. Bersabe L. de Rosas, et al. (including Wilson), March 3, 1877.
    Wilson and others were found in default for non-appearance.

21 *Daily Los Angeles Herald*, March 12, 1878.

CHAPTER 31

Conclusion

O f course history did not end when Wilson died. Here's what happened later to the people, places and things Wilson touched during his lifetime.

Margaret Wilson

W ilson's second wife, Margaret, grew distant from her daughters after her husband's death, absorbed by nervous disorders and "lost in fitful contemplations of Jesus."[1] She died on December 29, 1898, twenty years after the death of her husband, at her beloved Lake Vineyard home, with her son, Edward; her daughter, Ruth Wilson Patton; and her daughter-in-law, Sue Wilson Shorb, at her side.[2] Despite a life of chronic complaints about her poor health, she outlived both her husbands. She had shuffled along the North American frontier with a husband doomed to poverty only to marry, Cinderella-like, one of the richest men around. She had come to the nineteenth century American West before the covered-wagon era and died a year before the dawn of the twentieth century.

John Wilson

Benjamin Wilson's son John, whom Wilson had counted on to carry the Wilson name and legacy into future generations, was such a ne'er-do-well and drunkard that Wilson had disinherited the young man.[3] John ended his shattered life during his father's lifetime with a self-inflicted bullet in the hotel his father had once owned, the Bella Union. That bullet ended Benjamin Wilson's surname legacy. Don Benito's genes were carried forward in history by his daughters, but the lineage of his Wilson name was buried with his son.

The Patton Home

Around 1910 the Pattons moved out of the Lake Vineyard adobe into a new home next door, and had the Lake Vineyard adobe home razed. The 1910 Patton house still stands, at 1220 Patton Court in San Marino, on a street segment renamed in the family's honor. The twelve-acre Patton estate was subdivided into twenty-three lots in the early 1970s.[4]

Edward Sublette Hereford

Eddy Hereford, the child that Margaret Hereford dragged through Indian territory, across the Mexican Rockies, and raised in parts of Mexico when he was five and six years old lived on property adjacent to the Wilson estate in later life.[5] Wilson raised him as his own son, treating him equally with his own children in a will he drew up in 1853,[6] although he did not have that status in Wilson's later will. In 1870 the court took one hundred acres from his mother to settle a five hundred dollars debt that Edward had not repaid.[7] In her will she bequeathed to him the "farm . . . which he formerly owned and occupied, and which I now hold by deed from him."[8] He acquired the nickname "Judge" along the way, outlived his wife and child, and led an undistinguished life, dying suddenly of a cerebral hemorrhage on March 2, 1913.[9] He took "a particularly active interest in the welfare of the mission Indians, continuing their friendship and retaining their confidence until the time of his death," according to his *Los Angeles Times* obituary. Other than that, his life was notable perhaps only for its excess of alcohol.[10] Thus both Wilson's son and stepson, both raised strictly, suffered from alcohol abuse upon reaching their majorities.

City of Los Angeles

The City of Los Angeles has grown seventeen-fold in area and 2,294-fold in population since Wilson was mayor. Wilson is one of 494 to serve on its City Council.[11]

Mayor of Los Angeles

Some forty-three mayors have served since Wilson's term in 1851-52. As this is written the mayor of Los Angeles is Antonio Villaraigosa, the first Mexican-American mayor to serve the city since Don Benito's days and only the fourth in the city's history. Antonio F. Colonel, one of Wilson pallbearers, was the city's first Mexican-American mayor, serving in 1853-54. Manuel Requena filled the office as acting mayor briefly in 1856 and Cristobal Agujilar served 1866-68 and 1871-72.

Crime

Mayor Benjamin Wilson presided over the most dangerous city in the nation. Today the image of crime in the City of Los Angeles is magnified because of its role as a media capital, but among U.S. cities over 250,000 in population thirty U.S. cities ranked above Los Angeles in murders per capita in 2006, making Los Angeles a safer city than Phoenix, Minneapolis, Dallas, Nashville or Tulsa.[12]

County of Los Angeles

All 377 citizens who voted in Wilson's Los Angeles County would fit several times over in the meeting room where county supervisors do business today. Los Angeles County has been carved up with the creation of Orange, Riverside, San Bernardino, and Kern Counties out of the real estate it occupied in Wilson's early days on the Board of Supervisors. Today it is the most populous county in the country, its inhabitants outnumbering the residents of all but eight of the USA states.[13]

Bella Union Hotel

Don Benito's Bella Union Hotel, where his son committed suicide was the pueblo's original hotel, its stagecoach stop, the mansion of the last governor of Mexican California, the headquarters for U.S. troops during the Mexican War, the first American courthouse, and a structure of immense significance where much early Los Angeles history was written. It was torn down in 1939 to make way for a parking lot.[14]

Wilson's Pueblo Properties

Wilson's twelve-acre home site in the pueblo became for many years the Sisters of Charity's school and orphanage, named the Institute and Orphan Asylum. The sisters used his vineyard to help pay their expenses. The Institute was sold to Wilson's business partner, Dr. J.M. Griffin, who used the site for a lumber yard, before selling it to the Southern Pacific Railroad Company.[15] In 1939 Union Station was built there to consolidate passenger operations of the three railroads that served the city, Southern Pacific, Union Pacific and Santa Fe. Wilson's general store is gone and so is the land it was on. Wilson's other many properties in downtown Los Angeles have long since been reconfigured into other uses.

China

Wilson came to the West Coast seeking a ship to China. Only after he could find no such ship did he decide to buy property and settle in Southern California. He should have waited. After his death, the Chinatown section of Los Angeles formed on his old pueblo property, until the community was displaced once again for the construction of Union Station in the late 1930s. Today, his Lake Vineyard ranch has become the city of San Marino, where the majority of residents are Asian (mostly Chinese). Next-door Alhambra, which Wilson founded, is fifty-two percent Asian and thirty-eight percent Chinese;[16] and nearby Monterey Park is sixty-two percent Asian and forty-two percent Chinese, billing itself as "the most Chinese place in the United States."

Wilmington

There was no natural harbor for Los Angeles. In the eighteenth and nineteenth centuries, ships anchored in unprotected and shallow water off San Pedro, until Phineas Banning, in partnership often with Benjamin Wilson, developed the port of Wilmington and built a protective breakwater to create deep water. Wilson and Banning dredged the water, eliminated the mud flats and built a railroad to connect the port to Los Angeles. Around the turn of the century, long after Wilson and Banning died, Collis P. Huntington and other major figures tried to substitute Santa Monica as the port for Southern California. Congress resolved the epic fight over the port location in 1897, in favor of the San Pedro/Wilmington location, and in 1906 the City of Los Angeles annexed San Pedro.[17] Today the combined ports handle forty percent of the nation's maritime trade, and process as much tonnage every ten minutes today as the port handled the entire year when Wilson was mayor of Los Angeles in 1851. [18,19]

Wilson's Lake

The lake overlooked by Lake Vineyard was known at various times as Mission Lake, Wilson's Lake, Lake Vineyard and Kewen Lake. When its lifeblood streams were interrupted the once beautiful lake dwindled to an unsightly bog. In 1914 the remaining water was drained, the depression filled with ninety thousand yards of soil, and turned into a nine-hole golf course for the nearby Huntington Hotel. In 1925 the City of San Marino bought the land after the Huntington Hotel had been sold, planted nearly two thousand trees and shrubs there, and opened the land as the thirty-acre Lacy Park. Wilson Lake is remembered today by the road which led from the lake, up through Pasadena and Altadena to the mountains to its north, still called Lake Avenue.[20] The road was originally laid out by Wilson himself and called Lake Vineyard Avenue. In the late 1880s developers wanted to call an extension of the street up to Las Flores Canyon "Prospect Avenue" to appeal to buyers,[21] but the street remains Lake Avenue today throughout its length in Pasadena and Altadena. The San Marino portion of Lake Avenue is now named Virginia Road.

Mount Wilson

In 1887, nine years after Wilson's death, government officials announced what they felt was a more fitting name for Wilson's Peak, "Mount Kinneyloa." The new name would honor Abbot Kinney, an heir to a cigarette fortune and developer of Venice, California, who had been the first chairman of the California Board of Forestry. Reaction to the announcement in the Los Angeles Times on Feb. 18, 1887 was thundering. A government official struck back defensively, "Apparently somebody seems to be having a thorn in his side over our naming the mountain peak after your distinguished citizen, Abbot Kinney. The action of the Government is in recognition of the ardent services of the gentleman, as the official head of the Board of Forestry of California, in seeking to preserve the water sources and timber lands from spoliation and appropriation by lawless parties." The bombastic publisher of the Los Angeles Times, Harrison Gray Otis, responded, "A recognition of the distinguished services of Citizen Abbot Kinney would be all right, coming from the Government or from any other source, were it accomplished without an act of vandalism. But when an effort is made to set aside a time-honored and universally-recognized name in favor of a new one which contains a Sandwich Island graft upon the cognomen of Citizen Kinney, the proposition becomes odious in the extreme. Don Benito Wilson was in his day one of the foremost citizens of Los Angeles county and of Southern California. He was a pioneer among pioneers and a pathmaker no less than a pathfinder. He was noted for his farseeing enterprises and his rugged integrity. . . . Among his other enterprises he hewed out a trail to the summit of one of the notable peaks of the Sierra Madre chain, and brought out of the mountain fastness timber with which to build houses. Since that day the trail has been known as Wilson's Trail, and the mountain which it ascends has been called Wilson's Peak. These designations have been in use among the people of Southern California for upwards of thirty years. Old Don Benito Wilson earned them "[22] The vitriol heaped upon Mr. Kinney was so searing that within a week he asked that his name be withdrawn, leaving the mountain in Don Benito's name.

In May, 1889, eleven years after Wilson's death, Harvard University Observatory astronomers began use of a thirteen-inch telescope on Mount Wilson, mapping the sky and discovering stars. Mount Wilson had been chosen from among other local peaks in part because Pasadena business leaders promised to build a wagon road to that particular summit. Eighteen businessmen formed "The Pasadena and Mount Wilson Toll Road Company," but were slow in getting the road built so after only eighteen months Harvard dismantled their instrument and shipped it to Arequipa, Peru.

A year before the astronomers arrived, A.G. Strain had homesteaded on the north side of the mountain and became alarmed when Harvard and a tent camp operator, Peter Steil, infringed on what he deemed his private property. Strain built a fence across the trail and Steil tore it down, sending the matter to court. The judge noted that the trail had been open to the public since Don Benito built it in 1864, and thus it must stay open to the public. Strain and Steil's successors built ever larger facilities to attract visitors.

The toll road was finally finished, under a reorganized company, in July of 1891. With forty-four steep, hair-raising, hairpin turns hikers paid twenty-five cents and horse riders paid double that. The Mount Wilson Toll Road Company gradually bought up other commercial interests and paid the government for other rights until it gained complete control over Mount Wilson and the road. In 1905 the Carnegie Institution built an observatory on forty acres and the toll road firm opened a one-story hotel. After fire destroyed the hotel in 1913 it was replaced with a larger hotel. In 1907 Japanese and other laborers worked by hand to widen the six-foot toll road to accommodate automobiles, and a Franklin automobile with driver and passenger made the first trip. The passenger said, "Not for $500 would I make the trip again!" In 1917 it was widened again, to twelve feet, and the road saw increased auto traffic, staged auto races and service by the Mount Wilson Stage Line. The usual trip was two to three hours, although a Paige 6-66 set the record during a twenty-two-minute assent.

The public Angeles Crest Highway was finished in 1934 and in March, 1936, the now-obsolete toll road was closed and the toll road company became the Mount Wilson Hotel Company. The human-built forest of television towers was first planted in 1948 and in 1964 Metromedia bought the entire 720-acre holding of the former toll road company, and dismantled the Mount Wilson Hotel. Today the Mount Wilson towers of thirteen FM stations and seven television stations are clearly visible from Los Angeles below.

The largest telescopes in the world of their times were built on Mount Wilson, at sixty inches, then one hundred inches. Again and again Mount Wilson was the dateline of human discovery. Harlow Shapley mapped the globular cluster system of the galaxy, Edwin Powell Hubble discovered the expanding universe and Walter Baade first recognized the phenomenon of stellar populations. In 1926 the speed of light was calculated by Albert Abraham Michelson with mirrors on Mount Wilson and Mt. San Antonio ("Mount Baldy"), twenty-two miles away.

State Senate

Wilson's senate district included the vast, virtually empty reach of the state south of Tulare County. The state's population, and the power of the senate, was concentrated in the north. Today, sixty-five percent of the California senate, twenty-six of the forty districts, lies within the single district he once represented alone. When he was in the senate the population center of the state was farther north than San Francisco; today it is near Buttonwillow in Kern County, within Wilson's old district.[23] Today, each senate district in California represents 846,791 people, more than double the population of the entire state when Wilson served in the legislature. In his day the legislature wrestled with such questions as how to stimulate immigration into California, how to battle the hostile Indians, how to replace footpaths with wagon roads and how connect the state's communities with railroads. The issues of that faraway day are so remote from today's deliberations in Sacramento. Or are they? Today's legislature faces the challenges of immigration, maintaining highways, creating more rail links and the power of the Native Americans in the state.

Beverly Hills

After Wilson sold off his *Rancho San José de Buenos Ayres* in segments, the land passed to other owners over the years until bought by Burton Green, a director of the Amalgamated Oil Company, which had tried to find oil on the land but failed. Green subdivided the property and named his development for his Massachusetts home town of Beverly Farm. With 550 original citizens, the City of Beverly Hills was incorporated in 1914 and the area so long known for its bad luck has been associated with good fortune ever since. In 2007 the assessed value of Beverly Hills property was $17.7 billion, an increase in value of over four million fold over the four thousand dollars Wilson paid in 1854.[24]

Culver City

Asuccession of owners subdivided *Rancho La Ballona* in a number of schemes. In 1902 a failed vision called Port Ballona was resurrected as Playa del Rey, this time succeeding. On July 25, 1913, at the California Club in downtown Los Angeles, Harry H. Culver and directors and stockholders of his Culver Investment Company, celebrated the birth of a business and residential city to be named Culver City.

Oil

Fourteen years after Wilson died, Edward L. Doheny struck oil at 460 feet at the corner of Colton Street and Glendale Boulevard in 1892, making him a millionaire, and famous enough to be considered as a candidate for the vice presidency of the United States. The third largest oil field in the contiguous United States is the Wilmington Oil Field, under the land of Wilson and Banning. This oil field, with its 6,150 wells, will ultimately produce three billion barrels of oil.[25]

Lake Vineyard

Lake Vineyard was home to a large number of family members after Don Benito's death. The Pattons, who lived in Don Benito's house, and later in a new house a stone's throw away, accommodated Wilson's widow, Margaret; Nellie Patton Brown, George Patton II's widowed sister and her six children, Aunt Annie Wilson; Susan Patton, the unmarried sister of George Patton II; and Mary Scally, the family nurse and nanny.[26] A short distance away, was the Shorb household with its eleven children.

To maintain his regal lifestyle J. De Barth Shorb mortgaged Lake Vineyard. Even as his debts mounted he turned down offers from buyers believing in Southern California and being convinced that prices would go up.[27] He cajoled his wife into signing away her portion of the property by threatening to kill himself if she refused. He died deep in luxury but more deeply in debt. Soon after his death on April 16, 1896, his real-estate empire, the family real estate of Don Benito Wilson, began to unravel. Disease swept through the vineyards and drought plagued the land, but instead of reducing his gluttonous lifestyle or trimming back his real-estate holdings, Shorb simply borrowed against more and more of the family's holdings. By 1899, the long-time family friend and president of the Farmers and Merchants Bank, I. W. Hellman, could show the family no more leniency, and he foreclosed on the loans. The empire that Benjamin Wilson had so painstakingly built acre by acre over many decades toppled like so many stacked cards. George Patton II resigned his post as district attorney of Los Angeles County to devote full time to keeping the family fortune, but it was too late. In a few years the estate was lost. The duty of trying to literally save the farm was especially distasteful to Patton because of his bigotry towards the Mexican blood with which Sue Wilson Shorb had "polluted" the family lines, because of the Shorbs' Catholic religion and his social embarrassment of their large number of children. General George Patton carried this prejudice to the next generation rebuking the memory of J. De Barth Shorb as "either a fool or a crook." General Patton liked to quote a friend of his father's who commented that "God sent that young man to save the widow and orphan."[28]

The Shorb ranch was bought by Henry E. Huntington. The land in this ranch, along with that of the 100-acre Bean Ranch and L.J. Rose's Sunny Slope Ranch, were combined to form the incorporated city of San Marino in 1913.[29]

A final word

The world of Don Benito Wilson is long gone, but his legacy endures. His name is on Mount Wilson, Wilson Trail, Wilson Avenues in Pasadena and San Marino, Don Benito Elementary School in Pasadena and his Wilson's Lake is remembered in Pasadena's Lake Avenue.

His address book is today's atlas of streets and towns in Southern California: Pico, Sepulveda, Temple, Downey, Banning, Rose(mead), Arcadia, Alvarado, Vignes, Beaudry and Rowland.

A World War II Liberty Ship was named *S.S. Benjamin D. Wilson* in his honor. A million people live on property he once owned in Southern California. His golden wheat fields have turned to the real gold of Beverly Hills. His vast vineyards are the posh neighborhoods of San Marino. Twenty-six state senators divvy up the district that he once represented in Sacramento alone. Forty-three mayors have held the title since he presided over the tiny pueblo of Los Angeles. As a Los Angeles County supervisor he oversaw a Los Angeles County that included what is today Orange, San Bernardino and Kern Counties. His Wilson College was the predecessor of the mighty University of Southern California. Many of the railroads he helped bring to Southern California still haul freight over the original rights of way that he helped determine. Southern California will perhaps never again see a person who made such a mark on so many different fields as Don Benito Wilson.

Don Benito Wilson was a fur trapper, trader, merchant, cattle rancher, Indian fighter, Indian Agent, U.S. Army officer, POW, hotelier, agriculturist, vintner, citrus magnate, owner of gold and silver mines, manufacturer, oil company founder, railroad president, county clerk, city councilman, mayor, state senator, political leader in three parties and philanthropist. He was known by his peers for the noblest of qualities: integrity, tolerance, honesty, generosity, courtesy, intelligence. He is certainly worthy of our study and he deserves to be remembered by the world city of Los Angeles that he helped to create. We do well to remember Don Benito Wilson.

NOTES FOR CHAPTER 31

1 Patton, *The Pattons: A Personal History of an American Family*, 78.

2 *Los Angeles Times*, December 30, 1898.

3 In Wilson's probated will he left "All property, real, personal and mixed, to my three daughters . . . To my son, John B. Wilson, in view of his disobedience and undutifulness, I give nothing, further than the affirmance of such gifts and conveyances as I have made or may hereafter make to him during my life." Probate Court, Superior Court of Los Angeles County, #1030 Estate of B.D. Wilson.

4 Ross, *Side Streets of History*, 9 and 17.

5 Rose, L.J. *Rose of Sunny Slope*, 46. Also, Ward, "Some New Thoughts on an Old Mill," which cites a deed for the Old Mill, which describes that property as bounded by "the possession of B.D. Wilson, and E.S. Hereford."

6 Will of Benjamin D. Wilson, October, 1853, B.D. Wilson papers. However, Edward Hereford was not a beneficiary in the later will, which was eventually probated. See Probate Court, Superior Court of Los Angeles County, #1030 Estate of B.D. Wilson.

7 California 17th District Court action, re: $500 borrowed by E.S. Hereford from J.B. Caswell on July 1, 1870 at 2 percent per month. B.D. Wilson papers.

8 Will of Margaret Hereford Wilson, 1876, B.D. Wilson papers.

9 *Los Angeles Times* obituary, March 3, 1913.

10 Blumenson, *The Patton Papers 1885-1940*, 34.

11 Los Angeles City Clerk archive calculation, through March 2006.

12 InfoPlease.com Web site.

13 Los Angeles County Web site, February 2007.

14 de Packman, "Landmarks and Pioneers of Los Angeles," 86.

15 Newmark, *Sixty Years in Southern California 1853-1913*, 189.

16 U.S. Census, American Community Survey, 2006.

17 Port of Los Angeles, news release on 100th anniversary, January 1, 2007.

18 In 1851, less than five hundred tons per month was carried both ways between San Pedro and Los Angeles, according to *An Illustrated History of Los Angeles County*, 332.

19 Newmark, *Sixty Years in Southern California 1853-1913*, 189.

20 *The Golden Years*, a booklet produced by Turner and Stevens funeral directors in 1963, 14.

21 Reid, *History of Pasadena*, 358-359.

22 *Los Angeles Times*, February 21, 1887.

23 National Oceanic and Atmospheric Administration.

24 City of Beverly Hills Economic Development Division from data generated by the Los Angeles County tax assessor (August 2007).

25 White, *Formative Years in the Far West: A History of Standard Oil Company of California and Predecessors Through 1919*.

26 D'Este, *Patton: A Genius for War*, 35.

27 Dumke, *The Boom of the Eighties in Southern California*, 86.

28 D'Este, *Patton: A Genuis for War*, 42.

29 *The Golden Years*, 4-5.

Bibliography

The author has read extensively at The Huntington Library, where the papers of Benjamin Davis Wilson are contained, and credits those original papers for much of the information presented in this book.

The author has also read the pertinent nineteenth-century minutes of the Common Council of the City of Los Angeles, as well as the archives of the *Los Angeles Star* and the *Southern Californian*, plus many editions of the *Democratic State Journal* from the era when B.D. Wilson was in Sacramento.

His bibliography includes the following books, articles and theses:

Aitken, Melbourne F. "Benjamin Wilson: Southern California Pioneer." Master's thesis, UCLA, 1946.

Bacon, Walter R. "Pioneer Courts and Lawyers of Los Angeles." In *Annual Publication of the Historical Society of Southern California and Pioneer Register.* Los Angeles: Geo. Rice & Sons, 1906.

Barrows, H.D. "Los Angeles Fifty Years Ago." In *Annual Publication of the Historical Society of Southern California and Pioneer Register.* Los Angeles, 1905: Geo. Rice & Sons, 1906.

Barsness, Richard W. "Iron Horses and an Inner Harbor at San Pedro Bay, 1867-1890." In *Pacific Historical Review.* Berkeley: The Pacific Branch of the American Historical Association, Vol. 34, No. 3, August 1965.

—. "Los Angeles' Quest for Transportation, 1846-1861." In *California Historical Society Quarterly.* Vol. XLVI No. 4, December 1967.

Beattie, George William. "San Bernardino Valley Before the Americans Came." In *California Historical Society Quarterly,* Vol. XII, Number 2, June 1933.

Bell, Horace. *Reminiscences of a Ranger: Early Times in Southern California.* Norman: University of Oklahoma Press, 1881, 1999.

Benedict, Pierce E. *History of Beverly Hills.* Beverly Hills: A.H. Cawston and H.M. Meier Publishers, 1934.

Blumenson, Martin. *Patton: The Man Behind the Legend, 1885-1945.* New York: Morrow, 1985.

Brewer, William H. "Los Angeles and Environs." In *Up and Down California in 1860-1864: The Journal of William H. Brewer.* Berkeley: University of California Press, 2003.

California Research Bureau, California State Library. "California—One Hundred and Fifty Years Ago: 1856." On Library Web site *Studies in the News* (www.library.ca.gov/sitn), 06-39 / September 12, 2006.

California, State of. *Senate Journal: 1869-70.* Sacramento: State of California, 1871

Callahan, Ignatio. Oral History Project of the Friends of the San Marino Library. San Marino Historical Society, 1975.

Cameron, Tom. "Crime in the Early Pueblo Days" *Los Angeles Times.* June 23, 1957.

Carpenter, Edwin H. "Benito Wilson: Yankee to California." *The Downey Historical Society Annual,* Vol. 1, No. 1 1966-67.

The Catholic Encyclopedia. New York: The Encyclopedia Press, Inc., 1913.

Cleland, Robert Glass. *El Molino Viejo.* Pasadena: Many Moons Press, 2003.

Conde, Bruce. "Santa Ana of the Yorbas, Which Might Have Become Pastoral California's Greatest Semi-Feudal Hacienda." In *Historical Society of Southern California Quarterly,* June 1940.

Cooley, William C., Jr. *The Goodspeed History of Wilson County, Tennessee.* Originally published 1886. Reprinted by Woodward & Stinson Printing Co., 1971.

Core, Tom. "Bearly Remembered." *Big Bear Grizzly,* October 13, 2004.

Crongeyer, Sven. *Six Gun Sound: The Early History of the Los Angeles County Sheriff's Department.* Fresno: Craven Street Books, 2006.

D'Este, Carlo. *Patton: A Genius for War.* New York: HarperCollins Publishers, 1995.

de Packman, Ana Begue. "Landmarks and Pioneers of Los Angeles." In *Historical Society of Southern California Quarterly,* June-September, 1944.

DeVoto, Bernard. *Across the Wide Missouri.* Boston: Houghton Mifflin Company, 1947.

Dixon, Elizabeth I. "Recollections of Samuel Butler." An oral history interview, Oral History Program: UCLA, 1962.

Dryden, Gene, "Church of Our Savior: The Early Years (1853-1875)." In *The Grapevine*, San Marino Historical Society, Spring 2006.

Dumke, Glenn S. *The Boom of the Eighties in Southern California*. San Marino: Huntington Library, 1944.

Durham, David L. *California's Geographic Names: A Gazetteer of Historic and Modern Names of the State*. Clovis, California: Word Dancer Press, 1998.

Ferris, Jeri. *With Open Hands: A Story about Biddy Mason*. Minneapolis: Carolrhoda Books, 1999.

Fink, Augusta. *Palos Verdes Peninsula: Time and the Terraced Land*. Santa Cruz: Western Tanager Press, 1987.

Graves, J.A. *My Seventy Years in California: 1857-1927*. Los Angeles: The Times-Mirror Press, 1927.

—. *California Memories: 1857-1930*. Los Angeles: Times-Mirror Press. 1930.

Grivas, Theodore. "Alcalde Rule: The Nature of Local Government in Spanish and Mexican California." In *California Historical Society Quarterly*, Vol. XL, No. 1. March 1961.

Guide to the Historical Records of Los Angeles County. Los Angeles: Los Angeles County Task Force on Historical Records Preservation, 1991.

Guinn, J.M. *A History of California*. Los Angeles: Historic Record Company, 1907

—. "How California Escaped State Division." In *Annual Publication of the Historical Society of Southern California and Pioneer Register, Los Angeles, 1900*: Geo. Rice & Sons, 1901.

—. *Historical and Biographical Record of Los Angeles and Vicinity*. Chicago: Chapman Publishing Co., 1901.

Gunther, Jane Davies, *Riverside County, California, Place Names: Their Origins and Their Stories*, Riverside: J.D. Gunther, 1984.

Hafen, LeRoy R., editor. *Fur Trappers and Traders of the Far Southwest*. Logan, Utah: Utah State University Press, 1997.

Hamilton, Andy. "The Toughest Little Town." In *Los Angeles Times*, May 8, 1938.

Hereford, E.S. "The War Existing Between the Northern and Southern States." Essay written in an invoice book of Wilson & Packard, B.D. Wilson Addenda II, Huntington Library Collection.

Hirshson, Stanley P. *General Patton: A Soldier's Life*. New York: HarperCollins, 2002.

History of Los Angeles County. The Lewis Publishing Co., 1889.

Hittell, Theodore. *History of California*. San Francisco: N.J. Stone & Co., 1898.

Hornbeck, Robert. *Roubidoux's Ranch in the 70's*. Riverside: Press Printing Company, 1913.

Hummelt, Stephen; Cheryl Brown, and Bernadette McNulty, editors. *California State Blue Book: Sesquicentennial Edition*. Office of the Secretary of the Senate, 2000.

Hurt, Peyton. "The Rise and Fall of the 'Know-Nothings' in California." In *California Historical Society Quarterly*, Vol. IX, No. 1 and No. 2, 1930.

Ignoffo, Mary Jo. *Gold Rush Politics: California's First Legislature*. Sacramento: California State Senate, 1999.

James, G.W. *Through Ramona's Country*. Boston: Little, Brown, 1909.

Johnson, Allen. *Dictionary of American Biography*. New York: Prentice Hall, 1981.

Kelley, D.O. *History of the Diocese of California From 1849 to 1914*. San Francisco: Bureau of Information and Supply, 1915.

Kelsey, Harry. "A New Look at the Founding of Old Los Angeles." In *California Historical Society Quarterly*, Winter, Vol. XV, No. 4, 1976.

Klotz, Esther H. and Joan H. Hall. *Adobes, Bungalows, and Mansions of Riverside, California*. Riverside Museum Press, 1985.

Kroeber, A.L. *Handbook of the Indians of California*. Berkeley: California Book Company, 1953.

Krythe, Maymie R. "Daily Life in Early Los Angeles." In *Historical Society of Southern California Quarterly*, March, 1954.

Kurutz, Gary F. *Don Benito Wilson: A Pioneer in Transitional Southern California, 1841-1854*. Master's thesis, University of San Diego, 1972.

Lawrence, Eleanor. "Mexican Trade Between Santa Fe and Los Angeles, 1830-1848." In *California Historical Society Quarterly*, Vol. X, March, 1931.

Laycock, George. *The Mountain Men*. New York: Lyons & Burford, 1988.

Layne, J. Gregg. "Annals of Los Angeles: Part I." In *California Historical Society Quarterly*, Vol. XIII, No. 3., 1934.

—. "Annals of Los Angeles: Part II." In *California Historical Society Quarterly*, Vol. XIII, No. 4, 1934.

Lewis, Donovan. "'I Surrender Nothing!' Matt Harbin at the Battle of Rancho Chino." In *The Californians*, Vol. 12, No. 1.

Lindley, Walter, and J.P. Widney. *California of the South, Its Physical Geography, Climate, Resources, Routes of Travel and Health-Resorts*. New York: D. Appleton and Co., 1888.

Martinez, Frank T. *Facts About the City of Los Angeles*. Los Angeles: City of Los Angeles, 2006.

McDowell, Don. *The Beat of the Drum*. Santa Ana: Graphic Publishers, 1993.

Newmark, Marco R. "*Calle de los Negros* and the Chinese Massacre of 1871." In *Historical Society of Southern California Quarterly*, June-September, 1944.

Newmark, Maurice H. and Marco R. Newmark, editors. *Sixty Years in Southern California: Containing the Reminiscences of Harris Newmark, 1853-1913*. New York: Knickerbocker Press, 1916.

—. "Facts about the Census." In *Census of the City and County of Los Angeles For the Year 1850*. Los Angeles: The Times-Mirror Press, 1929.

Nunis, Doyce B., Jr. *A Southern California Historical Anthology*. Los Angeles: Historical Society of Southern California. 1984.

—. *Andrew Sublette: Rocky Mountain Prince*. Los Angeles: Glen Dawson, 1960.

O'Flaherty, Joseph S. *An End and a Beginning: The South Coast and Los Angeles 1850-1887*. Los Angeles: The Historical Society of Southern California, 1972.

Page, Henry Markham. *Pasadena: Its Early Years*. Los Angeles: Lorrin L. Morrison Printing and Publishing, 1964.

Patton, Robert H. *The Pattons: A Personal History of an American Family*. New York: Crown Publishers, Inc., 1994.

Pauly, Thomas H. "J. Ross Browne: Wine Lobbyist and Frontier Opportunist." In *California Historical Society Quarterly*, Vol. LI, No. 2, Summer 1972.

Peterson, F. William. "The Callahan Adobe Ranch House." Manuscript from San Marino Historical Society, 1973.

Phelan, Regina V. *The Gold Chain: A California Family Saga.* Prosperity Press, 1987.

Pinney, Thomas. "The Early Days in Southern California." In *Book of California Wine* by Doris Muscatine, et. al. Berkeley: University of California Press/Sotheby Publications, 1984.

Reid, Hiram A. *History of Pasadena.* Pasadena: Pasadena History Company Publishers, 1895.

Risher, Bruce D. *Alhambra: 100 Years in Words and Pictures.* Alhambra: City of Alhambra, 2004.

Robinson, John W. *Mines of the San Gabriels.* Glendale: La Siesta Press, 1973.

—. *Southern California's First Railroad,* Los Angeles: Dawson's Book Shop, 1978.

—. *The Mount Wilson Story.* Glendale: La Siesta Press, 1991.

Rose, L.J., Jr. *L.J. Rose of Sunny Slope.* San Marino, California: The Huntington Library, 1959.

Ross, Mrs. Ronald. *Side Streets of History,* pamphlet compiled for the Friends of the San Marino Library, 1979.

Rowland, Donald E. *John Rowland and William Workman: Southern California Pioneers of 1841.* Spokane: The Arthur H. Clark Company.

Sato, Stephen T. *San Pedro Bay Area Headlines in History.* Windsor Publications, 1990.

Spaulding, William A. *History and Reminiscences: Los Angeles City and County California,* Vol. 1. Los Angeles: J.R. Finnell & Sons Publishing Co., 1930.

Spitzzeri, Paul R. "'To Seduce and Confuse': The Rowland-Workman Expedition of 1841." In *Southern California Quarterly,* Spring, 1998.

Starr, Kevin. *California: A History.* New York: The Modern Library, 2005.

—. *Inventing the Dream.* New York: Oxford University Press, 1985.

Stephenson, Terry E. *Don Bernardo Yorba.* Los Angeles: Glen Dawson, 1941.

Sunder, John E. *Bill Sublette: Mountain Man.* Norman: University of Oklahoma Press, 1959.

Teiser, Ruth and Catherine Harroun. *Winemaking in California*. New York: McGraw-Hill Book Company, 1983.

The Golden Years. A booklet produced by Turner and Stevens Funeral Directors, 1963.

The Journal of San Diego History. San Diego Historical Society Quarterly, Vol. III, No. 3, July, 1957.

Truman, Maj. Ben C. *Semi-Tropical California*. San Francisco: A.L. Bancroft & Company, 1874.

Vestal, Stanley. *Jim Bridger: Mountain Man*. Lincoln, Nebraska: University of Nebraska Press, 1946.

Vickery, Oliver. *Harbor Heritage: Tales of the Harbor Area of Los Angeles, California*. Palos Verdes: Palos Verdes Book Company, 1979.

Vorspan, Max and Lloyd Gartner. *History of the Jews of Los Angeles*. San Marino: Huntington Library, 1970.

Vredenburgh, Larry M. "Fort Irwin and Vicinity History of Mining Development." On Vredenburgh Web site (www.vredenburgh.org/mining_history/pages/fort_Irwin.html), 1994.

Wagner, Walter. *Beverly Hills: Inside the Golden Ghetto*. New York: Grosset & Dunlap, 1976.

Waldron, Granville A. "Courthouses of Los Angeles County." In *Historical Society of Southern California Quarterly*, Volume 41, 1959.

Ward, Jean Bruce, and Gary Kurutz. "Some New Thoughts on an Old Mill." In *California History Quarterly*, Vol. 53, 1974.

Wayte, Beverly. "A History of the San Gabriel Cemetery." San Gabriel Valley Cemetery Association, 1993.

Weber, David J. "Louis Robidoux: Two Letters From California, 1848." In *Southern California Quarterly*. Los Angeles: The Historical Society of Southern California, Volume LIV, No. 2, Summer 1972.

Whelan, Harold A. "Eden in the Jurupa Valley: The Story of *Agua Mansa*." In *Southern California Quarterly*, Vol. LV, No. 4, Winter 1973.

White, Gerald Taylor. *Formative Years in the Far West: A History of Standard Oil Company of California and Predecessors through 1919*. New York: Appleton-Century-Crofts, 1962.

Williams, Mary Floyd. "Mission, Presidio and Pueblo: Notes on California Local Institutions Under Spain and Mexico." In *California Historical Society Quarterly*, Vol. 1, No. 1, July 1922.

Wilson, Benjamin Davis; edited by John Walton Caughey; introduction to the Bison Books edition by Albert L. Hurtado. *The Indians of Southern California In 1852: The B.D. Wilson Report and a Selection of Contemporary Comment.* Lincoln: University of Nebraska Press, 1995. (Originally published: San Marino, California: Huntington Library, 1952. The report, prepared in 1852, was originally published serially in the *Los Angeles Star*, July 18-Sept. 19, 1868.)

Wilson, John Albert. *History of Los Angeles County, California: with Illustrations Descriptive of its Scenery, Residences, Fine Blocks and Manufactories.* Oakland: Thompson & West, 1880.

Wolcott, Marjorie Tisdale, editor. *Pioneer Notes From The Diaries of Judge Benjamin Hayes 1849-1875.* Printed privately at Los Angeles, 1929.

Woodward, Arthur. "Benjamin Davis Wilson's Observations on Early Days in California and New Mexico." In *Historical Society of Southern California Annual Publication*, 1934.

Woolsey, Ron. "Crime and Punishment: Los Angeles County, 1850-1856," In *Southern California Quarterly*, Spring 1979.

Woolsey, Ronald C. "A Capitalist in a Foreign Land: Abel Stearns." In *Southern California Quarterly*, Summer 1993.

Workman, Boyle. *The City That Grew.* Los Angeles: The Southland Publishing Co., 1935.

Wright, Doris Marion. *A Yankee in Mexican California: Abel Stearns, 1798-1848.* Santa Barbara: Wallace Hebberd, 1977.

Wynn, Bob. "Salt Springs, Death Valley!" On *Ghost Town Seekers* Web site (www.robertwynn.com/SaltSprings.htm), 2004.

Yoch, James J. *On the Golden Shore: Phineas Banning in Southern California.* Wilmington, California: The Banning Residence Museum, 2002.

Index

ANGEL CITY PRESS